To Myra & Her
The proud
of the one + only
Matt Jeffers

Best wishes
Mitchell Whiteley

PULPIT POWER

Meaningful Sermons on Religion & Politics ... and Life

Rabbi Mitchell Wohlberg

EMEK Publishing LLC

Photography by Bradley Zisow • www.bradleyimages.com

Publication of this book was made
possible through the generosity of:

AHARON & RACHEL ע"ה DAHAN

AND

RICHARD & ROSALIE ALTER

Make for yourself a Rabbi and acquire for yourself a friend.
–Ethics of the Fathers

Every Rabbi should be blessed with friends like these.

FORWARD

I have known Rabbi Wohlberg since we were children together in the Borough Park section of Brooklyn, during the Golden Age of Modern Orthodox Judaism. His eminent father, Rabbi Harry Wohlberg Z'l, was one of my teachers. His brother, Rabbi Jeremiah Wohlberg, was my arch competitor in debating and basketball. His father's sermons were so mesmerizing that I would often sneak out at the synagogue my family attended to go listen to a brilliant Modern Orthodox rabbi, who had one foot in Eastern Europe, and the other foot firmly planted in contemporary America.

Rabbi Mitchell Wohlberg carries forward a great tradition. I have been privileged to hear and to read several of his sermons over the years. They inspire, provoke, challenge and persuade. Now Rabbi Wohlberg has gathered some of his most important sermons together into a book—a *sefer*. This too is part of a great tradition that goes back many centuries in many far-flung parts of the Jewish World—publishing the sermons and responsas of respected rabbinic leaders, so that future generations can experience them. Rabbi Wohlberg's collected sermons will allow future generations to benefit from his wisdom and insight. They are sermons that look to tradition to address contemporary problems. In that respect, they are lessons for the ages.

It is no secret that the kind of Modern Orthodox Judaism with which we grew up is an endangered species in many parts of the world. Rabbi Mitchell Wohlberg not only keeps it alive, he invigorates it with his brilliance, his energy, his wit and his commitment. When I read these wonderful sermons, I can hear Rabbi Wohlberg's voice. I can also hear the echo of his father's voice. But this book is not about our parents and grandparents. It is about our children and grandchildren.

Professor Alan Dershowitz
Felix Frankfurter Professor of Law, Harvard University

TABLE OF CONTENTS

INTRODUCTION

While campaigning against Barack Obama for the Democratic presidential nomination, Hillary Clinton told the workers at a General Motors plant: "Speeches don't put food on the table ... speeches don't fill up your tank or fill your prescription or do anything about that stack of bills." I beg to differ! Speeches have put a lot of food on my table, and they have helped me pay a lot of bills and certainly filled my tank!

I never really thought I would publish a book of my sermons because I always felt that they sounded better than they read. I think back to the nice, elderly woman who waited in the receiving line one Shabbos to tell me how much she loved my sermons and hoped that I would publish them in a book. I started to explain to her that I was a bit reluctant to do that — my father never did it, we always felt that sermons sound better than they read — but no matter what I said, she kept insisting. So, finally, just to keep the line moving, I said to her, "Well, maybe I'll publish them posthumously." And with a gleam in her eye, she replied, "Oh great! I hope it's real soon!"

I have now changed my mind. Perhaps it is because in the year 2008 we have discovered that what is said from the pulpit can have a dramatic affect on a national election. But more so, the year 2008 marks two milestones in my rabbinic life. In 1968 I received my rabbinic ordination at Yeshiva University and then, after serving congregations in New Bedford, Massachusetts, and Washington, DC, in 1978 I assumed the pulpit of the Beth Tfiloh Congregation in Baltimore, Maryland — and I have been delivering speeches ever since. That has been the easy part! The more difficult part is to get people to listen. Fortunately, I have been blessed with a congregation that has been most receptive to my words. Yet, today my words go way beyond those sitting in the synagogue; by way of the Internet, the words in the Ethics of the Fathers have come true: "What is said here is heard there." "There" has been anywhere and everywhere!

In my sermons I strive to speak about the present condition and what religion has to say about it. As a Modern Orthodox rabbi, I have tried to be both modern and Orthodox, bringing the lessons of the timeless Torah to events and challenges in the twenty-first century. For our well-educated generation, "Revelation" has little meaning, if not combined with relevance.

God has blessed me to be a rabbi at the most exciting and challenging time in the last 2,000 years of the Jewish people. At the same time, as Americans and as citizens of the world, there has never been another period in history when change has come as rapidly and as radically. Religion must speak to the times in which we live. Hillary Clinton told workers at the General Motors plant, "You can choose speeches or solutions." I do not know if my speeches have offered solutions, but I hope they have shed some light on the subject. That is what I think I am supposed to do as the rabbi of a people who are mandated to be "a light unto the nations."

I want to thank Gail Naron Chalew, whose copyediting translated my "Brooklynese" into coherent English; Arlene Abramson, my wonderful and devoted administrative assistant, for putting all my words down on paper for these past many years; Joan Feldman, Beth Tfiloh's Director of Communications and most especially, Lori Bernstein, for making me and this book look good; Melanie Kwestel for spending a weekend dotting my i's and crossing my t's; and Zipora Schorr for not letting this manuscript go to the printer before putting her final touches and corrections into place. I owe a special debt of gratitude to all my congregants for letting me know when they thought I was right, and to my entire family for letting me know when they thought I was wrong! My family is at the very center of my life. To them, I dedicate everything.

I have heard that God wrote a book –
The world;

And He wrote a commentary on the book –
The Torah

Rabbi Zadok HaKohen (Rabinowitz) of Lublin (1823–1900)

Part I:
Responding to Evil:
The Lessons of 9/11

What the World Needs Now, Post 9/11

I wish I was articulate enough to be able to put into words the empty feeling that enveloped all of us as we watched the terrorist attacks on Sept. 11th. If that is difficult for me, just think of my colleague who writes in an e-mail, "I have been running back and forth to two families whose children are missing and presumed dead in the World Trade Center. One was a new bride I married seven months ago. Halachic question: when do I do the funerals? After a body is found? Or, as I suggested, after all hope of recovery is lost, even with no body? Any advice is appreciated."

Who knows what to say? What should a rabbi say in a world where children in Israel go to school wearing bullet-proof vests and children in America go to school worrying whether their parents will come home at night from the office buildings where they work.

So I speak to you about here and there — America and Israel. I want to show you how the two are connected — and yet so different. To do so, I will not only draw on my own thoughts; rather, I base my thoughts on those of three other rabbis — all of whom are gone, but all of whose words live on: a rabbi in Jerusalem, my father, and a "giant" of our people.

There was a famous rabbi and preacher who lived in Israel by the name of Rabbi Sholomo Schwadron, known throughout the Jewish world as the Maggid of Jerusalem, the "speaker, the preacher of Jerusalem." He was a speaker from the old school: full of fire and brimstone, tears and laughter, but mostly stories. The one story with which he is most associated, his classic, is the story of Meirka. One day, Rabbi Schwadron was sitting in his home in Jerusalem when he suddenly heard a passing scream from the alleyway outside his window. In a moment, his wife ran into the house yelling that little Meir, the grandson of the Gabbai of their shul, had fallen and was bleeding profusely from a gash over his eye. The rabbi and his wife ran outside, and the rabbi picked up the child while his wife held a wet towel over the child's cut, trying to control the bleeding. Rabbi Schwadron began running through the alleyway to the main street, rushing as fast as his legs would carry him, to get the child to a doctor.

As they rushed up the hill, a pious, elderly woman was walking toward them, and she called out in Yiddish: "Reb Sholomo — Reb Sholomo — *ess is nit daw vos tzu daigen. Ess is nit daw vos tzu daigen.* There's nothing to worry about. You don't have to rush. *Der Ebeshter vet helfen.* God will take care of him." But, as the rabbi and his wife passed directly in front of this elderly woman, she looked down and realized that the bleeding child was her own grandson. She began to shriek uncontrollably, "Gevalt! Meirka! Meirka! Gevalt!" And she passed out. Rabbi Schwadron transformed that scream of "Meirka" into a catchword lesson. He would say, "If it's not my Meirka, it's easy to say, 'Don't worry, nothing is wrong, God will surely help.' But when it's my Meirka, it's a different story!"

What America confronted on September 11, the State of Israel confronts every day. Israelis have been living in a state of terror for years. But outside of Israel, few seemed to care; few seemed to understand. So much of what happened in America after the attacks of 9/11 brought to mind so much that happens every day in Israel. After the planes crashed into the World Trade Center and the Pentagon, it was hard to use your cell phone because everybody was calling their relatives and friends to make sure everything was okay. That happens every time a car bomb or suicide bomber or drive-by shooting takes place in Israel. The only difference is that Israel is such a small country that when you get through on your phone you discover that if you didn't know the person killed, your next-door neighbor most certainly did! After the twin towers fell, I got a phone call in the middle of the night. It was our friends in Israel making sure that my kids had not been in New York. They are the friends in Israel I call every time a bomb goes off there to make sure their kids were not hurt!

Tragically, on the night of September 11, Americans went to sleep for the first time understanding what everyday life in Israel is like. Suddenly it was our Meirka! Suddenly we understood what it feels like to be transfixed in front of your television, watching scenes of horror and destruction and senseless bloodshed being brought right into your living room. Israelis live with this every day! There is no country in the world that has been forced to confront what Israel confronts.

We, as Americans, have been devastated by the horrifying images brought into our lives from the crash scenes in New York, Pennsylvania, and Washington. In Israel, heart-wrenching, gut-wrenching scenes like these have taken place for years.

Scenes like those of Shalevet Pass. Shalevet was all of ten months old when her mother took her out in her stroller for a walk in Hebron. A Palestinian sniper put Shalevet in the crosshairs of his gun and killed her. Ten months old! They targeted a ten-month-old baby! It's hard to believe someone can hate so much to kill an innocent ten-month-old, but now as Americans we know it is possible. It has happened — to our Meirkas.

Or there is the story of Moti and Tzira Schiyveschuurder. One summer day they went to eat at Jerusalem's popular Sbarro pizzeria when the suicide bomber attacked. He killed Moti and Tzira and three of their children. The other two children were injured. One of them attended the funeral of her parents and siblings in a wheelchair while getting an intravenous drip. We all know how upsetting the horrifying scenes of carnage and destruction in New York and Washington were. Well, forgive me for upsetting you, but I have to describe to you the scene in the Sbarro pizzeria when the suicide bomber struck.

Jack Kelly, a reporter from *USA Today*, was sitting right across the street when that bomb in Sbarro went off. Here's how he described it on the front page of *USA Today*:

The explosion was deafening and sent out a burst of heat that could be felt far down the street. It blew out windows and threw tables and chairs into the air. Victims' arms and legs rained down onto the street. Three men, who had been eating pizza inside, were catapulted out of the chairs they had been sitting on. When they hit the ground, their heads separated from their bodies and rolled down the street. Dozens of men, women and children, their bodies punctured by nails from the bomb, began dropping in pain. One woman had six nails in her neck. Another had a nail in her left eye.

Two men, one with a six-inch piece of glass in his right temple, the other with glass shards in his calf, fell to the ground bleeding. A passerby tried to comfort them, but broke down crying. As he walked away, he tripped on a decapitated body and fell. Next to them, a man groaned in pain, "Help me, I'm dying," he said. His legs had been blown off and blood poured from where his torso had been.

Meanwhile, yards away, a little girl about three years old, her face covered with glass, walked among the bodies calling her mother's name. Seconds later, she found her. The girl told her mother to get up. But the mother, apparently already dead, didn't respond. The girl, still unaware of what had happened, was led away in hysterics by an Israeli policewoman.

Dozens of ambulances arrived over the next thirty minutes to cart off the dead and injured as relatives began arriving. Rabbis, with white gloves, raced around the street picking up pieces of flesh. One rabbi found a small hand splattered against a white Subaru parked outside the restaurant. "It's of a girl," Rabbi Moshe Aaron said. "She was probably 5 or 6, the same age as my daughter." He gently put it into a bag. "I wish I could say there won't be anything like this tragedy again," Rabbi Aaron said. "But it's just a matter of time until another bomber kills more of us. It will be like this until the end of time."

It was right there on the front page of *USA Today*, but nobody around the world wanted to believe these scenes were really happening. Nobody could comprehend that there could be such hatred. Nobody wanted to accept that there are people in this world capable of such cruelty and barbarism. Well, now we know! Our Meirka has been hit.

And in response you did not hear anyone in America calling for "negotiations" with Osama bin-Laden. No one said he should still be considered a "partner-for-peace." No one called for American concessions. No one urged "restraint." Instead the *Washington Post* op-ed page a few days after 9/11 contained articles with these headlines: "We must fight this war," "Destroy the network," "Hidden hand of horror," "American holy war," "To war, not to court," and "End of illusion." That is how Americans rightfully responded when our Meirka was hurt. But when the people of Israel fall victim to terrorism, there are always those around the world who will say, "You've got to sit down and negotiate, you've got to stop the settlements, you've got to pull back the borders, you've got to give up the land, you've got to accept their 'right of return' — then they'll be satisfied! Then they'll make peace!" Well, maybe now the world knows — maybe now it will see things differently.

Did you see those Palestinians dancing in the streets in celebration of the Pentagon and Twin Towers being blown up? That is how they dance every time they kill an Israeli. It was bad enough that the Palestinians killed two Israeli soldiers who made a wrong turn into Ramallah. Did they have also have to lynch them and tear them apart, limb by limb, and then throw them out of a second-floor window, with a crowd cheering them on? Did they have to hold up their blood-stained hands in glee? Bad enough that Palestinians killed fourteen-year-old Koby Mandell and his friend, Yosef Ishran, in Tekoa. But why did the murderers have to mutilate the bodies so badly that they could only be identified through their dental records? And in Egypt, a country with which we are supposed to be at peace and have normal relations, why is the number one hit song entitled "I Hate Israel"? Did the Egyptian press syndicate really have to give its highest honor to Ahmed Ragab, who published a column in the government newspaper *Al Akhbar* entitled "Thanks to Hitler," praising the Nazi extermination of the Jews? How come there is so much unmitigated hatred? This is because of "settlements?" Because we don't give them enough? Forget it! Maybe now the world understands that after Israel exited from Lebanon, after it signed peace treaties with Jordan and Egypt, after it offered to return 99 percent of the Golan Heights to Syria, after having offered a Palestinian state under the leadership of Yasir Arafat that would rule 98 percent of the Palestinian population, after being willing to share parts of Jerusalem — after all this, perhaps now the world understands: THEY STILL HATE OUR GUTS! Rabbi Schwadron was right: when it is your Meirka, you suddenly see things differently. Last week America came to the realization that its fight against terrorism is a battle that Israel has been fighting for a long time now.

Yet, having said all this, I am saddened to say the two situations are different. Here I turn to the wisdom of my father, of blessed memory. There is a famous verse in the Book of Lamentations describing the city of Jerusalem after its destruction: "*Bochah tivkah balailah v'dimata al lechayah ein la menachem mikol ohavehah* — she weepeth sore in the night and her tears are on her cheeks. She hath none to comfort her among all her lovers." Using this biblical verse, my father beautifully described the nature of the real tragedy. It was not simply that the Temple had been destroyed. It was not simply the city's "cries" at night. The real tragedy, the real source of anguish, was that the "tears were left on her cheeks, she had none to comfort her." Bad enough that the Temple was destroyed, with Jerusalem in ruins. Bad enough that the Jewish people were suffering. Yet, even worse was the fact that no one even came to offer a handkerchief to wipe away her tears. No one came to offer any comfort or consolation.

As bad as what the people of Israel have experienced this year, the worst part of it was the world's reaction to it. Look at what happened last week when terrorism hit us here in America. World leaders called with support. NATO offered to go to war. The European Union rallied around us. The UN Security Council immediately and unanimously sided with us. Yasir Arafat gave blood (who would want his blood!) From all over the world came expressions of sympathy, support, compassion, and understanding. But while Israel was under attack by terrorists, what did it get from the world community? You know how many terrorist attacks took place in Israel in 2001? Six thousand! From

Rosh Hashana to Rosh Hashana, 167 Israelis were killed by snipers, bus bombings, and at the hands of suicide bombers. Six hundred Israeli children became orphans. Thousands of Jews, many of them children, were permanently disabled. And the world could not care less. I want to know — WHY?

I prayed so hard for a peace agreement to come out of the Camp David Summit. I was prepared to accept most any and every Israeli concession in order to attain peace. Israel did, in fact, make just about every concession possible, offering the Palestinians a Palestinian state and the return of more than 90 percent of the territories, including parts of the Old City of Jerusalem and partial control of the Temple Mount. Yet, the Palestinians turned it down and made no counter-offer. It was sad; it was terrible. But the one consolation I had was to be able to say to myself that at least now the world knows who is at fault in the Arab/Israeli crisis. President Clinton and all his advisors went publicly on record as saying it was Arafat's fault. At least now, I felt, no matter what happens, the world will stand with Israel, recognizing the difficulty — if not impossibility — of negotiating with the Palestinian Authority. I was wrong! Terribly wrong! The world turned against us once again. The Palestinians reverted to terror and everything Israel did to protect itself was condemned by the Western governments. Blockade their cities? No good! Rubber bullets? No good! Shoot at their snipers? No good! Withhold their taxes? No good! Target their suicide bombers? No good! Seize their properties? No good! Every time Israel responded to a Palestinian attack, Western governments accused Israel's response of being "reprehensible," "excessive," "disproportionate," "provocative," "an escalation," etc., etc. On the same day that there were two car bombings in Jerusalem, Russia criticized Israel for the escalation of Palestinian/Israel violence. Russia annihilates countless Chechnyans, but it criticizes Israel. Britain sent hit teams to Gibraltar to wipe out members of the IRA, but it criticizes Israel. America bombed Qadafi. By mistake, we killed his daughter — yet that did not stop us from criticizing Israel, a country that is so careful and does its best to prevent civilian casualties. You will never read of Israel attacking crowded civilian centers, shopping centers, restaurants, or cafes. Yet, the Palestinians direct their acts to kill and hurt as many people as possible: men, women, children, and babies. And *Israel* is the one to be criticized.

America falls victim to terrorism, and everyone is sympathetic and understands. Israel falls victim to terrorism, and everyone criticizes and condemns her. Can you just imagine, under the circumstances, how Israel has felt this year? "She weepeth sore in the night and her tears are on her cheeks. She hath none to comfort her among all her lovers." The verse in Lamentations concludes so prophetically, "All her friends have dealt treacherously with her. They have become her enemies."

That is what happened to Israel, and I still find it hard to understand why! It was not supposed to be like this. This was supposed to be a "new world" in a new millennium. After the Holocaust, things were supposed to be different. After two thousand years of being called "Christ killers," now we were referred to as "brothers in faith," with a Pope standing at the Western Wall, our holiest shrine, asking our people's forgiveness. This was a different world from the one in which I grew up. As a child, whenever my brothers and I would walk past a church, we would cross the street. There was something very fearful to us when we would see the austere, rigid looking nuns and priests.

Now? A few years ago I was honored by Shaarei Zedek Hospital. Who else was honored that evening? Cardinal William Keeler! That night I told the story about two beggars sitting on a park bench in Mexico City. One is holding a cross and one a Star of David. Both are holding hats to collect contributions. People walk by, lift their noses at the man with the Star of David, and drop money in the hat held by the man with the cross. Soon the hat of the man with the cross is filled, but the hat of the man with the Star of David is still empty. A priest watches and then approaches the men. He turns to the man with the Star of David and says, "Young man, don't you realize that this is a Catholic country? You'll never get any contributions in this country holding a Star of David." The man with the Star of David turns to the man with the cross and says, "Moishe, can you imagine, this guy is trying to tell us how to run our business!"

I used to be afraid of priests, and now I am telling jokes about them to a Cardinal! And he is laughing — and lending his name in support of Shaarei Zedek Hospital. Indeed, it is a new world.

That is what I thought until now. Now I am not so sure. What the state of Israel has experienced, what the Jewish people have undergone, has forced me to stop in my tracks and look once again at a world and wonder: Are you with me or against me? What's your problem? Why am I feeling so insecure once again about you?

When Palestinian negotiators and religious spokespeople proclaim that the Temple never existed in Jerusalem, why hasn't the Christian world cried out? They know the truth! Jerusalem is also part of their history. If the Temple was never in Jerusalem, then where did Jesus walk?

Why did the Pope remain silent when he stood next to Syria's President Assad, who called on Christians and Moslems to join together against the Jews, "who tried to kill the principles of all religions with the same mentality which they betrayed Jesus Christ, and the same way they tried to betray the Prophet Mohammad." The Pope said nothing; the Vatican said nothing. The next day the Pope found his voice. Hearing that a Palestinian child had been killed, the Pope expressed his grief. Yet, when Syria's Minister of Religion tells him, "We must be aware of what the enemies of God and malicious Zionism conspire to commit violence against Christianity and Islam," the Pope says nothing; the Vatican says nothing. Again, nothing! Silence, again!

Do you remember when the Taliban in Afghanistan destroyed some ancient Buddhist sculptures? The Western world cried out in protest, asking how could the Taliban do that to age-old religious symbols. But when the Palestinians destroyed the ancient synagogue in Jericho, no one said a word. For thousands of years, we Jews paused during our High Holidays prayers to reflect on our matriarch Rachel, shedding tears at her burial place for her dispersed children. Now, every day Rachel's Tomb, one of our most sacred shrines, is under attack and gunfire by the Palestinians and no one says a word. Rocks are thrown at worshippers at the Western Wall and not a word — nothing! In Nablus, Joseph's Tomb is overrun and trashed, and the world remains silent.

And I want to know, WHY? Are not Jewish shrines sacred? Is not a Jewish life worth anything? The same day that a Palestinian shot ten-month-old Shalhevet Pass dead, Amnesty International called for observers to protect — the *Palestinians!* Why? I do not know. Is it possible that there is truth to the cartoon that appeared in an Israeli newspaper just two weeks ago showing bin Laden asking Arafat, "How come I get such bad press and you don't? After all, we do the same thing." And Arafat replied, "I make sure to only kill Jews." Is that what it's all about? I don't know! All I know for sure is, "She weepeth sore in the night and her tears are on her cheeks. She hath no one to comfort her among all her lovers."

Here I must say that my anguish over the behavior of the Moslem world for hating us and the Christian world for abandoning us is matched in some ways by my disappointment in the Jewish world. What happened to us? Where were we? Israel is *our* Meirka, our baby. Did we take care of her? Did we feel her pain? As Americans, we are all now ready to battle against terrorism. But as Jews, why did we wait until now? I was in Israel three times this year. There were so few tourists, so few Americans — it was heartbreaking. This summer my brother and sister-in-law went to Israel and stayed at the Sheraton Plaza Hotel in Jerusalem. She walked into the gift shop and saw a silver kiddush cup with eight little cups and she asked the woman in the shop how much it cost. When told $300, my sister-in-law said, "I'll take it." And the woman started to cry. It was her first sale in more than a week. Where were we?

Yet, I am prepared to defend my fellow American Jews. I have to be honest and say that I understand why they have not visited Israel. My family and I have been to Israel twenty-five to thirty times. We have been there during Scud attacks and terrorist bombings and a war in Lebanon, and we know that life in Israel proper goes on as usual — that at 2 o'clock in the morning on a Saturday night the discos are still full, the streets are still packed. But if you have not been there, how can you know that? And how can you go, when you read that your own State Department is telling American officials to be careful, to stay away from crowded places in Israel?

Yes, but then why didn't you take some action here in support of Israel — write a letter to the editor, make a contribution, attend a rally? Israel is under attack every single day, and its people have the indomitable fortitude to stand firm and not to panic. Even more, the people of Israel have the incredible ability to go on doing what they do best. In July 2001, millions of Americans watched a medical miracle broadcast on the *NBC Nightly News*: a nineteen-year-old paraplegic Colorado woman was using her own legs to move again after a car accident last year paralyzed her from the waist down. You know where they performed this groundbreaking surgical procedure? It did not take place at Harvard, or at the Mayo Clinic, or at Johns Hopkins. It took place in Israel, and it was developed by Michael Schwartz, professor of neuroimmunology at the Weitzman Institute of Science. While engulfed by terror attacks, the people of Israel continue to make breakthroughs in technology, science, and medicine. In this difficult, challenging, dangerous year, Israel still managed to resettle 36,500 Jews from the former Soviet Union and more than 3,500 from Ethiopia. The disgusting United Nations meeting in Durban so wanted to brand Israel as being a "racist" state. Yet, no African state, no Arab state, was willing to take in a single Ethiopian, even though these people are suffering from drought and famine! Only Israel took them in!

That is our people — the Jewish people. We are special, and that is why they hate us. But we are not the only ones who are special. The American people are also special, and that is why others hate us. Through the trying and difficult time that Israel lived through this year, sure, America voiced criticism of some Israeli actions. But, at the same time, America was the only country to extend any support or understanding. While everyone else was against Israel, only America stood with the Jewish people. America is not going to always see eye-to-eye with Israel; it hasn't in the past, and it won't in the future. America does have vital interests in the oil-producing Arab world! Yet, the fact is that the American media — with a few ignoble exceptions, like CNN and NPR — are most supportive of Israel. Congress strongly supported Israel, and Vice President Cheney and Secretary of Defense Rumsfeld went on public record as stating that it is understandable why Israel retaliates and defends itself the way it does. Indeed, the President of the United States, George W. Bush, refused to allow Secretary of State Colin Powell to attend the UN conference in South Africa. And when things really got ugly there for Israel, he ordered the American delegation to leave; it was the only country to join Israel in the walkout. You do not have to be a Republican to love George Bush for that action! If that is not enough, Mr. Bush, to his everlasting credit, still refuses to meet with Yasir Arafat — the only world leader willing to take such a stand.

And America is hated for these actions! Not just by our enemies, but by many of our so-called friends. Because the United States refuses to pressure Israel, the Foreign Minister of France accused the U.S. and President Bush of acting like "Pontius Pilate," washing our hands of the blood being shed in the Middle East. It was a shameful comment by that French "diplomat," but one that should come as no surprise. I was in France this past June. It was just after President Bush had visited Europe, and the French press, like much of the press throughout Europe, was critical of him and filled with anti-Americanism. They hate America because they envy America. There is no country as free, as successful, as the United States. This year, France was bumped from fifth place among the world's economies. You know who bumped it? California! California is a bigger economic power than France, which so wants to consider itself a superpower. It was no accident that the terrorists chose the Pentagon and World Trade Center as their target. These places represent the power of America: the Pentagon, our military power, and the twin towers, our economic power. How many countries have a 110-story World Trade Center — in fact, have two World Trade Centers dotting their skyline? And they hate us for that!

Similarly, it was no accident that the suicide bomber chose the Sbarro pizzeria in the heart of Jerusalem as his target. Anybody who has been on that street corner in Jerusalem knows that it symbolizes why Israel is head and shoulders above the other Middle Eastern countries and why it is hated so much. The corner of Neviim and Yaffo Streets where Sbarro's is located is the Times Square of Israel. You stand at that corner and you see Israel in all its excitement and diversity: the hustle and bustle of citizens with their different colors, different nationalities, and different backgrounds. And yet, the Israelis are the only ones in the entire Middle East who elect their own government. The other Middle Eastern countries still run themselves like banana republics. And that is why they hate us. They hate us because Israel does have a Sbarro pizzeria and a Home Depot and an Internet and a high-tech society that has brought Israel into the 21st century, while all of her Arab neighbors are still closed and backward in their thinking. In Egypt, they arrest homosexuals. In Sudan, they murder Christians. In

Saudi Arabia, women cannot drive a car. In Lebanon, Palestinians are not allowed to own land.

America is a beacon of modernity, liberty, and freedom throughout the world, and Israel is a beacon of modernity, liberty and freedom throughout the Middle East, and that is why we are both hated. But there is a big difference! America is the world's greatest democracy, whereas Israel is the world's smallest democracy. America is a mighty country with unlimited strength and resources; it is surrounded by Canada and Mexico — real friends and partners. Israel is not so blessed. Its resources are limited, and Israel is surrounded by neighbors still sworn to its destruction. For no one else is Israel their Meirka. Only for us Jews.

Make no mistake about it — not all Muslims are suicide bombers. Not all Germans were Nazis. Not all Christians consider us "Christ killers." There are good and bad among all people. Yet, ultimately, history has shown us time and time again that we Jews have got to take care of our own. Yes, we have our friends, most certainly here in the United States. "God bless America, land that I love!" At the same time, I have to accept the fact — we have to accept the fact — that while there are *some* in this world who would like to see the fall of "Satan America," *many* in the world would see the destruction of Israel as the solution to a problem. We are simply in the way and do not fit in. There are those who claim that Israel is responsible for the difficulty America is facing in creating a stronger coalition with Moslem countries in the war against terrorism. Yet, that is the way it has always been for our people. We are *always* in the way! We were in the way of the Babylonians and the Assyrians and the Romans. We were in the way of the early Christians and Mohammad and the early Moslems as well. In Europe, we were in the way of the French and the Germans, of the Fascists and the Communists. And eventually, Hitler rose to the challenge and proceeded quite methodically to eliminate this universal inconvenience.

So let all the Arabs and Palestinians remember, as Hirsch Goodman put it in the *Jerusalem Report*:

People smarter, more efficient, better equipped and more dedicated than them failed to destroy the Jewish people. And if the Germans couldn't do it, then the Palestinians are never going to be able to do it. Let the Palestinians see where the Jews were five short decades ago and think about where we are today. Let it sink into their heads — and into the head of every other Palestinian and Arab and Ayatollah and Hamas leader and neo-Nazi. They ripped the gold from our teeth and yet we've built a world-leading high-tech country. They can say we went like lambs to the slaughter, but now we have a country of our own that is a nuclear superpower. If Auschwitz couldn't destroy us, they never will. And the sooner they, and others, realize it, the better off the whole world will be.

Similarly, here in America, let the word go out to all those who hate us and seek to see us fall. We have been down before. Remember when Russia put up Sputnik? Remember when we used helicopters to flee from Saigon? Remember when Japan and Germany were producing the most advanced cars and cameras? Remember? Remember what people said? "America has lost it!" "America is not what it used to be! Others will soon surpass it." Remember what we did? We did what Americans do best. We picked ourselves up by our bootstraps and put American ingenuity to work. And now we are the only superpower in the world. You can bend us, but you will never break us! You can call us the "Great Satan," but we know that we are the greatest country on the face of the globe. Nobody has done what we — the American people — have done. As a Canadian television commentator, Gordon Sinclair, once put it,

It is time to speak up for the Americans as the most generous and possibly the least appreciated people on all the earth. Germany, Japan and, to a lesser extent, Britain and Italy, were lifted out of the debris of war by the Americans who poured in billions of dollars and forgave other billions in debts.... When France was in danger of collapse in 1956, it was Americans who propped it up and their reward was to be insulted and swindled on the streets of Paris.... When earthquakes hit distant cities, it is the United States that hurries in to help. This spring 59 American communities were flattened by tornadoes — nobody helped. The Marshall Plan and the Truman Policy pumped billions of dollars into discouraged countries.... I can name you 500 times when the Americans raced to the help of other people in trouble. Can you name even one time when someone else raced to the Americans in trouble? ... Stand proud, America. Wear it proudly.

We can stand proud as Americans! The day after the bombing of the Pentagon and World Trade Center, the Sbarro pizzeria in Jerusalem reopened. Israel rebuilt from its ashes, and America will do the same. But for now, where do we — as Americans and as Jews — go from here? We go to the wisdom of Rabbi Akiva, the great sage of the Mishna and Talmud. What Rabbi Akiva taught more than anything else was hope and love. Rabbi Akiva was an eternal optimist. When others cried when they saw wolves prowling the ruins of the Second Temple, Akiva was able to find in this scene a message of hope. When everybody else saw nothing but destruction and gloom, only Rabbi Akiva saw the arrival of the Messiah in Bar-Kochba, despite the iron hand of the Romans. Only Rabbi Akiva could begin to study Torah at age forty and become a Torah giant, because he believed. It was, of course, Rabbi Akiva who taught that you must love your neighbor as yourself, because hope and optimism have their roots in love. We are a loving people. Even when we struggle against a horrible enemy, we do not bomb their pizzerias, nor do we spray gunfire into their nursery schools. We do not preach hatred nor teach that heavenly rewards await the suicide bomber who kills as many Jews as possible. We are, thank God, a people of love.

Yes, we Jews *are* a people of love. And so are we Americans. There have been so many heartbreaking stories in newspapers and on television of people who lost relatives and friends on 9/11. One of the many that brought me to tears was the story of Howard Lutnick, the chairman and chief executive of Cantor Fitzgerald, a little-known firm but one of the more important ones in America's financial community. Cantor Fitzgerald has 2,300 employees worldwide. About one thousand worked at the company's headquarters on the 101st, 103rd, 104th, and 105th floors of One World Trade Center, the first tower hit in the attack. Of the 1,000 workers who were at work that morning, nearly 700 are still unaccounted for. Howard Lutnick, the chairman of the company, has lost nearly 700 of his employees, one of whom was his brother.

I watched this powerful executive crying his heart out on television, and I cried with him. I love my brothers so much that I could so feel his pain. He went on to tell how more than two hundred of his employees who had not been in their offices on that fateful day came to work two days later at a nearby hotel. That is the spirit of America! Mr. Lutnick addressed them. He did not call for vengeance. He did not cry out in anger. Rather, he said he would do everything humanly possible to make sure that the families of those who had died would always be provided for. *That's* the love of America. And then, he told his employees to go home. He said, "In the scheme of things, your jobs are not what's important. What's important is what you have at home. Go home and hug your children and your loved ones." That is the love of America. And that is what we, as Americans and as Jews, must do. We may never be able to change those "out there" who hate us, but we can most certainly draw closer to those closer to home who love us. Hug your children and spouses. Say thanks next time you see a policeman or fireman. In a world filled with so much hatred, we as individuals must show that we live by the words of the song, "What the world needs now is love, sweet love."

Stand proud with America, and purchase an Israel Bond to let the people of Israel know that you stand with them as well. These *are* historic times we are living through. These are challenging times — but we will rise to the challenge; as Americans and as Jews, here and there. And we, American Jews, are doubly blessed: blessed to be a part of a great country and blessed to be a part of a great people. By holding firm, by staying true to our democratic principles and values, by exhibiting "love, sweet love," both America and Israel will continue to be a blessing for all humankind.

Rosh Hashana, September 17, 2001

FUHGEDDABOUDIT!

I know you are going to find this hard to believe, but there are some people here in Baltimore who think that I speak with an accent! They don't actually tell me that, but I can sense it when I see the little smile that breaks out on their face when I say words like "chawklit" (chocolate). I don't know what their problem is!

But this I do know: the birthplace of my "perceived" accent has been the focus of the world's attention ever since that fateful September 11th day. New York is "ground zero." While all America — all the world — has been horrified by the destruction of the twin towers of the World Trade Center, no place is the devastation more keenly felt than in New York itself, where so many lives have been lost, so many businesses crushed, so many people affected. The whole country has stood in amazement at the ability of New Yorkers to cope and carry on, despite the disruptions in transportation, in communication, and in most every area of life. That ability comes as no surprise to me. New Yorkers have always been able to cope because they know a word that comes from New York and can best be expressed with a New York accent. It's a word central to our Day of Atonement. A word crucial for everyone to know in confronting life and all its challenges. A word that runs counter to where many people put their emphasis these days.

But first, a story and then a few questions. The story: there were these two elderly people living in Florida. He was a widower and she was a widow. They had known each other for a number of years. Now, one evening there was a community supper in the big activity center. These two were sitting at the same table, across from one another. As the meal went on, he made a few admiring glances at her and finally gathered up his courage to ask her, "Will you marry me?" After about six seconds of "careful consideration," she answered, "Yes. Yes, I will."

The meal ended, and with a few more pleasant exchanges, they went to their respective homes. Next morning, he was troubled: "Did she say 'yes' or did she say 'no'?" He could not remember. Try as he would, he just could not recall. With trepidation, he went to the phone and called her.

First, he explained to her that he didn't remember things as well as he used to. Then he reviewed the lovely evening past. As he gained a little more courage, he then inquired of her, "When I asked if you would marry me, did you say 'yes' or did you say 'no'?"

He was delighted to hear her say, "Why, I said, 'Yes, yes I will,' and I meant it with all my heart." Then she continued, "And I am so glad that you called, because I couldn't remember who had asked me!"

Now, let me ask you a couple of questions. Do you sometimes find yourself standing before the open refrigerator just staring inside, wondering what it was you were looking for in the first place? Or have you ever heard a voice answer the other end of the telephone and you have forgotten whom you called? Do you increasingly have trouble remembering where you put your keys or your glasses? Has any of this happened to you? Well, if you are younger than forty, you might not know what I am talking about. But just you wait! You'll find out! We have a nice name for this: it is called having a "senior moment." But it is no joke! When it happens, as it inevitably does, something inside of us starts to wonder: is this a warning sign that I am on my way to having Alzheimer's disease, and even if not, is it going to get much worse as I get older?

Preserving our memory has become a major issue in the 21st century; in fact it is now a multi-billion dollar industry. Bookstores bulge with memory improvement guides; perhaps the most interesting one I saw advertised is entitled *How You Too Can Develop A Razor Sharp Mind and A Steel Trap Memory, and Perhaps Even Improve Your Sex Life and Extend Your Days!* All for $29.95! (I would tell you how to get it, but I forgot where I saw the advertisement!) Wherever we look, improving your memory is Topic A. The Web is filled with memory sites. Numerous hospitals and private therapists teach memory courses. Health food stores sell over-the-counter products to improve your memory— products like ginkgo. Taking it may increase the risk of internal bleeding, but at least you will remember what caused the major surgery you are about to undergo!

Certainly, the Jewish tradition understands the importance of remembering. What better example can I give you than to simply point out that one of the names for Rosh Hashana is *Yom Ha-Zikaron* — the Day of Remembrance. God remembers. And so must we! What happened on September 11th in the year 2001 — and those who perpetrated such a dastardly act — must never be forgotten! We are told in the Torah, *"Zachor et asher assah lecha Amalek . . . lo tishkach* — Remember what Amalek did to you — don't forget!" As a nation we are warned to never forget those who sought our destruction: whether it is the Jewish people's "Remember Amalek," or the American people's "Remember Pearl Harbor," or in our day, remembering September 11th. These memories must be permanently etched into our consciousness, for as the philosopher George Santayana taught, "Those who forget the lessons of history are condemned to repeat them."

Yet, I tell you that there are times in life when forgetting is absolutely crucial for our well-being, when forgetting is considered a blessing from God. Nobody knows this better than New Yorkers.

Long before September 11th, living in New York was not easy. Life there is a constant challenge. You are packed together like sardines on the trains, with people bumping into you. You find yourself, at times, stepping over people sleeping on the street. You have to encounter panhandlers and constantly be on the lookout because people do not always curb their dogs. Your taxi drivers do not speak English. Other drivers think their car is a Sherman tank. So watch out! Living in New York sometimes feels as if there are daily assaults on your personal dignity and divine image. And yet, in recent years New York has blossomed, the crime rate is down, and its economy is up! And some of that is the result, in part, of New Yorkers having developed the ability to confront all of the assaults on their dignity by echoing one word. The word is spelled: F-U-H-G-E-D-D-A-B-O-U-D-I-T, and it's pronounced *Forget about it!*

Sure, there are some things that we must always remember! That is the message of Rosh Hashana, Yom Hazikaron — the Day of Remembrance. Amalek, Pearl Harbor, September 11th — we must always remember. But there are also things that we must forget. That is the purpose of Yom Kippur — a day of forgiveness, a day of reconciliation. Yom Kippur is not a day of dealing with international conflicts. It is a day of individual healing. It is the day of dealing with each other, and in dealing with those who are nearest and dearest to us, the ability to say FUHGEDDABOUDIT becomes an absolute necessity. In dealing with the pain others have caused us, FUHGEDDABOUDIT does not mean that one totally forgets, that one must develop amnesia. What it means is that happiness can only come if we are able to work through our anger and frustration and put them aside. It can only come when we do not allow personal slights and hurts to become the center of our existence, to dominate our thoughts.

So many heartbreaking stories have come out of the terror catastrophe of September 11th. Let me share one that I read in the *Washington Post*: Candy Glazer tells how early that morning, her husband had called her from Boston's Logan Airport to let her know that he had arrived in time to catch his American Airlines flight — the flight that ended up crashing into the World Trade Center. Dazed and numb, at the end of that horrible day, Cathy finally dozed off in her bed. At two o'clock in the morning, her four-year-old son, Nathan, came in and jumped on his father's side of the bed. She had not told him anything yet about what had happened, but then she said, "Honey, Daddy's been in an accident." Nathan looked at her and asked, "What do you mean?" And she said, "Daddy's dead." The boy started sobbing, "Can't we fix him?" he asked.

God, do I wish we could, but it is too late for that. Yet, now that all of us collectively have confronted the frailty of life, I want to make sure that we do everything possible to fix those relations of ours that may be broken, but that *can* still be fixed. To do that, more and more people are going to have to start using this word from the sidewalks of New York: FUHGEDDABOUDIT.

Let me tell you about two people who recently came to my office, but indeed, people like these come to most every rabbi's office.

One of my members comes to ask me if I would please do the funeral for her husband, who has just died. I say, sure, but I would like to first meet with you and your children — when can we get together? And then there is a long silence, and finally she says, "That's not going to be easy." I ask, "Why? Are they out of town?" And she says, "No, they are in town but they haven't spoken to each other in many years. In fact, I'm embarrassed to tell you this rabbi, but they are planning to sit shiva in two different places." "But it's their father," I say. The woman says, "I know, but what can I do? They really despise each other." I then meet with the sons separately. Each tells me he intends to sit in different rows at the funeral and go their separate ways after the service. It is as if an invisible *Mechitsa* — a physical divider — has separated these children from each other for something that was said or done years and years ago.

And then I meet with the divorced mother of an upcoming Bar Mitzvah. She is in tears of anger when she says to me, "I don't want my ex to have an aliyah. He doesn't deserve an honor. He hasn't done right by me all these years, and he left me.. . . I don't want him up there." And she turns to her son and says, "You don't really want your father up there with you, do you?" The boy stares at the floor in my office and then grunts and says, "It doesn't matter to me. I don't care." He cares! Believe me, he cares!

The famous restaurant on top of the World Trade Center was called "Windows on the World." I have come to realize that a rabbi's office is also a window on the world from which I see so many people who are hurt and divided, fighting a never-ending battle — when they would all be so much better off if they could just get themselves to say that one word: FUHGEDDABOUDIT!

Yes, I know that you cannot turn back the clock, you cannot reverse the past, you cannot completely erase from memory. But you can put it aside. You can let go of it. You can forgive. You can seek reconciliation. And we must learn to do this in three crucial areas of our lives.

First, on the Day of Atonement when we ask God to forgive us, we must learn to forgive God. Many of us are angry with God, questioning God. Many more do not believe in God. We speak of God as being just and compassionate and righteous, but many of us see little justice or compassion or righteousness in the hurt and suffering we experience. And it is not only when we collectively witness the utterly senseless and unexplainable deaths of more than 3,000 people in one tragic moment. So many of us experience ill health, business reverses, tormenting family problems, the untimely death of a loved one. "Why, God?" you ask. "Why me? What did I do to deserve this?"

As a rabbi, I say, don't blame God. It's not His fault! Don't blame yourself! It's not your fault! I know that is not what Pat Robertson and Reverend Jerry Falwell would tell you. Those two always have the knack of saying the wrong thing at the wrong time. They reached their pinnacle — or I should say, their low point — when they explained the terrorist attack on the United States as being God's punishment for "the gays and the lesbians . . . the ACLU, People for the American Way — all of whom have tried to secularize America."

Unfortunately, Christians do not have a monopoly on foolishness in some of their religious leaders. A couple of months ago, a terrible tragedy took place in Israel when the Versailles wedding hall in Jerusalem collapsed, causing the death of 23 Israelis, with another 377 injured. It was a horrible tragedy, but let me tell you what made it even more horrible. It was the fact that the rabbi who officiated at the wedding that evening, Rabbi Reuven Levy, told a Jerusalem newspaper that the floor collapsed because mixed dancing was taking place at the wedding, and mixed dancing is a form of sexual immorality that is punishable by death. That was a horrible thing to say!

But then another Israeli rabbi said something even more horrible. The twenty-two teenagers and young adults who were killed by a suicide bomber at the Dolphinarium on a Friday night in Tel Aviv — do you know why they died? He said, because they were out partying when they should have been at home observing the Sabbath.

As if all this was not enough, some weeks later Yitzhak Vaknin, Israel's Deputy Minister of Labor and Social Affairs and a member of the ultra-Orthodox Shas Party, declared that the sex channels now available on cable television systems in Israel were responsible for the high number of car crashes that had taken place in June. Now, even I would have to admit that if you were watching one of these sex channels while driving, it might lead to a car accident. But these people's idea of cause and effect defies understanding! The Versailles wedding hall collapsed because of faulty construction! The twenty-two people and young adults died because of a suicide bomber! Road accidents take place because of reckless drivers! These deaths are not caused by acts of God, and they are not meant as God's punishments for our sins. That is not the way the system operates.

The Talmud makes clear the way the system operates in a famous story about a man who sends his son up a ladder to fetch eggs from a bird's nest. The son climbs up, and in so doing, he is fulfilling two positive commandments from the Torah. He is fulfilling the commandment to honor his father, and in chasing away the mother bird, he is fulfilling the humane mitzvah of "shiluach haken," not taking a mother bird and its baby together. These are two commandments for which the Torah tells us the reward is length of days. But lo and behold, as this child climbed down the ladder, he fell and died. The rabbis tried to explain what went wrong. One says that maybe the story never really happened. Impossible, says a rabbi — he saw it. Well then, maybe, says another rabbi, this child was thinking evil thoughts or even idolatrous ones. No, that cannot be the reason because he was on his way to doing a mitzvah and that would have made him immune from harm. And then along comes Rabbi Eleazar, and he gives the real reason why the child fell. He fell, said Rabbi Eleazar, because it was a rickety ladder. That is why he fell — it was not because of God's punishing the child for anything he had done. It was a rickety ladder!

So, forgive God for creating a world that stands on a rickety ladder, a world filled with malignancies and genetic disorders and drunk drivers and plane crashes and terrorists and so much that is beyond our ability to prevent or even comprehend.

Let me tell you about one person who understands this and lives by it. His name is Matthew Jeffers. He is a student in our day school who spent this entire summer recuperating from surgery on his legs. In a school of more than one thousand students, Matthew stands out because he is a dwarf. This year I was called to his class to listen to Matthew's presentation about himself. And this is what he said:

A Little Bit About Dwarfism

When I was one year old, the doctors told my parents that I had a kind of dwarfism and that I would always be smaller than other people my age. Dwarfism is a word that is used to describe people whose bones do not grow at the same rate as others. It might be hard for you to imagine what it is like being small, so I thought you would like to learn more about it.

There are over 200 types of dwarfism, but I do not fit exactly into any of these types. I have been told that the way I am happens only once in 100,000 births, so that makes me really special. The most important thing to remember is to treat me according to my age and not my size. I am just like the rest of the kids in my class in every other way except I am not as tall.

Sometimes kids want to pick me up, but I do not like that and it could be dangerous. Also, people like to pat me on the head and it makes me feel like I am a furry animal. One of the things I do not like about being a dwarf is having surgeries. I have already had operations on my legs and I know that I will need more.

Another thing that bothers me is that sometimes I have a hard time reaching things that my friends can reach easily. A lot of times people tease me and it hurts me when they do. Also, people who do not know me stare at me like I am from outer space. If you have ever been stared at, you will know it is not very fun and I wish I could say something to them to make them understand who I really am.

I like to be treated like every other kid – I like to do the same kinds of things as other kids. I like basketball, soccer, baseball, music, playing video games, and lots of other things just like my friends. This is the way Hashem made me and I am thankful for so many things. I might be small, but that doesn't stop me from having a great life.

You know what? In my eyes Matthew is a giant! He has lots to complain about and could ask lots of questions of God. Instead, he says, "This is the way Hashem made me and I am thankful for so many things." We can all learn from him. None of us is spared the challenges; life certainly is not easy. Let us forgive God for creating an imperfect world. Let us forgive God for all the unfairness in this world, for the sickness and the accidents and the fact that other people are born luckier and better looking and more talented than we are. It isn't fair and I suspect that God knows that, but we have to learn to forgive Him for creating a world that stands on a rickety ladder.

Reb Levi Yitzchok of Berditchev used to say that the most meaningful prayer and dialogue with God he ever heard came from a poor, simple tailor in his town, who said the following words in front of the Holy Ark before Yom Kippur:

> Dear God, I know that I have sinned in the past year. There were times when I spoke badly of others. There were times when I did not fix and mend a suit or dress as well as I could have. There were times I may have even shortchanged a customer.... I have sinned. But look at what you have done in the past year, dear Lord. You have caused such grief. You have made so many sick. So many became widows and widowers because of you. So many suffered sleepless nights because of your actions. So, I'll make a deal with you, God. You forgive me, and I'll forgive you!

Yes, my friends, on this day as we ask God's forgiveness, let us at the same time forgive God.

The second area of our lives where the ability to forget and forgive is crucially important is in our relationship with others. So many of us have been hurt by the actions of others. We are angry and resentful; how could they do this to me? We carry this deep hurt and resentment in our hearts, in the end hurting no one but ourselves.

To overcome this anger, the first thing we must do is to make sure that we, in fact, are not the guilty party. Do you remember the scene in the movie *Avalon*? There is a Thanksgiving dinner and one of the uncles comes late, and he is the one who traditionally cuts the turkey.

The other family members get tired waiting for him, so someone else finally cuts the turkey. And as soon as he does, the uncle arrives and says, "You cut the turkey without me?" From then on, there is only acrimony. Never again does the family sit down to eat at the same table, never again until death brings them together. But by then it is too late. At the shiva table, they cry for all the meals they could have had together before this one — and all the years they wasted just because somebody cut the turkey too soon.

I know lots of families that have uncles like that; once you cut the turkey before he got there, or once you sat him at the wrong table at a wedding or Bat Mitzvah. And he was never able to see that no one meant him any harm, that no one wanted to wrong him, that it was just one of those things. But he just could not let go of the hurt. To him, everyone was out to get him, when it was only that he was the one who was hurting himself because he was unable to simply say FUHGEDDABOUDIT!

I told this story to a woman who came to my office to complain about her daughter-in-law. She cannot warm up to her, she does not feel that they have much of a relationship, and she tells me, "Rabbi, it all started from the very beginning when she wouldn't call me 'mom.'" I know lots of sons-in-laws and daughters-in-law who cannot get themselves to call their in-laws "mom" or "dad." I know a lot of mothers-in-law and fathers-in-law who are called by their children-in-law "Hi," or "How are you?" The fact of the matter is that "mom" and "dad" are emotionally packed words, and it is hard for some people to say them to anyone who is not their real mother and father. But does it really matter what they call you? What matters is that they call! Our children have enough pressures on their marriages without us imposing our own hang-ups. What do you think I told the woman who complained that her daughter-in-law wouldn't call her "mom?" I told her one word: FUHGEDDABOUDIT!

And so many would be better off if they could utter this word, not just in terms of their sons-in-law and daughters-in-law but also in terms of their own flesh and blood — their own sons and daughters. I know parents who have cut themselves off from their own children. These are parents who are still angry years later over what their children did or did not do that they should have or should not have done. And

I know parents who are on talking terms with their children, but they have a strained relationship. The parents feel the children don't call enough, or they don't visit enough — or some other slight. When they tell me about it, it is always followed by the words, "And after all I've done for him ..." FUHGEDDABOUDIT! How does it go? One parent can take care of ten children, but ten children cannot take care of one parent. That is just the way it is! Forgive your children for not living up to your expectations of them.

Remember, our children are not perfect, but neither are we. Our children are no saints, but let us not blame them for all that might be missing in our relationship. We have to look at ourselves as well and make sure we are not part of the problem, that we are not the guilty party.

I read a cute story on the Internet: David invited his mother over for dinner. During the course of the meal, his mother could not help but notice how pretty David's roommate was. She had long suspected that there was a relationship between the two, and this meal had only made her more curious. Over the course of the evening, while watching the two interact, she started to wonder if there was more between David and his roommate than met the eye. Reading his mom's thoughts, David volunteered, "I know what you must be thinking, but I assure you Rachel and I are just roommates."

About a week later, Rachel came to David saying, "Ever since your mother came to dinner, I haven't been able to find those beautiful silver candlesticks. You don't suppose she took them, do you?" "Well, I doubt it," he responds. "But I'll write her, just to be sure." So he sat down and wrote:

> Dear Mother, I'm not saying that you *did* take the candlesticks from my apartment, but I'm not saying that you *did not* take the candlesticks. But the fact remains that they have been missing ever since you were here for dinner.
>
> Love, David

Several days later, David received a letter from his mother that read:

Dear Son, I'm not saying that you *do* sleep with Rachel, and I'm not saying that you *do not* sleep with Rachel. But the fact remains that if she was sleeping in her own bed, she would have found the candlesticks by now!

Love, Mom

Yes, a lot of times before we accuse others of doing us wrong, we should make sure that we are not the wrongdoers. And if after looking in your heart, you are sure that it is, in fact, the other who has hurt you, scorned you, and disappointed you — it is then that I would tell you: FUHGADDABOUDIT! Get over it and go on, forgiving the one who has hurt you. Not every business partnership can last forever, and not every friendship was meant to be. Not every relationship is cast in stone and can last until eternity. But why not forgive, forget, and go on.

I guess by now you know the one word I told that Bar Mitzvah mother in my office who did not want her ex-husband to have an aliyah. And when I told her that word, she says to me something like this: "He walked out on me. He left me and the kids with nothing. He ruined our lives. And you want me to forget about it? You want me to forgive him for what he did to us?" So I repeated to her the words I read in a book by Rabbi Harold Kushner:

I want you to forgive him, not for what he did to you. Not to approve of what he did, not to condone it, not to excuse it. I want you to forgive him as a way of saying that he has no right to live inside your head anymore than he has a right to live inside your house. A guy who would be that thoughtless and selfish does not deserve the power to mess up your head and dominate your thoughts, and does not deserve the power to define you as a rejected woman. But that's the power you are giving him! He doesn't deserve it!

Forgiveness does not mean pretending everything is fine when you feel it is not. FUHGEDDABOUDIT does not mean it never happened. Forgive and forget have nothing to do with deserving! As someone once pointed out, "The single most important lesson to learn about forgiveness is this: FORGIVENESS IS FOR THE *FORGIVER*, NOT THE

FORGIVEN." In the act of forgiving another, we free *ourselves* from the debilitating effects of chronic anger and resentment. Forgive not because the person who has hurt you deserves to be forgiven. Maybe he does and maybe he does not! But that is not the issue. The person who has hurt you does not deserve the right to continue to hurt you. It is not good for the liver — in both senses of the word!

This is why the cardinal rule of forgiveness is this: no matter what someone else has done to you, the only person hurt by your anger and resentment is you. Life is too short, too precious to waste by simply giving it away to someone who hurt you. FUHGEDDABOUDIT! And if I tell this to a spouse about someone he or she has divorced, how much more so is it necessary to say this word to our husbands and wives to whom we are still married.

I officiated at the wedding of a lovely bride and groom from our synagogue. They had asked, and I had agreed, to let them say a few words to each other during the ceremony. In front of some two hundred family and friends they addressed each other, and it was really beautiful. Each of them had tears in their eyes as they spoke. They spoke with such love, with such happiness that they had each other for the rest of their lives. I have officiated at hundreds of weddings, but for some reason this really moved me — so much so that I found it necessary to stop the ceremony and say these words to everyone who was assembled there: "My friends I want us to pause at this time. All of you who are sitting out there who have husbands and wives — I want you to reflect on the beautiful words and feelings this bride and groom just expressed toward each other. And I want to remind you: there was a time all of you felt that way about each other as well."

Yes, we all start out feeling that way, but as time goes by in our lives, our memory causes us some real problems. You see, doctors and scientists have shown through research that our memory has a tendency to be stronger in remembering bad things that have happened and weaker in remembering the good things. As time goes by, in most every marriage, there are inevitably those bad memories that keep piling up of hurtful words, of disappointments, of anger and anguish. And then, any time and every time something goes wrong, those memories come to the fore and are used as daggers to stab into each other's hearts. That is no way to live! No one can live well with another person if they carry around with them at all times that kind of baggage, ready to dump it on their partner at every opportunity. How much better off we would all be if we could just learn to say that word: FUHGEDDABOUDIT!

I guess you know by now the word I told those two brothers who were going to sit in separate rows at their father's funeral because of some misunderstanding they had had years earlier: FUHGEDDABOUDIT! You are saying good-bye to your father. Do you think he wants to hear it from separate rows? Do you think that is the way he wants to leave this world?

There was a man who lived a long, full life. He was not very wealthy, but he left three successful sons. In his will, he divided his estate equally among the three of them, but he put a certain amount of money aside for each of them to use in a specific way. This is what he wrote in his will:

> Every year on the day of my Yahrzeit, if you will come to shul and say kaddish for me, that would be nice. If you give charity in my memory, that would be okay. But what would be most important for me is, if every year on my Yahrzeit, you use some of this money for the three of you to get together to go out for lunch. Knowing that you are together would be the greatest honor you can ever pay me.

So I tell you, brothers and sisters, husbands and wives, parents and children — if you're on the outs with each other, in these moments before Yizkor, honor those who preceded you by forgiving each other.

And there is one more area in our lives — perhaps the most important area — where we must learn to forgive and forget. And that is in dealing with ourselves. The fact of the matter is that often our greatest hurts and biterest disappointments are self-inflicted. You remember the line from that song from some years ago: "Learning to love yourself is the greatest love of all?" That is true, you know. But many of us just are not able to do that.

Much has been written recently about "survivor's guilt." Amidst the joy and exhilaration expressed by those who were fortunate enough to have survived the attack on the Pentagon and World Trade

Center, many of these survivors are also feeling guilt. "Why did I survive and others die?" "Why didn't I help others out?" "I didn't deserve to survive." While it has been noted that these feelings are common among survivors of the Holocaust and of earthquakes and natural disasters and war and terrorism, from the window of my office I have seen that these feelings are also common among survivors of the natural assaults that life inevitably brings. There are a lot of people who are never satisfied with themselves, who are always trying to live up to the expectations of others, and no matter what these people have done or have not done, they are always haunted by a sense of their own shortcomings. Says Dennis Shulman, a New York psychoanalyst, "From outside these people look anything but fragile. But inside they feel hollow and empty."

I see a lot of people who are like this; on the outside they are strong and successful, but on the inside they feel hollow and empty — never able to forgive themselves for not living up to their expectations of themselves or what others expected of them, always looking back on their failures and flaws. Let me tell you who some of those people are. They are the person you are living with! There are a lot of American homes where the husband thinks he is married to a strong-willed, independent career woman — when, in reality, he is married to a little girl who has her fears of insecurity and inadequacies, who desperately needs some emotional understanding and sensitivity from her husband. There are lots of homes with wives who think they are married to a real macho man — a rugged, know-it-all, high-pressured businessman — who is really a little boy who worries if anybody really cares about what he does and who he is. And who desperately needs some hugging, some words of reassurance, some "Yes, Tattelah, everything's going to be alright." We all, at times, feel inadequate and insecure. How can we not? We live in an age that has been described by one social analyst as the age of "unreasonable expectations." We are taught and implored to expect so much of ourselves that it is almost inevitable that we are going to fall on our faces, ending up thinking little of ourselves. One wrong move, one wrong turn, one wrong decision, one wrong step — and our confidence is shattered, our self-image diminished. All because we cannot forgive ourselves and just say FUHGADDABOUDIT!

God did not create a world of angels, just of human beings with human foibles. All of us have made our mistakes. All of us have our regrets — something we so wish we could undo. All of us have our dark moments that shame us. We should learn from them and correct them. But we must not let them haunt us! At some point, we have to FUHGEDDABOUDIT and move on. Don't let the past warp your future.

I know that, in these moments before Yizkor, many of you carry the guilt expressed in the words, "I should have . . . I could have . . . If only I would have. I should have come to visit more. I could have called more. If only I would have realized." That all might be so, but what purpose does it serve feeling that way now? FUHGEDDABOUDIT. Let it go! Now is as good a time as any to forgive yourself if you were not the perfect child to your parents. And now is as good a time as any to forgive your parents if they were not the perfect mother and father to us.

There are people who are still arguing with their parents, still hungering and longing for their approval for twenty or even thirty years after they are gone. Some of us are angry with parents who are still alive, unable to forgive them for doing something that hurt us. I meet with widows and widowers who are planning to get married. I ask how many people are going to be at the wedding. Often when I ask that question, there is a silence in the room. Finally, one of them tells me, with considerable embarrassment, that his or her children are not coming to the wedding. They tell me that the children are boycotting the wedding because they do not approve of Daddy or Mommy remarrying so soon after the death of their parent. "So soon" may be one year or two years or ten years — it doesn't matter. For these children, for a parent to remarry is an act of betrayal. And for them to attend the wedding is an act of disloyalty.

Forgive your parents for being mortal! Maybe someday you will understand they meant no disrespect to your late mother or father. They loved them too! But maybe someday you will understand what it means to have lonely days and lonely nights and to want companionship.

Even if we are convinced, and properly so, that our parents are the cause of some of our problems to this day, FUHGEDDABOUDIT! They — like us — did the best they could under the circumstances. For the worst criminals, there is a statute of limitations; aren't our parents entitled to some forgiveness?

Let us make this our purpose for the day of atonement, the day of reconciliation, not just for those who are gone but for those people who are part of our lives and are still with us. Let us do it while we can! Mitch Albom, author of the book, *Tuesdays with Morrie*, writes,

> I watched my old college professor, Morrie Schwartz, who was dying from ALS, break into tears when he told me of an old friend with whom he had lost touch. Once they had been so close. But a silly little argument had split them apart. "I found out last year," Morrie said, "that this friend died of cancer." He began to weep openly. "I never had the chance to make it up to him. I never had the chance to say 'I'm sorry.' Why did I let that stupid argument separate us for all these years?" I watched Morrie cry. He could no longer move his arms or legs, he was weeks away from death, but he wept not for his weakened health, but for the missed opportunity. He wept for the days, weeks, and years that he could have spent in loving companionship with a friend, but instead lost to stubbornness. "If there's anyone you care about that you're fighting with now," Morrie told me, "let it go. Say you were wrong — even if you think you're right. Because I promise you, when you get to this point in your life . . ." He nodded to his dying body . . . . "You won't care who was right or wrong. You'll only want to savor every minute you had with them."

I thought of Morrie's words while reading and crying through an article that appeared in the *Sunday New York Times* on the weekend after the terror attack on our country. The article was entitled "Last Words." It was a collection of the last words expressed by some of those who died on September 11th. As you know, many of those on the hijacked airliners and many of those in their offices at the Pentagon and World Trade Center, knowing that they were about to die, spent their final moments on their cell phones or at their computers sending emails with their last words. In these moments before Yizkor we should remember their words:

• The words of 32–year–old Stuart Meltzer, who told his wife, "Honey, something terrible is happening. I don't think I'm gonna make it. I love you. Take care of the children."

• The words of Kenneth Van Auken, from the 102nd floor of the World Trade Center, who called home and left these words on the answering machine to his wife, "I love you. I'm in the World Trade Center and the building was hit by something. I don't know if I'm going to get out, but I love you very much. I hope I'll see you later. Bye."

• The words of Mark Bingham from United Airlines Flight 93, who called his mother and said, "I love you, I love you, I love you."

• The words of 38–year–old Brian Sweeney, a passenger on Flight 175, who left a message for his wife Julie on their answering machine, "Hey, Jules. It's Brian. I'm on a plane and it's hijacked and it doesn't look good. I just wanted to let you know that I love you and I hope to see you again. If I don't, please have fun in life and live your life the best you can. Know that I love you and no matter what, I'll see you again."

• The words of 28–year–old Veronica Bowers, whose mother recalled the conversation in these words, "She called me and said, 'Mommy, the building is on fire. There's smoke coming from the walls. I can't breathe.' The last thing she said was, 'I love you, Mommy. Goodbye."

• And then there are the words of Jeremy Glick, one of the heroes who helped bring down United Flight 93 in the fields of Pennsylvania. His wife described their last conversation in these words, "We said 'I love you' a thousand times, over and over and over again. And it just brought so much peace to us. He said, 'I love Emma' who is our daughter, and to take care of her. And then he said . . . 'whatever decisions you make in your life, I need you to be happy and I will respect any decisions that you make.' His wife added, "I think that gives me the most comfort."

As painful as they are, I repeat these words to you because I want you to go home tonight and call your loved ones and tell them the same words that all these people spoke as their "last words." Because who knows? They just might be our last words! Who knows? Tuesday's *New York Times* told the story of a woman who keeps replaying in her mind the argument she had with her husband on the morning of September 11th. It was a silly spat over where they would meet that evening. Her husband left in a huff without kissing her or saying goodbye. Within hours he was buried in the rubble of the World Trade Center!

This world does stand on a very rickety ladder. Every conversation should be treated as our last words. They should be filled with words of love and words of gratitude and words of encouragement and words of understanding. And these words have to be spoken not only to those who are nearest and dearest to us. They also have to be spoken to those who are distant from us, to those with whom we are on the "outs." Remember the words of Morrie: "If there's anyone you care about that you're fighting with now, let it go. Say you were wrong, even if you think you are right. Because I promise you, when you get to this point in your life . . . you won't care who was right or wrong."

So yes, whether in relation to God, others, or ourselves, let us speak the words that need to be spoken while there is still time. As Rabbi Kushner put it, speak the words of forgiveness, of reconciliation, and accept the fact that in return you might not hear the words you need to hear because the person at the other end of the conversation just doesn't get it — and never will! And that would be too bad. But we cannot control what other people will do. We can only control what we do.

I am so sorry for four-year-old Nathan Glazer, who lost his father on that flight from Boston. I am sorry your daddy's dead — and we cannot fix him! But we *can* fix our relationships with those who are gone. You remember these words from *Tuesdays with Morrie*: "Death ends a life; it doesn't end a relationship." The last words we spoke with our parents and others who are gone have not really been spoken yet. That is what Yizkor is all about. It provides us with the opportunity for one last phone call, one last opportunity to communicate with those who have been taken from us.

In the moments of Yizkor, our challenge is to spell out our appreciation to them, to speak the words now that we may not have been able to speak then. To thank them where they deserve to be thanked and to forgive them where they need to be forgiven, even as we would like to be thanked when we deserve it and forgiven when we ache for forgiveness. Speak the words that need to be said. For every one of us, the words will be different, the memories will be different, but the stories will be similar — bonds of love, bonds of gratitude, tears of understanding that maybe we were not capable of years ago, but that we have learned to shed since.

If we can meet this challenge concerning the people closest to us, the living and the dead, and, indeed, in terms of ourselves; if we can heal old wounds and forgive old hurts, then we will in fact become new people: more open, more loving, and more confident, as we step forward into this New Year.

Yom Kippur, September 27, 2001

WHERE WAS GOD ON SEPTEMBER 11, 2001?

It took place on a Saturday night when ESPN was broadcasting the semi-final game in the Little League World Series, and twelve-year-old Micah Golshirazian was sitting in the dugout as his New England champion team was playing. Micah was sitting on the bench not because he was not good enough to play, but because it was Saturday night — it was still Shabbos — and Micah is Sabbath observant. He could not play until 8:43 that evening. ESPN had a clock counting down the minutes for the national TV audience to watch — and then 8:43 arrived. It was during the fifth inning, and Micah, to the cheers of all the fans, entered the game as a pinch runner. Nice story. A seventh grader at Maimonides Day School in Boston thus sanctified God's name by remaining true to his faith. But then comes the dangerous side of the story. As soon as Micah entered the game as a pinch runner, he was thrown out at second base! "Ha-shofet kol ha-aretz lo yaaseh mishpat? Shall the judge of all the earth not deal justly?" Is there a God in this world? And if there is, then why wasn't Micah safe at second?

Perhaps on no other day of the year is this question more appropriate than Shemini Atzeret. For what is this holiday all about? Unlike most other festivals, it has no special ceremony, nor does this day mark any historic occasion. Shemini Atzeret is a holiday unto itself — independent of Succot and independent in its manner from any other major observance. So why this holiday and why now? Our sages delved into God's psyche, so to speak, and explained this holiday accordingly: for nearly a month now, the Jewish people and God have been drawn together by Rosh Hashana, Yom Kippur, and Succot. Now, when the Jew is about to go back to business as usual, God established one more holiday saying, "*Ikvu imi od yom* — stay with me another day. *Kasheh alay pridatchem* — your parting is difficult for me." It is on this day that God shows His full love for the Jewish people. He loves us so much that He does not want to let go of us. And if that is the case — if God loves us so much — it is only fair to ask, Why does He allow such terrible things to happen to His children? Why did He allow Micah to be thrown out at second? And why does He allow things so much worse than that?

This question is not a new one. It is a question Abraham asked. It is a question Moses asked. It is a question Job asked. Yet, it is a question that has taken on new life in the post-9/11 world.

Where was God on September 11th? How did He allow it to happen? Or as one of our congregants recently wrote me, "I don't understand how we can pray to a merciful, loving God and be intellectually honest. We all want to be children and to have a father in Heaven who loves us and will protect us, but in the face of history and the human condition, how can we put our heart and soul in that belief? Nu? So how do you do it?" This question has been on the minds of many Americans since September 11th. Americans have responded to this question in the way they respond to so many things: they have written books about it! Shortly after 9/11, seven of the ten nonfiction books on the *New York Times* best-seller's list were on the subject of September 11th.

A whole series of books have been written to try and explain where God was on September 11th, and they range from the ridiculous to the sublime. The ridiculous? Father Thomas Keating, the Trappist monk and expert on meditation, in his book explained that watching people jump from the towers — and I quote — "opens up the possibility of a universal experience of the redemptive force of love and transformation." Would someone please tell me what in the world that means?

The sublime? Yittah Halberstam, in her book, *Small Miracles for the Jewish Heart*, tells the story of a small synagogue near the twin towers where many Jews who worked in the towers would gather every morning for Shacharit services. For some reason, on the morning of September 11th, only nine men showed up. And so they waited and waited for a tenth. After a long wait, which meant they would be late for work, someone whom they had never seen before entered the room, saying he came because he had to say kaddish. They invited him to lead the services, and he proved to be a very slow at it, which made things even later — so late that while they were praying, the first plane crashed into the Twin Towers. All those present had the same feeling: were it not for our having to wait for the tenth man and for his having prayed so slowly, it could have been us. They turned to thank this mystery man who had saved their lives, but the story concludes by telling us, "When they turned around to embrace him, the man was gone, his identity forever a mystery."

This story is but one of many that explain God's presence on September 11th as being made manifest in the thousands and thousands of people who survived the collapse of the twin towers. That is where God was! But that explanation lets God off the hook too easily. Elie Weisel, in writing of God, so properly proclaims: "To thank Him for Jerusalem and not question Him for Treblinka is hypocrisy." To say that God was with those who were saved on September 11th but not with those who were killed on September 11th leaves more questions than answers. To say that He was in the room with those ten people who prayed in the minyan while the twin towers were hit, but was not in the room in the minyanim that took place earlier that day defies belief.

So how do we understand it? Well, I am not going to write a book, but I will tell you what it says in *the* Book — in the second sentence of the Book, right after we are told, "In the beginning, God created the heavens and the earth." We are then told, "The earth was unformed and void and darkness was upon the face of the deep . . . *V'ruach Elokim m'rachefet al p'nei hamayim*. And the spirit of God hovered over the face of the waters, the waters which then covered the entire earth" (Genesis 1:2). Our sages were fascinated by the description of God as being *m'rachefet* — "hovering" over the world. What does that mean?

And they found the answer in the one other place in the Torah where that word appears. It apears toward the end of the Torah where we are told, *"K'nesher yair kino al gozalav y'racheyf* — as an eagle arousing its nest, hovering over its young"* (Deuteronomy 32:11). The biblical commentator, Rashi, explains that the eagle "does not press heavily upon its children, but hovers above them — touching them and yet not touching them. So too, the Holy One, Blessed be He" does with His children.

Rashi is telling us that God's involvement with His children is like that of the eagle with its children — "hovering," "touching and not touching." The eagle wants to protect its young so it stays fairly close on top of them. But it is also afraid, because of its great weight, that if it would actually rest on them, it would smother them. It is mother love, but it is careful not to be "smother" love. If you want your children to fly, you have to let them do it on their own — even if they are going to fall to the ground. That is the only way they are going to learn. And if God wanted His children to have free choice — the freedom to eat from the tree or not to eat from the tree — then all He could do with His children was *m'rachefet*: hover. Hover but not smother. Direct, guide, help — but not control.

That is where God was on September 11. At every minyan, at the twin towers, and at every place else on earth — yes, even on a Little League field — "touching and not touching." Does God know everything that we are doing? For sure! It is one of Maimonides' principles of faith that God also knows everything that we are *going* to do. Are there things that we are going to do that He does not like? For sure! Then why doesn't He stop us? Because He is "hovering," allowing us another basic principle of our faith: that every person has the free will to act as he or she chooses. Sure, there are "acts of God," but any time the human element is involved, whether the speed of the running of Micah or the murderous designs of an Osama bin Laden, then, for the most part, God's hands are tied. Or better yet, He ties His own hands.

So what is the good of belief in God? Not that such belief will spare you harm. You can believe all you want, you can be Sabbath observant, come to synagogue every day, live morally, and give charity, but if a Hitler comes along or if a drunk driver crosses your path, tragedy may follow. What belief in God can do is give you the faith and the strength to overcome a tragedy when it hits you, to let you know that you are not alone in this world, that God is hovering over you and loves you.

I know it is not always easy to have this faith. We all see and experience so much pain, grief, loss, and disappointment in our personal lives and in our collective lives. Ultimately the choice is ours — to believe or not to believe. But who is better off? Several months before the twin towers fell, thirteen Israeli soldiers were killed in a battle in a Jenin refugee camp. Two days later there was an article in the *Jerusalem Post* about the funerals that had taken place for these fallen soldiers. These are the exact words in which two of them were described. First there was the story of Gadalyah Malik, all of twenty years old. His father, Simcha Malik, was abroad working for the Jewish Agency when he heard the news of his son's death. He returned for the funeral, and standing in the cemetery ready to say goodbye to his son, he said, "It's not clear that we are parting one from the other. What does that mean? Who understands the way of God? Yesterday when his mother called with the news, she said, 'God gave us a gift and now we have returned it.' Thank you, God, for the gift we received," his father said.

Then came the funeral of Sgt. Major Avner Yaskov, where these words were recorded: "Speaking yesterday at the funeral of her husband at the military cemetery in Beersheva, Penina Yaskov asked God: 'Why did you take him from me? I don't believe in you anymore and I am no longer going to pray to you.'"

Two reactions of families to a similar circumstance: the loss of a loved one taken all too soon. And both reactions are understandable. In confronting death, which is to be our reaction? We can either cry out and curse God for what He has taken from us, or we can bless and thank God for what He gave us. The choice is one that each of us has to make for ourselves. We have to make that choice every time we are about to recite Yizkor, recalling to memory the loved ones taken from us. So many, in confronting the death of a loved one, strike out and complain bitterly and unceasingly about the utter injustice of it all. We are angry with the doctor, we are angry with the patient for not taking care of him- or herself, and we are angry with God. The thought of it all brings tears to our eyes — tears of sorrow.

Yet, there are also tears of joy that are available to us. The joy in recalling what we had for as long as we had it. The joy we feel in thanking God for the blessing that He gave us and for the blessings that have been and shall ever remain.

It is not a matter of what He has done for us; it is a matter of what He means to us and how much we need Him — like a parent, hovering over us. In the words of the prophet, "*K'ish asher imo t'nachamenu kein anochi anachemchem* — as a mother comforts her children, so shall I comfort you, says the Lord. Your sun will set no more, neither will your moon be withdrawn for the Lord will be your enduring light and the days of your mourning will come to an end. He will destroy death forever. The Lord God will wipe away tears from every face" (Isaiah 66:13, 25:8)

Shemini Atzeret, October 9, 2001

Part II:
Intersection of Religion and Politics

Vote Early and Vote Often — And Keep Israel in Mind

Even though it happened many years ago, I remember it like yesterday. It was the first week of November 1980. That Monday, my father, of blessed memory, underwent quadruple bypass surgery. I had come to New York on Sunday to be with him and my mother and brothers. The doctor told us it would be twenty-four hours before we would know if things were okay. Finally, early Tuesday afternoon, the word came: all was well! That day was November 4th, 1980, Election Day, when Ronald Reagan was running against the incumbent Jimmy Carter.

I did not like Jimmy Carter. It ends up that most of America did not like Jimmy Carter as president. But my wife Sherry, she should live and be well, never met a conservative Republican that she liked. My wife is every liberal Democratic candidate's dream. So I called her that day and said, "Sherry, look I feel bad that I'm not home and I can't vote. But you know I would vote for Reagan, as I know you would vote for Carter. Do me a favor and don't vote this year. That way, it will be a wash, and I can stay here with my father in New York." And Sherry, in her sweet, charming manner said to me, "FUHGEDDABOUDIT! I'm a citizen of the United States; it's my obligation as a citizen to vote and I am going to vote." I then told Sherry how impressed I was with her sense of patriotism (or something to that effect), and we hung up. And I took a Metroliner home so that I could vote.

That incident still remains part of our family lore; it is just another example of how Sherry and I see eye-to-eye on every subject! Yet, the fact is, in a sense, she was right. As citizens of the United States, we are not only privileged to vote; I believe we are *obligated* to vote. The 2000 election showed how every single vote counts! Your vote may choose the next president!

When Abraham pleads with God to save the city of Sodom, he says, "*Ulai yesh chamishim tzadikim b'toch ha-ir* — perhaps there are fifty righteous people in the city." The question then arises: had there been fifty righteous people in the city, would not Abraham had known them? Wouldn't Abraham have heard of them? Fifty righteous people in a city like Sodom — surely a man the stature of Abraham should have known them.

The answer to this question was given by the Chassidic master, Reb Simcha Bunim who said, "Perhaps there were fifty righteous people, but they weren't '*b'toch ha-ir'* — they weren't in the midst of the city." They were not involved in making the city a better place to live. They were never heard from. Such a city was worthy of destruction. We — the good citizens of Maryland — have an obligation to be "*b'toch ha-ir* — in the midst of the city." We have an obligation to have our voices heard. In a democracy, the way for your voice to be heard is through the ballot box.

As Americans, we are obligated to vote because the American voting record brings shame to our country. On the average, fewer than half of the citizens of the United States vote in a presidential election, as opposed to the voter turnout in countries like Germany and Israel, which is as high as 80 to 90 percent. In the 2000 election, only 51 percent of the eligible voters voted. In the 2002 election, that figure was only 37 percent! America has one of the lowest voting percentages of any democracy in the world. We, members of the greatest democracy who are supposed to be a shining example to others, do not even exercise the most basic and fundamental right that a democracy brings — the right to choose who will lead our country. While in previous elections that has been a disgrace, in the next presidential election it can prove to be extremely dangerous.

Our country — our world — is involved in a war on terrorism. One of the most important ways we have of fighting terrorism is to make sure that the dictatorial countries that breed these terrorists turn democratic; to make sure that people in the Middle East feel that they have a say in their government and need not resort to terrorism to bring about change in their lives. We also believe — with good reason — that democratic countries do not go to war against their neighbors. We have good reason to believe that because the record speaks for itself. Look at the world in which we live: Canada and America do not go to war, and France and Germany no longer go to war. The threats of war come not from democracies but from an Iran and a North Korea, and they used to come from a Libya and an Iraq. So you tell me, How can we encourage others to turn to democracy when we, as shown by our voting record, do not exercise our own democratic privilege? Democracy has its faults, but as Thomas Jefferson said, "Democracy is the worst form of government except for all others that preceded it."

We as Jews must vote for several reasons. First, we must vote because I believe that Jewish law obligates us to vote. You know the "Prayer for the Government" we recite every Shabbos at our services? We recite that not because it is a nice thing to do or not because it is the patriotic thing to do. We recite that prayer because it is the Jewish thing to do! We are told to do it! Right there in the Ethics of the Fathers we are taught,"*Hevay mitpallel b'shlomo shel malchut* — pray for the welfare of the government." We Jews have a concept, "*dina d'malchutah dina*" — the law of the land is the law. We are obligated as Jews to support the government of the country in which we live. Support of the government is made manifest by our vote.

We Jews have an obligation to vote in this year's presidential election for yet another reason. We have an obligation to vote because the lives of millions of Jews might be at stake. I specifically refer to the Jews living in Israel. Now, I know a lot of people have a problem with what I just said. The *Baltimore Jewish Times* quoted one rabbi as saying, "All presidents since 1948 have been supportive of Israel." So it really does not matter who is elected and therefore we should "leave Israeli politics to Israel and vote for what's best for America." I disagree with just about every word in that statement. On its simplest level, those words could be used to make an argument that American Jews should not spend their money purchasing Israel Bonds — they should only be purchasing U.S. Savings Bonds. On another level, the words can be taken to mean that what is in the best interest of America is not necessarily in the best interests of Israel. I do not believe that is true!

What I do believe is that those who say that American Jews as Americans should not place too much emphasis on a candidate's position on Israel are going against everything that Jewish tradition teaches and that a Jewish heart should feel. Ever since our first Babylonian exile in 586 BCE, when Jews started living in a Diaspora, ongoing physical, financial, spiritual, and political forms of support have come from diverse Jewish communities throughout the world to help the people in Israel. Without that support, whether it was in the time of Mordechai and Esther, or the Rothschild family, or Theodore Herzl, there might never have been a reborn state of Israel.

I am concerned when many American Jews seem to place greater importance on most any and every issue than on Israel. According to a poll of American Jews, when asked, "Which two of the following issues/areas would be most important to you in deciding how to vote for a candidate for president," Israel was mentioned by 15 percent of the respondents, while 19 percent said Social Security and Medicare, and 42 percent said the economy and jobs. I am afraid that many Jews have come to think that placing Israel on the top of our priorities makes us too narrow- minded, too parochial in our interests. I disagree!

And I think most Americans disagree with that perspective. During the 2000 election campaign, *Time* magazine had an interview with Sumner Redstone, the American media giant and chairman and CEO of Viacom. When asked about politics, he said, "There has been comment upon my contribution to Democrats like Sen. Kerry. Sen. Kerry is a good man. I've known him for many years. But it happens that I vote for Viacom.... Viacom is my life and I do believe that a Republican administration is better for media companies than a Democratic one." So, Sumner Redstone chooses his president based on his position regarding Viacom. Many Roman Catholics choose a president based on the candidate's position regarding abortion. Many Hispanics do it on the basis of issues of immigration and Cuba. AARP, of which I am now a full-fledged member, sends out information limited to the candidate's positions on drugs and Medicare and Social Security.

So, what is wrong with me, as a Jew, making a candidate's position on Israel central to my vote? Many will be voting on the basis of Iraq. Iraq — yes; Israel — no? Many vote on the basis of the economy. Well, I am one of those who does not mind paying taxes. They are a small price to pay for living in the greatest country on earth. As for the economy itself, during the course of my lifetime it made no difference who was president — my lifestyle did not change one iota. Yet, if something were to happen to Israel, I would never be the same. When I wake up early in the morning, the first news I look for is not in regard to the ozone layer, and not in regard to the Dow-Jones average, and not in regard to employment, and not in regard to gay marriage. It is in regard to the war on terrorism and the war that Israel is fighting. To me, the two go hand in hand, because Israel is on the frontline of the war on terrorism.

Even if it were not, Israel would still play a central role in my voting decision. I do not want to be guilty of the same mistake our forefather, Abraham, made that could have led to the end of the Jewish people. It took place when God told Abraham to sacrifice his son Isaac. Suddenly Abraham's two loves are in conflict. Abraham loves God, and he loves his son. Yet, Abraham immediately decided that he must slaughter his son. Why? Why didn't he argue with God the same way he argued with God when God was about to destroy the city of Sodon? He certainly had a good argument; he could have said to God, "You promised that I'll be the father of a great nation. How can you now ask me to slaughter my only son?" But Abraham remained silent. I guess he felt that he had no choice. After all, as against an individual son who is only a tiny speck of humanity, he had to, by necessity, prefer God who is universal and all-embracing. His son was a private interest, his own flesh and blood. Abraham must have thought that he had no choice but to prefer God who is the totality of all nature.

Abraham thought he had chosen wisely, but God did not! God tells Abraham, "Do not touch the lad." God is telling Abraham that He may be greater and more universal, but that does not necessarily mean that you have to suppress a father's natural love for his child. Quite the contrary, because of your great love for God, your love for those near and dear to you should be even greater. Taking care of your own is the means by which one achieves the deepest love of God. Love of individuals is the anchor from which one searches to discover and fulfill even more universal loves.

My love for Israel is not in conflict or at the expense of my love for America. Those words from the *Baltimore Jewish Times* — "We should leave Israeli politics to Israel and vote for what's best for America" — are extremely dangerous and downright destructive. They lead to the conclusion that America and Israel's interests are not the same, when in fact our own government says they are! Israel — the only democracy in the Middle East — is the only guaranteed ally of the United States in that explosive region. America, for all practical purposes, is Israel's only trusted ally in the entire world. My concern about Israel does not come at the expense of my concern for America. In supporting Israel, America tells the whole world that we are a principled country; we do what is right, not necessarily what is popular. The fact is that I love America more and more because of its support for Israel. America's support for Israel does not make our country loved throughout the world. It could easily sell Israel down the tubes, just as the European countries are prepared to do. Yet, America has not done that. Because of that support, Israel can stand up to a hostile world surrounded by treacherous enemies and still feel safe and secure.

In the coming weeks, months, and years, Israel is facing challenges that can very much threaten its survival. Sure, the whole world is concerned about that bomb, but it is only against Israel that Iran has threatened to use it. And what if Israel decides to destroy Iran's nuclear capacity as it had done in Iraq? How will the world react? That we know! How will the United States react? We have no way of knowing for sure. But who will be president then will certainly make a difference.

America — whether it be led by a Republican or a Democrat — supports Israel. Yet, that does not mean that it makes no difference who the president is. In 1973, when Israel's very survival was at stake during the Yom Kippur war, Richard Nixon — no great friend of the Jews — approved a massive airlift of arms to help save the beleaguered Israel. If George McGovern had been president, would he have done the same? I don't know, but I am glad we did not have to find out!

Similarly, in 1991, George W. Bush pounded on his podium at a White House press conference, complaining about the strength of the Jewish lobby on Capitol Hill. On another occasion he reminded his critics that the U.S. gives "Israel the equivalent of $1000 for every Israeli citizen," a remark that many took as an allusion to the stereotype of Jews as money obsessed and greedy. Had Michael Dukakis been president, would he have reacted the same way? I do not know, but I would have liked to have found out!

Sure, it makes a difference who is president! Which candidate is better for Israel? There is really no way of knowing for sure. One really never knows. In the 2000 election I can tell you that I voted for Gore and Lieberman. I certainly felt that they would be better for Israel. I was sure that Bush — as a Bush — would be a disaster for Israel. I was wrong! Each of us must make the best choice that we can and hope for the best.

Israel should play a central role in an American Jew's presidential choice. No, it is not the only issue, for there are many issues to be taken into consideration. But let all of us as Americans vote for what's in America's best interests. For Sumner Redstone that relates to Viacom; for me, that relates to Israel.

America's support for Israel is in America's best interests. That is not my opinion; that is God's opinion! It is right there in the Torah when God first appears to Abraham and tells him, "*V'avorcha m'vorechacha u'm-kallelcha a-or* — those who bless you, I will bless and those who curse you, I will curse" (Genesis 12:3). The friends of the Jewish people are blessed by God. And in this world, the Jews have no better friend than the United States.

"*Havey mitpallel b'shlomo shel malchut* — let us pray for the welfare of our government," and let our prayers be manifested by our ballots. As Americans and as Jews, keep in mind what they used to say in Chicago: "Vote early and vote often!"

October 30, 2004

PESACH, POLITICAL CORRECTNESS, AND THE "PEACEFUL RELIGION"

Most everyone knows that the word "Pesach" means "to pass over." As the Torah tells us, God intended to destroy the first born of the Egyptians; the Jews are then to slaughter a lamb and place its blood on their doorposts: "*u'fasachta aleichem*, And I will pass over you . . . when I strike in the land of Egypt." Yet, there is another meaning of this word "Pesach," a meaning that takes on deep significance in our day and age. For we are living in the day of Political Correctness.

For a New Yorker to be "politically correct" means not to call your mother "Bubba!" But for most Americans, it means much more than that. Political correctness dictates that you must be careful of every word that you say to make sure nobody is being offended. So our whole lexicon has evolved. You do not say, "housewife"; instead you say "domestic engineer." You do not call someone "poor"; you say he is "economically unprepared." You do not label a child "learning disabled"; instead you say, she possesses "self-paced cognitive ability." It is no longer a "slum"; it is now an "economic oppression zone." You do not say someone is "lazy"; instead he is "motivationally deficient." No person is "overweight"; he is just "gravitationally challenged."

All this is innocent enough, but at times this need to be politically correct can be extremely harmful and may inhibit someone from telling the truth, from telling it like it is.

President George Bush knows exactly what I mean. When he referred to the countries of Iran, Iraq, and North Korea as being an "axis of evil," his words were immediately denounced. The French Foreign Minister called them "simplistic." The European Union's External Relations Commissioner called the phrase "deeply unhelpful." Past President Jimmy Carter said it would take years to undo the harm caused by that phrase.

Of course, none of his critics could question the validity of Mr. Bush's assertion. Everyone knew that Iraq had gassed and tortured its own people. Everyone knew that North Korea is allowing its people to starve while spending a fortune building and selling ballistic missiles and other highly dangerous weapons to countries like Iran. And everyone knew that Iran was suppressing its moderates and building a nuclear reactor while exporting its revolution and funding and supplying terrorists throughout the Middle East.

No, it was not that what President Bush said was not true; his mistake was that he was not politically correct. His mistake was that he told the truth in the most certain terms. And that is not acceptable in our day and age — a day and age where terrorists have to be called "activists" so we should not be seen as being judgmental of their actions.

The fact of the matter is that political correctness can be downright dangerous! During a visit to France in 2002, Israel's Foreign Minister, Shimon Peres, told reporters, "I am certain that France is not anti-Semitic neither historically nor currently," and he went on to say, "I am convinced the French leadership is staging a serious and determined battle against anti-Semitism in France." He said this on the very same day that the *New York Times* had a long article describing the rise of anti-Semitic incidents in France and how the government is denying that there is any problem.

In his desire to be politically correct and not ruffle the feathers of French officials, Mr. Peres turned a blind eye to dark periods of French history. Theodore Herzl wrote that his Zionist dream was conceived when he saw the depth of anti-Semitism at the trial of Captain Alfred Dreyfus. No history of anti-Semitism in France? Tell that to Dreyfus. Tell that to the thousands of Jews who lost their lives because the

French Vichy government collaborated with the Nazis during World War II. Tell that to the Jews living in France today when every Jewish building in Paris requires protection and every Jewish gathering is a cause for concern. France, which is home to the third largest Jewish community outside of Israel, suffers from the highest level of anti-Jewish violence of any Western nation. But in Mr. Peres's desire to be politically correct — to not offend his hosts — he forfeited the freedom that was his as the then-Foreign Minister of the State of Israel.

For what, in fact, does it mean to be "free" from the Jewish perspective? The answer is found in the Pesach experience. We are told that when the Jews left the land of Egypt, they first encamped in a place called *Pi ha-chirot* — the literal translation of which is "Mouth of Freedom." It is so called because this is where the opening occurred — the beginning — of the freedom for the Jewish people. Yet, our biblical commentators give us a deeper insight into the name of this location, *Pi ha-chirot*. According to many biblical commentators, *Pi ha-chirot* was originally named "Pitom," the location where the Jews were first enslaved. Remember the Bible tells us, "Therefore the Egyptians set over the Jews taskmasters to afflict them with their burden.... *Vayiven orai miskenot l'Pharaoh et Pitom v'et Ramses* — and they built for Pharaoh the cities of Pitom and Ramses" (Exodus 1:11).

The Jews' enslavement began in Pitom, a name our sages read as being made up of two Hebrew words — *Peh satom* — meaning "their mouths were closed." When we speak of the place where our enslavement started, we do not focus on the physical labor our people suffered, but on the place where *peh satom*, our mouths were closed. The Jews lost their right to express their feelings. They could no longer speak up for themselves and for their rights. It was only 200 years later, after the exodus, that the very same spot was renamed "*Pi ha-chirot* — mouth of freedom," for once again the Jews were able to open their mouths in freedom and speak out as Jews.

So what does it mean to be free from a Jewish perspective? It means the most basic of all freedoms — freedom of speech. It means that you must be able to speak out for your rights; it means that no one can force you to be politically correct. You must tell it like it is and not feel inhibited because of the way others may hear it.

Do you know who understands this concept?   Reverend Pat Robertson! Rev. Robertson is frequently found to be suffering from "foot in mouth" disease. He always seems to be getting into trouble for the things he says, and often his words are worthy of condemnation. Rarely do I have a chance to defend the words of Rev. Robertson, so let me not pass up this opportunity. Mr. Robertson came under attack for his recent statement that Islam is not a peaceful religion. The criticism of his words was best summed up in an editorial of the *Washington Post* entitled "Mr. Robertson's Incitement."   The editorial asked, "Is Mr. Robertson trying to start a pogrom?" And it went on to accuse him of using his "national television platform to incite hatred."

Is it true that Islam is not a peaceful religion? No. Yet, it certainly is not 100 percent true to proclaim, as President Bush did, that Islam *is* a peaceful religion. President Bush's words may have been politically correct — but they were not factually correct! There is in Islam a deep thread of intolerance toward unbelievers. The fact of the matter is that Islam divides the world into two regions: *Dar Al Harb*, the "House of War" containing all territories ruled by non-Muslims, and *Dar Al Islam*, the "House of Islam," which is destined to dominate the former. Historian Paul Johnson points out that the word "Islam" does not mean "peace," but "submission." Johnson calls Islam "an imperialist religion." If he can say this, why can't Pat Robertson?

Bernard Lewis, the great scholar of Islam, writes,

> There is something in the religious culture of Islam which inspired in even the humblest peasant or peddler a dignity and a courtesy toward others, never exceeding and rarely equaled in other civilizations. And yet in moments of upheaval and disruption, when deeper passions are stirred, this dignity and courtesy toward others can give way to an explosive mixture of rage and hatred which impels even the government of an ancient and civilized country — even the spokesman of a great spiritual and ethical religion — to espouse kidnapping and assassinations and try to find in the life of their prophet approval and indeed, precedent for such actions.

If Bernard Lewis can write that, then what is wrong with what Pat Robertson had to say? Other than it not being politically correct!

Let the record speak for itself. Under the banner of Islam we have gone from the assassination of Anwar Sadat to the fatwa against Salman Rushdie to the terrorism of bin Laden to the destruction of ancient Buddhist statutes to the persecution of women by the Taliban to the World Trade Center massacre to suicide bombers — and through it all, Muslim leaders have for the most part remained silent. Islam is a peaceful religion? Tell that to Chanah Nechmad. The Nechmads are a religious family living in Rishon Litzion. They had decided to spend last Shabbos in the ultra-Orthodox Beit Yisrael neighborhood in Jerusalem — the neighborhood where, as the Shabbos ebbed, a suicide bomber walked directly toward a group of women standing with their baby carriages and blew himself up. The next day Chanah Nechmad stood in the cemetery and watched the caskets go into the ground — the caskets of her son and her daughter-in-law and five of her grandchildren. One after another, the seven members of her family were buried in the cemetery, victims of a suicide bomber whose religion promises him a reward for his action of seventy-two virgins in Paradise.

I have some bad news for that suicide bomber. First, I read that modern scholars question whether the passage in the Koran about virgins really means that. The Arabic word there is "hur," which some translate as "virgin," but others say really means "raisins." That is what the suicide bomber is going to get! Not virgins — but raisins! Let me tell you something else. Only in Islam is there the belief that the suicide bomber is going to Paradise. Most every other religion would agree that he would be going to the hell he deserves.

The *Washington Post*, in its editorial criticizing Rev. Robertson, wrote, "There are Muslims who justify violence with reference to their religion. There are Jews and Christians who do the same." That is a nice politically correct statement that does not offend one religion at the expense of others, that makes all religions in equal possession of virtues and faults. Yet, the fact is that the statement is an outrageous lie! I will leave it to a priest or minister to defend his religion, but speaking on behalf of the Jewish people, let me say that I know of no Jew who allows his children to strap on explosives to murder civilians. I know of no Jew who would slit the throat and cut off the head of a Daniel Pearl, as the Muslim extremists did. Contrast the picture of what took place in the West Bank and in Jerusalem after the suicide bombing of Chanah Nechmad's family. In Ramallah, the home of Yasir Arafat, Palestinians cheered in the streets, calling for more blood. And in the streets of Beit Yisrael? It was right there in the *New York Times* — a headline read, "For Israelis New Tragedy Is A Challenge Sent by God."

Sure, we have had our religious extremists — our Meir Kahanes and Yigal Amirs and Boruch Goldsteins — but they were a handful and they were condemned by the broadest spectrum of the Jewish world. In the Muslim world, tens of millions of children are sitting in Islamic schools being taught hatred of the Western world, denial of the Holocaust, and the importance of Jihad — of holy war — and genocide of the Jews. Much of this education is paid for by the Saudi government, the "defenders of the faith."

To say all this may not be politically correct, but sad to say it is all true. And if we want to be a free people, we have to act as free people do; that is, to have the courage of our convictions, to tell it like it is, to stand up for truth. Whether it is anti-Semitism in France or Islamic terrorism worldwide, it will not stop as long as the many good people — Jews, Christians, and Muslims as well — sit back and remain silent. We must raise our voices, as Americans and as Jews. We must do it for our sake — and for theirs as well.

Let us remember the other definition of the word "Pesach." The Kabbalists note that it is a contraction of two words — *peh* and *sach* — which mean "a mouth that speaks." That is what freedom means. Let us as Americans and as Jews never be reluctant to speak the truth. For, in speaking the truth, we will be doing our share — more than our share — for the cause of freedom around the world, but most especially in the two countries we cherish. Where? The concluding words of each country's national anthem tell it all: " in the land of the free and the home of the brave" and *"l'hiyot am chofshi b'artzeinu b'eretz tzion v'Yerushalayim* — to be a free people in our land, in the land of Zion and Jerusalem."

Pesach, March 9, 2002

Money

Let's talk about money. The truth of the matter is that it is highly unlikely that one would ever hear a priest begin a sermon with those words. It was Jesus who taught in the New Testament that the chances of a wealthy person getting into heaven were like that of a camel passing through the eye of a needle. In the church the religious leader takes a vow of poverty. No religious leader in Judaism takes such a vow. God forbid! It might work out that way, but not as a religious requirement. And certainly not for me, thanks to you. No, there is a vastly different attitude within Christianity and Judaism when it comes to money. Perhaps this difference is best expressed in the sign hanging over a Jewish-owned bank that reads, "Jesus saves — Moses invests!"

In the eyes of the world, Jews have always been associated with money — usually in a negative sense. Many languages have their own disparaging slurs associating Jews with money:

• In Spanish, it is said, "A real Jew will get gold out of straw."

• The Polish expression is, "Bargain like a Jew but pay like a Christian."

• For the Hungarians it is, "Money is the God of the Jews."

• Our good old friends, the Germans, say, "The interest rate of a Jew and the price of a prostitute are both very high."

• In America they are kinder; Americans just talk of "Jewing you down."

Many of these statements are based on envy, with history showing that down through the ages our people have had a higher rate of financial success than most other ethnic groups. Credit for this, to some degree, must be given to both the Jewish and Christian traditions. The Jewish tradition of teaching children Talmud at an early age made things like interest rates and futures and options and stocks more than abstract concepts. The intellectual discipline of studying Talmud helped them understand such complex abstractions. As for the Christian contribution to our financial success, in the Middle Ages, the Jews were forbidden by the Church to own land, so they were forced to turn to moneylending to survive. Since the Jews were damned and money was damned, the Church concluded that a marriage of the two was entirely fitting and appropriate. With Jews being denied entry by the Church into guilds, there was little else for our people to do but become doctors or lawyers and, for the brilliant ones, to become rabbis!

So our association with money goes way back in time. This is nothing to be ashamed of, particularly when we recall that twenty-one Jews have been winners of the Nobel Prize in Economics. We are 0.25 percent of the world's population, but we have won 41 percent of the world's Nobel Prizes in Economics!

I gave lots of thought to money when I was invited to be part of a rabbinic delegation to France in March 2003. At the time, I asked myself this question: Should I use my money now to buy a ticket on Air France to travel to Paris? I asked the question as an American and as a Jew. As an American, we had not simply witnessed France recently undermining all of our efforts at the United Nations to disarm Iraq, but we had seen France do it with a certain glee. Of course, there are many countries who opposed our efforts, but somehow we as Americans expected something a little different from France. After all, there are many American imports in France. I saw them in one of my unforgettable moments overseas — when I traveled to Normandy and saw the American cemetery there, with its seemingly endless lines of crosses and Jewish stars on the graves of American soldiers who had fallen on D-Day and thereafter in the battle to liberate France. France has a short memory, indeed! One suspects that as a declining world power, France will do whatever it can to assert itself. And who better to do it to than to America? After all, in 2002, the year before France opposed the efforts to disarm Iraq, it was bumped from fifth place among the world's economies. And do you know who bumped it? California! California is a bigger economic power than France, which so wants to consider itself a superpower.

But we Jews have even bigger problems with France. There was a time not so long ago when France was Israel's largest arms supplier. Indeed, it was France that made it possible for Israel to have a nuclear reactor. But then Israel did something horrible in French eyes: it won the Six-Day War. When Israel's very existence was at risk, Charles DeGaulle slapped an arms embargo on Israel that is still in place and proclaimed the Jews to be an "elite people, sure of themselves and domineering." Things have gone downhill ever since, with France siding with the Palestinians, releasing terrorists, and having a foreign policy hostile to Israel while playing up to its Arab oil interests.

But nothing prepared us for what we had seen in France in recent years. There has been an outbreak of anti-Semitism on the streets and in the media of France unlike anything seen since the Dreyfus Affair — all of which had led the American Jewish Congress last year to publish a series of advertisements suggesting that American tourists "consider not visiting France."

And so, I asked, as an American and as a Jew, at this point in time, should I spend my money on a visit to Paris? I decided to do so, but I went to France not *despite* the anti-Semitism in that country, but *because* of the anti-Semitism in that country. I was going as part of a delegation of rabbis sponsored by the North American Boards of Rabbis and the World Jewish Congress to meet with the leadership of the European Catholic Church; this meeting was hosted by Paris's Cardinal Jean-Marie Lustiger, one of the world's leading Catholic leaders and a born Jew himself. We met with the Cardinal and other church leaders to discuss possibilities for joint efforts at reconciliation and stemming the tide of anti-Semitism in France and throughout Europe. So yes,

I was going to France, but because my trip was sponsored by those Jewish organizations, I was not paying for it out of my own pocket.

But what about everyone else? As Americans and Jews, how should we be spending our money these days — should we be visiting countries with anti-American and anti-Israeli positions and sentiments? For us as Jews, that is not an easy question to answer because if we only go to countries that support Israel, we will soon find ourselves asking how many times can we visit Mauritania!

But the question runs deeper. So many European businesses, industries, and universities are calling for boycotts of Israel. Some universities have fired Israeli teachers and refused to be involved in any research with Israeli institutions. At one point the European Parliament called for a suspension of trade agreements with Israel. For a while, even Britain's famous Harrods had removed Israeli goods from the shelves.

How are we as Jews to react to these boycotts? If the Europeans are using their dollars to hurt Israel, what should our reaction be?

An answer can be found in the Torah portion of *Ki Tisa*. In the description of the commandment to give toward the building of the Temple, our sages noted something that caught their eye. In the verse containing this commandment, God says, "*Zeh nitnu* — this they shall give. Everyone that passes among them that are numbered half a shekel after the shekel of the sanctuary" (Exodus 30:13). Why the emphasis on God saying, "*this* they shall give"? Our sages explained this phrase by noting that God showed Moses the actual coin because he did not fully understand this commandment.

In his book, *Understanding Judaism*, Rabbi Benjamin Blech explains just what was so difficult about this commandment that it defied Moses' understanding. What caused confusion in Moses' mind? Explains Rabbi Blech, what Moses could not grasp is that for the construction of the sanctuary itself, God commanded something as seemingly secular as a half-shekel. How could money be introduced into the holy sanctuary? Says the Medrash, "God then showed him the shekel — a coin of fire." What does the Medrash mean by "a coin of fire?" And why then did Moses understand the commandment?

Because God was telling Moses that fire is to be the symbol of money. Fire destroys, but it also creates. Fire may burn, but it can also warm and serve the most beneficial purposes. So, too, can money! Precisely because it has this quality of being both destructive and beneficial, it becomes doubly holy. When we choose to use a potentially destructive object in a positive and productive manner, we have learned the secret of true holiness. Yes, money is like fire; many people get burned and destroyed by it. But money is also like fire in the sense that it can be used creatively and serve a positive purpose.

We as Americans and as Jews have the opportunity these days to use our money for a positive purpose — to use it to make statements that will resonate. I do not like advocating boycotts because they can be a double-edged sword and have been used enough times in the past to hurt the Jewish people. Yet, I do think that we should "consider" not traveling to France or other countries that have turned on us, unless it is absolutely necessary that we do so. We can decide not to purchase goods from countries whose foreign policies we do not like. We can stop buying Norwegian salmon and Danish herring and Belgian chocolates and French champagne — our great-grandparents lived all their lives without these foods — and so can we.

Our money can make an important statement not only in what we *do not* buy but also in what we *do* buy. Do you know who Jeffrey Swartz is? He is the president and CEO of the Timberland Company — a $1.1 billion footwear, apparel, and accessory company. Timberland operates six stores in Israel; their Jerusalem store had to close due to poor sales, but Swartz wants to see more stores open there. When asked if his Board of Directors might have a problem with his strong support for Israel, he responded, "Sure. But I owe this to my children, to my family, to you and to the nation of Israel." He went on to say, "The Godfather was wrong when he said, 'This is nothing personal, it's just business.' This is deeply personal." So, next time you are looking for boots or other apparel, a good place to spend your money would be at Timberland.

And if you want to smell good and look good, try some Estee Lauder products, which is the parent company of Presciptives, Mac, Bobby Brown, Aramis, Aveeda, and Bumble & Bumble. Do you know that the Estee Lauder Corp. is being boycotted by a loud and ambitious campaign waged by the world's Arab and Muslim communities because of the strong support for Israel of its president, Ronald Lauder? Lauder has helped, through his financial support, revitalize Jewish communities in Eastern Europe. He has served as president of the Conference of Presidents of Major Jewish organizations and has been a strong voice of support for Israel. He pays a price for that in business lost in Arab countries. Think about that the next time you walk past an Estee Lauder counter. Remember, money is like fire: it can burn, but it can also warm and create — and make you look and smell good as well!

And then there is Leslie Wexner. Wexner is the owner of The Limited, and his company also includes Express, Bath & Body Works, Henri Bendel, and Victoria's Secret. He has been listed among Forbes' wealthiest Americans, and he has used his wealth for good. In Columbus, Ohio where he lives, he is among the major supporters of the Jewish Federation, the Jewish Student Center at Ohio State University, the Jewish nursing home, the Columbus Torah Academy, the Columbus Jewish Day School, the JCC, and a variety of local synagogues and other Jewish organizations. On a national level, he has created a series of programs designed to enhance the quality of Jewish leadership among communal professionals, volunteer leaders, and Israeli public officials. Some of our synagogue's leaders are graduates of Wexner programs. He has used his money for us, so why don't we do the same for him? So I appeal to all the men in our synagogue this morning: the next time you have a chance, go to Victoria's Secret and get a little something nice for your beloved. And when she asks you why you did it, just tell her: the rabbi made me do it! Remember in doing all this we are not only supporting our supporters but we are also supporting the American economy.

And let me add that it is not just the Swartzs, Wexners, and Lauders who deserve our support. Thank God, our people have lots of friends who are not Jewish. Right here in our community, many of the major banks have purchased millions of dollars worth of Israel Bonds to put into their investment portfolios. And in case you have not noticed, the CEOs of these banks have names that sound nothing like Swartz or Cohen or Goldberg. But they have made good names for themselves in investing in our people. And yes, "Moses invests," and we — his people — should know where to put our money as well.

Before the beginning of every new month, we recite a prayer in which we make all sorts of requests from God: for a long life, a good life, a peaceful life. In the blessing we also ask God for a life that will be blessed with *"osher v'kavod* — wealth and honor." The fire of the shekel reminds us that money can burn, yes. But it can be used most creatively if our wealth — our *osher* — is connected with *kavod* — honor. Wealth is honorable if it is earned with honor and if it is spent with honor. Let us as Americans and as Jews do just that. Then we can hope for the fulfillment of the concluding words of our monthly prayer: we will be blessed with a *"chayim sh'yemaleh mishalot libeinu l'tovah"* — a life in which all the desires in our heart will be fulfilled for good

March 1, 2003

CHANUKAH WITH A BUSH

There is no way of knowing for sure, and I was not present to be able to testify to it, but I have reason to believe that I know exactly what George and Laura Bush said to each other when they woke up on Monday, December 10, 2007. One, I am sure, turned to the other and said, "Oh God, what are we going to wear? What are we going to serve? The Wohlbergs are coming to dinner tonight!"

On December 10, 2007 – the seventh night of Chanukah – Sherry and I were invited to the White House for the President's annual Chanukah party. Abe Foxman, from the Anti-Defamation League, was there, syndicated columnist and media personality Dennis Prager was there, Malcolm Hoenlein from the Conference of Presidents of Major Jewish Organizations was there, Senator and Mrs. Joseph Lieberman were there – and the Wohlbergs were there! It was quite an evening being in the White House with the President and his wife having the Chanukah menorah lit by the parents of Daniel Pearl. And then the hundreds of invited guests were served a massive buffet dinner – strictly kosher – of lamb chops, roast beef, chicken, and, of course, jelly doughnuts!

As I was roaming through the historic rooms of the White House, I could not help but think of the two or three people who had told me that they would not have accepted the invitation because of the disaster George Bush had been as president. I thought back to when I entered the rabbinate as a rabbi in New Bedford, Massachusetts. It was a small congregation that met in a renovated house, and there was a huge Conservative synagogue in the community. I used to deliver sermons then about the "edifice complex" — how unimportant size was when it came to synagogues and how obsessed American Jews had become with the money they put into their synagogue buildings. Of course, as soon as I became rabbi of Beth Tfiloh, I started singing a different tune! So, yes, I understood that those who told me they would not have accepted the invitation had, in fact, not received an invitation.

But I did receive one — and I had accepted. Do you know why I accepted the invitation? Not simply because I have not seen George Bush in the negative light that many others have. I accepted the invitation because I had *received* the invitation! For centuries, when a Jew was asked to appear before the leader of the town, or village, or city, or the government, the Jew immediately had to make sure all of his affairs were in order because he knew he had no choice but to go. And he did not know if he ever would return. Here we live in such a great country that when the President of the United States invited me to his Chanukah party — just imagine the President has a Chanukah party! — the only choice I confronted was what tie to wear!

And what does the President of the United States do at a Chanukah party in his home? You are going to find this hard to believe, but he stands in line for what had to be at least two hours to pose for a photo with each and every person who was invited to the party! To make matters even more surprising, his wife Laura stands with him for all the pictures. To make matters even worse, we were told that during this holiday season President and Mrs. Bush did that on twenty-four different occasions for parties that took place at the White House. That is some job he has! Under those circumstances, would you want to be President of the United States? Would you want to be married to the President of the United States? In fact, when Sherry and I were introduced to the Bushes, the first thing I said to Mrs. Bush was, "I'm sure you're going to miss doing this when your husband is out of office." She laughed!

And what did I say to the President? First, I told him he had a pretty nice house! Then, I told the President that I believed that he would always have a special place in the annals of our people for the support he has provided to the state of Israel. And then I recited a blessing: "*Boruch attah Hashem Elokeinu melech ha-olam she-chalak mikvodo l'vasar v'dam* — Blessed art Thou, O Lord, our God, King of the Universe, who has given a portion of His honor to human beings." That is the blessing that Jewish tradition has one recite when meeting a ruler. I had recited it once before when I met the Pope. Jewish tradition expects, indeed commands, that we extend respect to a leader, irrespective of what kind of leader he may be. This is the basis for the "Prayer for the Government" we recite every Sabbath in the synagogue. The Jews of Austria prayed for the welfare of Franz Joseph; the Jews in Russia prayed for the sake of the Czar, just as we pray for the welfare of the president of our country. This prayer is always recited standing as a sign of respect — not so much for the *person* as much as for the *position*. The moment someone becomes a leader, that individual is no longer a private person but now represents an entire nation, and his or her honor is the nation's honor.

This tradition has one of its roots in the Torah in that famous confrontation between Aaron, Moses, and Pharaoh, King of Egypt. Aaron and Moses tell Pharaoh, "Let my people go." Pharaoh then asks, "Who is this God that I have to listen to?" (Exodus 5:2). And they respond, "The God of the Hebrews appeared to us. Let us please now go for a three-day journey in the wilderness and we shall sacrifice to the Lord our God, lest He encounter us with the plague or the sword." What does this mean: "lest He encounter us with the plague or the sword?" If you do not let us go, Pharaoh, God is going to encounter the *Jews* with a plague or a sword? The biblical commentator, Rashi, points out that, no, it was not the Jews who were going to be so afflicted; it was Pharaoh. In Rashi's words, "They should have said to him, "lest he encounter YOU — God is going to afflict YOU — *elah sh'cholku kavod l'malchut.*— they accorded honor to royalty." We learn from this that you do not go around threatening royalty; you do not go around being disrespectful to the leader of a country, even if he is as wicked as Pharaoh.

I tell you all this because I find disturbing the trend in our country to ridicule and belittle not only the President of the United States, but all those who are running for office as well. There is a way to express one's disagreement; there is a way to point out the flaws in others. But it should be done in a respectful manner because we are talking about leaders of our country.

I find disturbing the way our leaders are referred to. I am not simply talking about the Rush Limbaughs who make a living out of being disrespectful. I am talking about a person like Maureen Dowd. Maureen Dowd writes a column on the op-ed page of the *New York Times*. The *New York Times* prides itself on being what its motto proclaims: "All the news that's fit to print." However, I am not sure that Maureen Dowd's habit of referring to leaders of our country by nicknames is really fit to print: Rumsfeld becomes "Rummy," Gingrich becomes "Newt," Wolfowitz is called "Wolfie," the former President Bush is referred to as "Poppy," and this one is "W." I have been reading the *New York Times* for a long time. I remember when they had giants writing on their editorial pages: people like James Reston and Abe Rosenthal and William Safire and Arthur Sulzberger. They took the leaders of our country to task, but it was always done with a certain respect for the office.

Believe me, this has nothing to do with defending the honor of President Bush. The same is true in speaking of Hillary Clinton. What did this woman ever do that evokes such spiteful, hateful comments, references, and innuendoes? She has served as a Senator of the United States while being a devoted mother and daughter and having to live with quite a *tzatzka* for a husband! One does not have to agree with any of her policies to respect her as a person. If we were commanded to show respect to the leader of a country that enslaved us, then what should we say in regard to the leaders of this great country of ours? And great it is!

Let me tell you a little something about the country in which we live. What is the one thing that we Jews have always been accused of? It was put into writing in the fraudulent *Protocols of the Elders of Zion*, but it has been part of the belief of anti-Semites since time immemorial. It is the accusation that Jews are trying to control the world's economy, that Jews control the banks, that Jews only care about money. Yet, who did George Bush appoint to head the World Bank? A man by the name of Robert Zoellick — a Jew. Who did he choose to replace him? Paul Wolfowitz — a Jew. Who did the President of the United States appoint to head the Federal Reserve? Ben Bernanke — a Jew. And who did he replace? Alan Greenspan — a Jew. The four most significant and important appointments in regard to money and finances have been made to Jews. In some ways the major control of the American economy and the world's economy has been put into the hands of Jews. Did you know that? Did you hear any complaints in our country regarding these appointments? Were there any editorials or outcries or protests that Jews are taking over the world? Did the President have to stop and pause for a second and say, I better not appoint another Jew? No, he went ahead and appointed as the new Attorney General another Jew. And except for some lunatic fringe Web sites, nobody seems to see anything unusual about these appointments. That is America — the land of the free and the home of the brave!

Jeff Jacoby, the syndicated columnist for the *Boston Globe*, was one of those who had been invited, and was present, at the White House Chanukah party this year. These are some of the words he used in a column to describe his feelings:

On the night of Chanukah in 1944 my father was in Auschwitz. He had been deported with his family to the Nazi extermination camp eight months earlier; by Chanukah, only my father was still alive. That year, he kindled no Chanukah lights. In Auschwitz, where anything and everything was punishable by death, any Jew caught practicing his religion could expect to be sent to the gas chambers or shot on the spot. So, I strolled about the White House last week gazing at the portraits of past presidents and first ladies and listening to the Marine Band play "I Have a Little Dreidel." By the light of the White House menorah, I thought about my father and about the unimaginable distance from the hell he knew in 1944 to the place of joy and warmth where I found myself standing in 2007. I was overcome with a feeling of gratitude so intense that for a moment I was too choked up to speak. To be an American and a Jew is truly to be doubly blessed.

Celebrating Chanukah at the White House really was something special, and because of it, it is with a special feeling that every Shabbos I recite the "Prayer for the Government," which includes these words: "Bless thou the constituted officers of government in this land. Set in their hearts a spirit of wisdom and understanding to uphold peace and freedom."

December 29, 2007

THE WOHLBERG PEACE PLAN

Everyone thinks they know the key to ending the Arab/Israeli conflict. There have been UN resolutions, the Road Map, the Saudi Peace Plan, the Geneva Accords, etc., etc. Nothing seems to work, so it is now time for all the parties involved to consider the Wohlberg Solution. And here it is: the conflict in the Middle East can be resolved if all the countries involved come to better understand the true meaning of our synagogue's name. First, let's begin at the very beginning.

With so much blood having been shed in the Middle East, it might be helpful for us to study the root cause of the first bloodshed in history. Right at the very beginning of the Torah, we are told, "And Cain said to his brother Abel . . . and when they were in the field, Cain set upon his brother Abel and killed him" (Genesis 4:8). At the dawn of creation blood is being shed. And it is brother against brother, and no one is even sure why one kills the other. Did you notice in that verse — "And Cain said to his brother Abel . . . and when they were in the field Cain set upon his brother Abel and killed him" — the Torah never tells us what Cain said to his brother Abel. The Torah never tells us what was the root cause of their conflict.

Yes, the Torah does not tell us this important information. But our sages made many attempts to fill in the gap, and the reasons that they offered for what happened then are just as relevant now.

According to Rabbi Yehuda, "The argument was over the first Eve." They fought over their mother! They both wanted to reproduce with their mother! According to Rabbi Yehuda, the cause of the first conflict in history was a sexual one. Hello, Sigmund Freud, who saw so much conflict in our time as having a sexual connotation. Perhaps had he known of the words of Rabbi Yehuda, he might have named his famous complex the "Cain and Abel complex," and none of us ever would have known who Oedipus was.

A second talmudic sage offers a very different explanation for the conflict when he writes, "What was the argument about? They said, let us divide the world. One takes the land and the other takes the movable property. This one said: the land you are standing on is mine. That one said: What you are wearing is mine. One said: strip! The other said: get lost! In consequence, Cain set upon Abel." Hello Karl Marx! It's all economic! What he saw in the twentieth century as the conflict between Communism and capitalism has its roots in the Cain and Abel story. They fought over real estate; they fought over material possessions! That is what brings people into conflict. Or, to put it into the words of the battle cry that brought Bill Clinton to office, "It's the economy, stupid!"

Yet, there is a third opinion expressed in the Midrash that might be the most relevant of all. Said Rabbi Joshua of Sikhnin, "Both of them possessed land and movable property, so what was the dispute about? This one said: the temple will be built on my land. That one said: no, on my land." Talk about contemporary relevance! According to Rabbi Joshua, right at the dawn of creation the first conflict in history is the one we are living through today. Blood was shed back then for the same reason that it is being shed today: to determine who would own the Mount on which the Temple was to be built. After all the other issues in the Middle East today are negotiated, this is the one that seems to defy any resolution: who should control the Temple Mount. Blood is being shed for a patch of land that is considered holy.

The idea sounds so absurd — to kill for a piece of land that is supposed to be holy? Holiness is meant to elevate us human beings, to make us better people. For this you kill? For this you shed blood? It cannot be! And it is not!

There is another story in rabbinic lore regarding where the Temple was to be built. Admiel Kosman, writing in the Haaretz newspaper, pointed out that this second story is also about two brothers and about a dispute regarding a piece of land — but what a difference! The Midrash tells the story of two brothers who worked together on the family farm, tilling the field. One was married and had a large family; the other was single. At the day's end, the brothers shared everything equally — both produce and profit. Then one day the single brother said to himself, "It's not right that we should share equally the produce and profit. I'm alone and my needs are simple." So each night he took a sack of grain from his bin, crept across the field between their houses, and dumped the grain into his brother's bin. Meanwhile, the married brother said to himself, "It's not right that we should share the produce and profit equally. After all, I'm married and I have my wife and children to look after me in years to come. My brother has no one and no one to take care of his future." So each night he took a sack of grain, walked across the field, and dumped it into his single brother's bin. One night, in the darkness, their paths converged. The brothers, each realizing his sibling's noble intentions, fell into each other's arms and burst into tears. And according to the Aggadah, "God desired this place where two brothers thought fine thoughts and performed good deeds. Thus it has been blessed by the people of the world and chosen by the children of Israel to be the home of God."

So there you have it! Here are two stories our rabbis tell about how the land for the Temple was chosen. In both stories the central players are two brothers. In both stories the location is the same. But in the biblical story, they fight over who is to control the Temple Mount. In the rabbinic story, there is no conflict. Quite the contrary — *because* there is no conflict, because there is harmony among brothers, that site in the rabbinic story is considered the proper place for God's Temple.

What a powerful lesson these ancient stories bring to our contemporary condition. Cain and Abel, and so many like them today, consider land holy and are willing to kill for it. But the rabbinic story corrects this mistaken notion. From the perspective of our sages and from the perspective of our tradition, it is not the *land* that is holy – it is *people* who must be holy! The land absorbs its holiness from them.

Ours is a society that puts all the emphasis on the material, not the spiritual. The solution to all problems is found in "things," not in people. If there is violence, ban a gun. If there is promiscuity, hand out a condom. An unwanted pregnancy? Take a pill! Immorality? Hang the Ten Commandments on a classroom wall! All material solutions – though some of them are important and significant. But ultimately, it is *people* who have to change, not *things*.

The conflict in the Middle East will never be resolved if all the peace process does is center on things: on territories, on settlements, on security posts, on borders, on debating which is holier, the Al-Aksa Mosque or the Holy Temple. It is not the "things" that count. It is the people. One of the great rabbinical thinkers and commentators of the twentieth century was Rabbi Meir Simcha Hakohen of Dvinsk. Listen to his words found in his classic biblical commentary, the *Meshech Chochmah*: "Do not imagine that the Temple and Tabernacle are intrinsically holy. Far be it! The Almighty dwells amidst His children and if they transgress His covenant these structures become divested of all their holiness." Those are powerful, all-important words. It is not the Temple, it is not the land – it is the people who bring holiness. Brothers cannot fight over the holiness of the land. Only when brothers act as brothers can a land take on holiness.

I know that I speak from the biased perspective of a rabbi, a Jew, a lover of Zion, but for me – and I believe it should be true for all the world – the facts are there for all to see. In every which way, the people of Israel have tried to change themselves, to reach out to their Arab cousins, to see things from their perspective, to share more of the land with them. The people of Israel have changed their textbooks to include a more positive picture of the Palestinian people. The people of Israel have established countless programs bringing Arabs and Israelis together to help change the image they have of each other. On a website I came across a list of names of some of the programs taking place in Israel that are meant to foster better understanding between Arabs and Israelis:

A Bridge for Peace

A Bridge to the Present through the Study of the Past

A Creative Treatment Project for Children of Drug Abusers

A School Community of Difference

Afternoon Workshops for Jewish and Arab Children

Arab and Jewish Cooperation in Acre: School-Family-Community
    Partnership for   Literacy Development

Arab and Jewish Meetings Program

Arab and Jewish Women's Coexistence and Leadership Forum

Arab Language Materials on Epilepsy and Children

Arab-Jewish Cooperation for Cleaning up the Galilee Landscape

Arab-Jewish Dance Troupe

Arab-Jewish Outreach Project

Arabic-Hebrew-English Language Learning Center Programs

Art and Culture for Coexistence

Artistic Enrichment for Children in Arab Group Homes and
    Collaboration with Jewish Group Homes

Beyond Words: Enhancing Dialogue in Israel through Dance and
    Movement Therapy

Bilingual Education in Israel

Bridgebuilders

Building a Common Language

Building Cultural and Environmental Trails

Calansuwa - Ramat Hasharon

Camping and Wilderness Survival Combined with Social Activities for
    Physically and Emotionally Challenged Children and Youth of the
    Arab Sector

Care Force: Advanced Early Childhood Caregiving Certification and
    Community Activist Task Force

Changing Society

Children Teaching Children

City at Peace

Coexistence Among Arab and Jewish Kindergarten Children

Coexistence and Tolerance: An Educational Approach

Coexistence as an Occupation

Coexistence Training for Teachers

Community Building

Continuing Employment of an Arabic Speech Therapist

Cooperative Democratic Leadership Training for High School
    Students

Cultivating Coexistence

Dialogue: The Name of the Game...

Discovery Program in Arab Communities

Dramatic Cooperation

Early Lessons in Coexistence

Economic Development Training Program for Jewish and Arab Local
    Town Councils in Northern Israel

Education Against Racism

Education for Peace

Educational Activities for Coexistence and Children's Rights

Encounter for Peace

Encounters between Arab and Jewish Kindergarten and Elementary
    School Teachers in Arad and Kseife

Enhancing Humanistic Education and Coexistence through Holocaust
    Study

Enhancing Jewish–Arab Coexistence through a Joint Battle against
    HIV/AIDS

Environmental Protection

ERAN Emergency Hotline in Arabic

Establishing Small Business Training Clubs for Jewish and Arab
    Women

Establishment of Bedouin Schools – Kaye College Partnership

Facilitators Training Program

Family Nursery Project in Rahat

Festival for Local Creativity

General Support and Annual Progress Report

Good Neighboring

Good Neighbors Summer Programs

Hand in Hand

Hope and Peace

Identifying and Assisting Victims of Domestic Violence: Emergency Room Educational Pilot Program

Improvement and Advancement of Educational Level in the Bedouin Township of Hura

Increasing Understanding and Tolerance

Integrated Kindergarten Program

Inter-Cultural Bridges: Ethiopian Jews Meet Arab Israelis

Intergroup Processes in the Jewish-Arab Context

Israel Heritage Center in Jisr Az-Zarqa

Jewish Muslim Beit Midrash-Madrasa

Jewish-Arab Common Roots

Jewish-Arab Youth Circus

Junior Achievement Israel - Company Program

Just Do 'Shalom'

Kaleidoscope: Educating Young People

Leadership Development Programs

Learning to Lead

Learning to Mainstream

Learning Together

Living with Conflict

Local Early Educational Leadership

Making Music in the Galilee

Meet the Neighbors

Meetings between Russian and Arab Journalists

Multicultural Encounters for Youth

Music as a Language to Promote Coexistence

Muslim Scout Movement

Neighborhood Home

Neighbors: A Model School Program for Jewish-Arab Coexistence

Networking to Create a Guidebook of Model Jewish-Arab Coexistence Projects

Northern Jewish/Arab/Druze Outreach

Ombudsman for Children and Youth in the Arab Sector

Opening Windows: Windows Magazine for All Children

Outreach to Arab Children and Youth in Nazareth

Outreach to Arab Women

Pairs on the Narrow Bridge: Growing in a Multicultural Society

Partners in Coexistence

Photography Training Program and Traveling Gallery Exhibit
    Documenting Coexistence in Israel

Publication of A Taha Hussein Reader in Hebrew Translation

Publication of Folder and Maps of Arab Villages

Recognition of Bedouin Traditions by Medical Staff in Soroka
    Medical Center

Rim — The Girl from Ein Hod: A Bilingual Storybook for Arab and
    Jewish Children

Schenim (Neighbors) and Coexistence

School Pairing Project

School-Family-Community Partnership for Literacy Development
    in Acre

Science and Engineering Studies for Bedouin High School Students

Seminar for Arab and Jewish Instructors

Shchenim (Neighbors) and Coexistence

Small Business Development Center Network in the Israeli Arab
    Sector

Staff and Volunteer Training towards Coexistence and Dialogue

Student Council: Coexistence and Democracy (II)

 Student Council: Coexistence and Democracy

Teaching for Peace and Coexistence

Teenagers Speak Peace

Tennis 2000

The Folklore of the Other

The Image of Abraham

The Interreligious Beit Midrash (Learning Community)

The Multicultural Resource Center

The Promotion of Educating Illiterate Arab Children

Theater as a Way to Communication and Dialogue

Through Art We Communicate

Through the Camera

Tolerance Training for Israel's Border Police

Traditions Teach Tolerance

Training for Early Childhood Educators

Training Local Government and Municipal Officials in Bedouin
Communities

Training Professionals in Jewish-Arab Relations

Understanding Ourselves, Understanding Each Other

Volunteer Development for Strengthening Coexistence

We All Eat the Same Bread

Women in a Democratic Society

Women's Health Newsletter in Arabic

Women's Studies

Young Leadership Training Program

Your Culture/My Culture: Art As the Common Denominator

Youth Encounters

Youth for Peace

Now listen to the names of programs that have been initiated in
Arab countries to foster closer relations between Arabs and Israelis.
Are you ready? Listen! (Silence) Do you get it? Well, they still don't!
There has been no reciprocity from the Arab side. Israel still does
not exist on Arab maps, the Arab media are still anti-Semitic, and
Arab children still attend mosques where so-called holy men call upon
them to conduct a holy war and encourage them to "kill the Jews." No
Jewish children have ever attended a synagogue where a rabbi called
on them to kill anyone. No Jew was ever called on to fight a "holy war"
because war just is not holy!

Recently, I read a heartbreaking story in the *New York Times*. It
was a story of a Palestinian child, Muhammad Rayyan, all of twelve
years old, who was shot dead by Israeli soldiers during a violent
demonstration at the Netzarim junction in Gaza — the scene of the
most violent Palestinian-Israeli conflicts. It is heartbreaking to think
of a twelve-year-old child being shot by an Israeli soldier, but it was
even more heartbreaking to read how that child got there. Every day
his father would give him and his brothers three shekels so that they
could take a taxi to be at the Netzarim junction to "join in the battle
for Jerusalem." What a tragedy! What Jewish parent would give their

children money to be in the line of fire in a battle for what? A holy city? It is not holy if that is the way you get it.

And that brings me to the name of our synagogue. The name is *Beth Tfiloh*, meaning "a house of prayer," certainly an appropriate name for a synagogue. However, the name has a biblical context that, if understood, could bring peace to the Middle East. It is the prophet Isaiah who refers to the Temple in Jerusalem as being a *beth tfiloh*, a house of prayer. He says it in a most famous verse, which is emblazoned on the front wall of the synagogue: "*Ki beiti beit tfiloh yikareh l'chol ha-amim*" (Isaiah 56:7). Listen carefully to the translation of that verse: "For my house (which means the Temple in Jerusalem) will be called a beth tfiloh, a house of prayer for ALL THE PEOPLES." Do you realize what that verse says? That this particular kilometer of land, which is the most sacred space in the Jewish religion, someday will become a house of prayer for *all* the nations of the world – it will be shared with all humankind. Then it will truly be a *beit mikdash* – a holy temple. We do not tell Yasir Arafat to "go to hell" like he told Prime Minister Barak. No, we say "Go to Jerusalem," but know that you are going to have to come with Ariel Sharon! Only when brothers and cousins reach out to each other and share with each other will the land truly become holy.

In every fiber of my being, I believe the people of Israel are prepared to do this. I pray that the Arabs will someday be prepared to do the same. Only then will we be able to see the fulfillment of the prophetic dream, "Nations shall not lift up sword against nation, neither shall they know of war anymore."

October 28, 2000

Images of Abuse in Iraq ... and Israel

I want to draw your attention to one person who died on Shavuot and one person who was supposed to be born on Shavuot but never had the opportunity. Although separated by thousands of years, their stories speak so clearly to the contemporary situation we confront these days as Americans and as Jews.

It is said that "one picture speaks a thousand words." If that is the case, the photographs of prisoner abuse that came from Iraq spoke volumes. Although we know that "war is hell," that every war brings with it incidents of shame, and that prison abuse is nothing new — it takes place in civilized and uncivilized countries, among superpowers and Third World nations alike — nothing could fully prepare us for the pictures that came out of Iraq. Prisoners with dog leashes around their necks, bodies piled together in provocative sexual displays, a prisoner with a hood covering his head and electrodes attached to his body — there really are no words to describe the pictures. But we do not have to use words for a picture speaks a thousand words. The pictures themselves said it all.

The question that is always raised when acts that go against the norms of society take place is whether the fault lay with a few individuals who perpetrated such acts or if something even more dangerous was involved. Perhaps the acts are endemic to the society

attack perpetrated the day before while we Jews here were celebrating Mother's Day.

The Hatuel family lived in one of the settlements in Gaza, and Tali Hatuel was driving her car with her four daughters when shots rang out. She was immediately hit and died in front of her daughters. Two terrorists then approached the car as the four girls were screaming and crying, with their mother's blood spread on the front seat. Through the window of the car, the two terrorists then systematically shot each of the children three times in the head. The last to die was Meirav, the youngest child, all of two years old. She was strapped in her car seat for safety sake. But shoulder straps and car seats cannot protect you from a killer's bullets.

So there was the picture of the Hatuel family in five caskets, which really should have been six, for Tali was pregnant and in her eighth month, expecting her first boy, who was scheduled to be born on Shavuot.

When seeing the pictures of the abuse of Iraqis, the world was "outraged," "appalled," "revolted." Why did not the picture of the Hatuel family evoke a similar response? I do not know — but this I do know: the people responsible for the murder of the Hatuels were not just those two terrorists. It was the entire society that spawned them. Did you hear any Palestinian or Arab leaders express outrage, revulsion, or disgust over the inhuman killings of little children? Sure, war is hell. But even in war, there are certain rules of conduct — soldiers just do not go around killing innocent civilians and most certainly not women and children. And to add inhumanity to inhumanity, while the Hatuel family's funerals were taking place, Arab snipers started shooting at the mourners. This is barbaric! This is inhuman!

Yet, not only do the Palestinian murderers perpetrate inhuman acts like this, and not only do their leaders not denounce them, but the Arab people actually applaud these actions! Different groups rush to take "credit" for these actions! Let me just remind you: this is not the first time we have seen such barbarism by a collective people. A few years ago when two Israeli soldiers mistakenly drove into the Palestinian city of Ramallah, they were lynched, dragged through the streets, torn to pieces — with their murderers marching through the streets showing their blood-covered hands to the cheers of the masses. Let me just remind you that it is not just the Palestinians who act like this! Remember in Iraq at the end of March, 2004 when the mutilated bodies of four Americans were hung up in the public square near Fallujah. Somehow, the same Iraqis who were outraged when their prisoners were humiliated lost their voices when it was Americans who were being mutilated. And we cannot forget the beheading of Daniel Pearl. All these are not just the random acts of a few terrorists and murderers. They stem from a society that has risen within the Islamic world that encourages children to be suicide bombers, that shows no remorse for acts of inhumanity, that cheers terrorists who march around with severed body parts as trophies, that sees nothing incongruous in cutting a man's head off while proclaiming "God is great," and that celebrates death over life.

Does this mean that all Arabs, all Muslims, are "bad?" Certainly not! There are good and bad among all people. We Jews have our own "rotten apples." But contrast our reaction to them to the Arab reaction to theirs. Years ago when Boruch Goldstein went on a rampage, killing Palestinians at the "Cave of the Patriarchs," every single responsible Jewish leader throughout the world denounced him, with Prime Minister Rabin leading the way, in proclaiming: "I am ashamed over the disgrace imposed upon us by a degenerate murderer ... sensible Judaism spits you out. You are a shame on Zionism and an embarrassment to Judaism." Have you heard similar sentiments expressed by the "good" Arab people regarding the degenerate behavior of the murderers in their midst? What's the good if the good remain silent? And what's the good when it is beginning to become obvious that the "good" silent ones are not the majority?

To some degree, the support of the Palestinians for terrorism explains the fence that Israel is now erecting, separating itself from the Arabs on the West Bank. On one level — the physical level — that fence is meant to keep out suicide bombers and those who would randomly kill Israelis. Yet, I think that fence has a psychological purpose as well. After Oslo, many in Israel thought there was going to be a "new" Middle East; the walls separating Israel from its Arab neighbors — physically and psychologically — would come tumbling down, no different from the wall that divided Berlin and that divided East and

West. But now we know that was all a dream. We talked of peace, but they planned for war. We spoke of friendship, but they taught hatred in their schools. We talked of our right to exist, but they insisted on their right to return. We talked of life, but they talked of death. We said that war is hell, but they spoke of Jihad, that war is holy.

Of a video shown on television in which a Palestinian mob was seen mutilating the body parts of the six Israeli soldiers killed in Gaza, Israel's Major General Dan Harel, head of the Southern Command, said, "It made me sick to my stomach. It is unbelievable that human beings could reach such lows. The video I saw emphasizes the difference between us and them." Similarly, Colonel Eyal Eisenberg, Commander of the Givati Brigade that saw eleven of its soldiers blown to bits, was quoted in Israel's *Maariv* newspaper:

> I haven't told this to anyone but in the midst of this operation, we assisted a baby being born and evacuated an elderly Palestinian woman who was injured and summoned a local ambulance for her. Terrorists ran and fired from behind the ambulance. Therefore, I do not want to make any comparison between our scale of values and theirs. If my soldiers can assist a Palestinian woman giving birth when six of their comrades have been blown to bits in the street but, at the same time, they fire at us from behind an ambulance, you must understand that we are at opposite ends of the scales of values. They are at the very bottom.

Yes, they have left us no choice but to build a wall to make sure that *we* never become like *them*. That *their* way will not become *our* way. We are building a fence not just to keep their murderers out, but to keep the mores of their society out as well.

Do you know what? The United States is on our side of the fence — not theirs. Europe? I am not so sure. I guess the Europeans are doing the thing they usually do: sitting on the fence! The President of the United States — the most powerful country on earth — has apologized for the acts of abuse of individual Americans. Why is there no head of an Arab country or a Muslim leader capable of doing the same?

The pictures we as Americans — and as Jews — have seen from Iraq and from Israel have been painful, indeed, downright ugly. But how different is our reaction from the reaction of others — those others on the other side of the fence. Ours is a reaction in keeping with the spirit of King David, who begins his Book of Psalms with these immortal words: "Happy is the man that hath not walked in the counsel of the wicked nor stood in the pathway of sinners nor sat in the seat of the scornful. But his delight is in the law of the Lord" (Psalms 1:1–2). In these dark times, we can pause to rejoice in the knowledge that the American people and the Jewish people are united in their dedication to upholding the law, at all times and under all circumstances, in the hope that some day we will be privileged to witness the fulfillment of the words of David, *"Yitamu chataim min ha-aretz u'reshaim od einam* — when sinners will be obliterated from the world and the wicked shall be no more" (Psalms 104:35).

May 22, 2004

SENATOR OBAMA — WRIGHT OR WRONG?

In light of recent events, I do not think it is unreasonable of me to expect all of you who are members of Beth Tfiloh to wake up every morning and, after saying the *Modeh Ani* prayer, thanking God for keeping you alive, adding a little prayer thanking God for bringing Rabbi Mitchell Wohlberg into your lives. For those of you who are not members, that statement might sound a little smug and self-centered. Yet, given the recent news, the members of Beth Tfiloh *should* express gratitude to God for my being their rabbi. After all, it is a lot better having me than having the Reverend Jeremiah Wright as your pastor, as did the congregants at Chicago's Trinity United Church of Christ — where Senator Barack Obama is an active member.

The controversy that erupted over Rev. Wright's hate-filled, anti-American sermons not only put Senator Obama in an awkward position; it put every member of a church or synagogue in an awkward position as well. It raised many uncomfortable questions. Are you to be held responsible for what I say from the pulpit? What happens if you disagree with what I preach? What are you to do? And is it possible that someone who has been a member of a congregation for twenty years really does not know what his rabbi, pastor, or priest's position is on some of the most challenging subjects of the day?

Sen. Obama knew that he had to respond to these questions, and he did it in a talk that was truly thought provoking, something rare for a political speech. The talk covered a lot of territory, and it answered many questions — but it also raised a few others.

What did Sen. Obama learn from his relationship with his pastor? Did he learn to refer to the United States as the "U.S. of KKK-A" as Rev. Wright did? Did he learn to refer to our country with the words, "God damn America," as Rev. Wright did? Did he learn to believe that the AIDS virus is part of a government plot to get rid of black people, as Rev. Wright claimed? The answer is, No, no no! Anyone who questions Sen. Obama's patriotism is wrong, wrong, wrong! Those sending around e-mails claiming that Sen. Obama is really a Muslim are wrong, wrong, wrong! Those who take some sort of perverted pleasure in underscoring that his middle name is Hussein should remember how we felt when Rev. Jesse Jackson referred to New York as "Hymie town." To hold Sen. Obama accountable for everything his pastor said, to think that he believes everything his pastor says, would mean that you would have to be held accountable for everything I say! And even I do not always feel comfortable doing that!

Unfortunately, Sen. Obama's otherwise eloquent speech did indicate that there is a certain "something" that he indeed learned from his pastor. And that is a dangerous "something": it is the concept of moral equivalence.

The phrase "moral equivalence" is not a new one. Some attribute it to William James, who wrote an essay in 1910 entitled "The Moral Equivalent of War." Others attribute its popularity to Jeane Kilpatrick, who served as the U.S. Ambassador to the United Nations during the Reagan administration. "Moral equivalence" has become a popular phrase in our time. What it means is a blurring of differences, a blurring of all distinctions. It is like saying there is no difference between an ice cube and boiling water — it's just a matter of degrees! It means that in every conflict, there is no real right and wrong: they are just two sides of the same coin. Rev. Jeremiah Wright displayed this way of thinking when, in a sermon he delivered on September 16, 2001, he said the United States had brought the death and destruction of 9/11 on itself. In his words, "It was chickens coming home to roost." He went on to say, "We nuked far more than the thousands in New York and the Pentagon and we never batted an eye … we have supported state terrorism against the Palestinians and black South Africans and now we are indignant because the stuff we have done overseas is now brought right back to our own front yards." Do you understand what he is saying here? That what Osama bin Laden did on 9/11 was no different than what the U.S. did to Japan. That what bin Laden did on 9/11 was no different than what Israel is doing to the Palestinians. And he said this while the bodies were still being pulled out of the wreckage of the twin towers.

That people in his church did not find this sentiment offensive perhaps is not surprising, because others were saying much the same thing. Noam Chomsky and many other so-called enlightened thinkers in America were expressing similar beliefs. We got what we deserve! *They* may be guilty, but so are we! Leave it to the great thinker Woody Allen to express it best. In an interview in *Der Spiegel*, Germany's most important magazine, Mr. Allen dismissed the events of 9/11 in the following manner: "The history of the world is like: he kills me, I kill him … only with different cosmetics and different castings. So in 2001, some fanatics killed some Americans and now some Americans are killing some Iraqis. And in my childhood, some Nazis killed Jews and now some Jewish people and some Palestinians are killing each other."

You see? It is all the same! A best seller in Germany claims the actions of the Allies were no different than the atrocities of the Nazis. They are all morally equivalent! Do you know that some Jewish religious leaders have fallen into this same trap of moral equivalence?

The Reconstructionist movement in Judaism is the smallest Jewish movement in America, but it has always been at the forefront of change. It was the first to have a Bat Mitzvah, the first to have women rabbis, the first to sanctify gay marriages. And here is another first: a few years back the Reconstructionist movement printed a new Haggadah that includes a reading on behalf of the "dispossessed" Palestinian people, a reading that was written by Raymonda Tawil, who had been arrested several times by Israeli authorities. She also happens to be the mother-in-law of Yasir Arafat. The editors of the Haggadah felt that including the reading was appropriate because the plight of the Palestinians today is comparable to the plight of the Jews in Egypt in ancient times. That is like saying that what Churchill did and what Hitler did are the same. Indeed, that is exactly what Mahatma Gandhi said! That statement is a moral equivalency that is dangerous and downright wrong. The plight of the Palestinians is a sad and tragic one. But let us remember that it was caused when in 1947 the Arabs refused a two-state solution that would have given both the Jews and the Palestinians a homeland. Let us keep in mind that it is Palestinians who are responsible for the most despicable terrorist attacks. They are the ones who blow up the buses and stores and schools, killing countless innocent Israeli citizens. And while Israel's treatment of the Palestinians has at times been harsh, it has been much more benevolent than that of any other occupied nation, and it is disgraceful to cast it as equivalent to how the Egyptians treated the Jews. Even to this day, while Israel seeks to make peace with the Palestinians, 86 percent of the Palestinian people are in favor of the recent terrorist attack that killed eight Yeshiva students in Jerusalem — 86 percent! Do not put them in my Haggadah! Their story is not the moral equivalent to our people's story.

Moral equivalency is wrong, and it is dangerous. And that is why we have the Jewish dietary laws found in this morning's Torah portion. There are few things that underscore the uniqueness of the Jewish people more than our laws of kashrut, which dictate that certain animals you can eat, and certain animals you cannot eat. Yet, according to many commentators, when God created the world, He intended that no animals should be eaten. Look in the story of Creation, and you will see that Adam was told to eat from the herbs of the fields, from the vegetation. There is no mention of eating animals. It is only after the flood that God tells Noah that animals can be killed and eaten. What happened? Why the change?

The rabbis explain that when humankind was told that neither humans nor animals should be killed, people made the mistake of thinking, Well, if that is the case they are morally equivalent; there is no difference between a human and an animal. Indeed, there are some people who feel that way today. And what is so terrible about that belief? Well, to early humankind if both people and animals were equivalent — if you could not kill one, then you could not kill the other — then do you know what happened? If you could make love to one, you could make love to the other! That is just what humanity started to do! Only then did God say "No!": people and animals are different — one can be killed and one cannot. They are not morally equivalent.

In his speech, Sen. Barack Obama fell into the moral equivalence trap of his pastor and mentor when he said, "I can no more disown [Rev. Wright] than I can my white grandmother." That is a moral equivalency that holds no water! His grandmother had expressed a fear of black men who passed by her on the street, an attitude that Jesse Jackson has said he understands. Rev. Wright accused the United States of being guilty of, among other things, Hiroshima and Nagasaki, giving drugs to blacks, and spreading AIDS throughout the black community. Are those things morally equivalent? Is it morally equivalent to compare what your grandmother says in private to what a religious leader says in public, to a cheering crowd?

Do you know what else, Senator Obama? Your pastor and your grandmother are not morally equivalent! How does it go — you can pick your friends, but you can't pick your family! That is very true. We do not get too many grandmothers during the course of a lifetime. For that matter, we do not get too many members of a family during the course of a lifetime. When it comes to family, "It is what it is!" You cannot throw a member of your family out with the trash, even if their *talk* is trash! Yet, when it comes to your rabbi, pastor, minister, or priest, you can vote with your feet. In fact, according to a recent survey, 45 percent of the American people have switched their religious affiliation. I know of no one who has switched his or her grandmother! It is not the same!

It is also not the same to claim, as Sen. Obama has done, that Rev. Wright is like "an old uncle who says things I don't always agree with." That is a moral equivalency that has no basis in reality. We all may have had a crazy uncle who said the most outrageous things, but everyone in the family knew he was crazy and no one took him seriously. No one is saying that Rev. Wright is crazy: he was the minister of 8,000 church members, and people took very seriously his hate-filled words that were being passed on to a new generation that should know better, that must know better. Rev. Wright is not a crazy man. Rev. Wright is a dangerous man because he is not just someone's crazy uncle — he is thousands of people's reverend.

In our Torah portion this morning we read of the tragic and sudden death of Nadav and Avihu, the two sons of Aaron the High Priest. They were killed while performing the Temple service. They were reverent, serving the Lord, and yet what they did found disfavor in the eyes of God. What was it that they did? From the words of the Torah, it does not seem as if they did much: they brought an *eish zarah* – a strange fire – to the altar. What was so strange about the fire they brought? According to some sages, the only thing that made it strange was the fact that it did not come from the altar. According to other sages, the only thing that made their action strange was the fact that they had not been commanded to do it. Okay, but what is so terrible about that? What was so terrible was that they were leaders in the Temple, and everyone was watching what they were doing. Even the slightest incorrect step could not be allowed, could not go unpunished, because everyone else would feel free to do the same. Religious leaders have a special responsibility and have to be held to a higher standard, because their behavior influences others.

Here is another place where Barack Obama fell into the trap of moral equivalency. In speaking of Rev. Wright, he said, "Did I strongly disagree with many of his political views? Absolutely – just as I'm sure many of you have heard remarks from your pastors, priests, or rabbis with which you strongly disagreed." Sure, religious leaders of every persuasion have said foolish things, stupid things, controversial things, with which their congregants have disagreed. I am sure that is true of the members of Beth Tfiloh! I know some of you have disagreed with my positions on President Bush and Christian evangelicals and intermarriage and many other things. It is impossible for an entire congregation to agree with everything their spiritual leader says. Indeed, truth to tell, I've disagreed with some of the things I have said!

But let me tell you something: nothing I – or any other religious leader I know – said is comparable to what Rev. Wright has said! It is one thing to disagree with the positions of your spiritual leader. It is quite another to have a spiritual leader like Rev. Wright who preaches hatred, racism, and disloyalty. It is Rev. Wright who calls Louis Farrakhan "a twentieth and twenty-first century giant." That is the same Farrakhan who called Jews "bloodsuckers" and Judaism a "gutter religion." It is Rev. Wright who traveled with Farrakhan to Libya in

1985 to visit Col. Qadahfi — at a time when Qadahfi was considered the chief financier of international terrorism, including the Munich Olympics massacre, for which America had banned Libyan oil imports and branded Libya a "rogue state." It is Rev. Wright who used his church bulletin to reproduce articles from Hamas, a sworn enemy of Israel and the United States.

I cannot speak for priests or pastors, but I can tell you that I do not know of a single rabbi who ever stood in the pulpit and delivered a sermon proclaiming, "God damn America!" as Rev. Wright did. No rabbi would say it, and no congregation, no synagogue would tolerate it! We Jews have known from persecution! No, our American experience cannot be compared to the slavery and lynching, the pain and degradation of the black experience, but nothing was handed to us on a silver platter. Many of us American Jews share an experience no different from that of the man Mark Steyn wrote about in the *New York Sun*. This man was born and raised in Siberia until the Cossacks came and ravaged his village. His family immigrated to the United States, and he grew up in the poverty of New York's Lower East Side. He made it big, but he still suffered slights as a Jew. When he married a Park Avenue heiress, she was expelled from the Social Register. And in the '30s, her sister moved in with a Nazi diplomat and proudly flaunted a diamond swastika in front of him. But that did not stop Irving Berlin from proudly and unashamedly writing, "God bless America, land that I love ..."

I am sure Barack Obama, who spent his childhood in Indonesia and ended up a graduate of Harvard, shares those sentiments as well. Is it asking too much to not only expect every political leader in our country to feel the same, but every religious leader as well?

Barack Obama represents the American experience at its best — Rev. Wright at its worst. Barack Obama should be worshiping at a religious institution like ours. When members from the Trinity United Church of Christ in Chicago are asked what their pastor preached that morning, they have to say, "God damn America." If anyone asks you what Rabbi Wohlberg preached this morning, you can tell them, "Oh, just ... God bless America!"

March 29, 2008

CHRISTIAN EVANGELICALS: FRIEND OR FOE?

There is a book that has become popular in England. It is not a very big book; in fact, it is its small size that has made it so attractive. This book is called *The 100-Minute Bible*. It only has sixty pages, each designed to be read in less than two minutes. There are other books like it, including *The Light Speed Bible* and *The Bible in 90 Days*. All these books attempt to do the same thing: make the Bible easier to read by removing verses that seem outdated or meaningless. I have not seen any of these Bibles, but I can tell you with an absolute certainty that they all leave out one particular verse, a verse that on the surface adds nothing to our knowledge. Indeed, one of the kings of Israel sought to remove it from the Bible for that very reason! Yet, according to our sages, while on the surface this verse appears to be meaningless, on closer study its importance is most significant in our day and age. In fact, if it had been taken to heart 2,000 years ago, there may never have been a Christmas.

In the Second Book of Kings, we are told of a wicked man named Menasheh who reigned as King of Judah for fifty-five years. He turned against God and ridiculed the Torah and, in a sense, he tried to write his own "100-Minute Bible" by leaving out verses that he claimed had no meaning. According to the Talmud, the first verse he offered up for ridicule was one from the concluding part of the Jacob/Esau narrative:

it describes how, after fleeing from Esau because Esau has threatened to kill him, Jacob comes home, and the story draws to an end with the two brothers standing together as they bury their father, Isaac. Then the Torah, which is careful with every word, spends the next forty-three verses telling us the lineage of Esau, with verses like: "And these are the generations of Esau," "Esau took his wives of the daughters of Canaan" (Genesis 36:1-2), "And these are the generations of Esau, the father of the Edomites. These are the names of Esau's sons, Eliphaz the son of Adah, the wife of Esau; Reuel the son of Basemath, the wife of Esau. And the sons of Eliphaz were Teman, Omar, Zepho and Gatam and Kenaz. And Timna was concubine to Eliphaz, Esau's son" (Genesis 36:11-12) To which King Menashe said, "Did Moses have nothing to write in the Torah other than such useless trivia as Latam's sister was Timna and Timna was a concubine of Eliphaz? Who needs such information? What purpose can it possibly serve?"

But along come the rabbis to tell us that there is an important lesson found in the last verse. The rabbis tell us that Timna, described as being a concubine to Eliphaz, was no ordinary woman. According to tradition, she was a product of a royal family. She sought to convert to Judaism, as in the words of the Talmud: "She came to Abraham, Isaac and Jacob for that purpose. V'lo kibluha — but they refused to accept her. She thereupon went and became a concubine of Eliphaz, the son of Esau, saying, 'It is better to be a maidservant to this nation than to be a princess to any other nation.'" Do you know what happened after she became Eliphaz's concubine? She and Eliphaz had a child. What was the child's name? Amalek — the arch-enemy of the Jewish people. The Talmud concludes this story by telling us that Amalek became our eternal enemy as a punishment to us for having rejected his mother.

The rabbis of old understood that this seemingly meaningless and insignificant verse about Esau's progeny was a very important one, containing within it a most important lesson: be careful when you reject someone. It might come back to haunt you!

I thought about this when I read of two pronouncements made by two nationally recognized Jewish leaders; one by Abraham Foxman, the national director of the Anti-Defamation League, and the other by Rabbi Eric Yoffie, the leader of the Union for Reform Judaism. Both of them were addressing a national gathering of their respective organizations, and both chose to speak about the greatest threat that is confronting us as Jews in America. What is that threat? Evangelical Christians! Mr. Foxman described them as having "built infrastructures throughout the country intending to Christianize all aspects of American life, from the halls of government to the libraries to the movies to recording studios to the playing fields and locker rooms of professional, collegiate and amateur sports, from the military to SpongeBob Squarepants."

This list of charges against Evangelical Christians was not enough for Rabbi Yoffie. During a Shabbos morning sermon he delivered at the Biennial Convention of the Union of Reform Judaism, Rabbi Yoffie referred to those on the religious right as being "zealots" who were guilty of "blasphemy" and "bigotry." In speaking to the delegates about the Christian Evangelical approach to gays, he described it as "hateful rhetoric that fuels the fires of anti-gay bigotry" and was similar to what Adolf Hitler did when he came to power in 1933.

I view Christian Evangelicals from a very different perspective — a perspective with which many Jews disagree. And that is their right! But let us assume for argument's sake that I am wrong. Let us assume that I was wrong when I pointed out what marvelous friends the Evangelicals have been to Israel — how they come to Washington to lobby for Israel, how they send millions of dollars to help resettlement in Israel, how when many Jews were afraid to go to Israel, they kept coming on pilgrimages. Let us assume Israel's Bibi Netanyahu was wrong when he recently said that the Evangelicals are the best friends Israel has in the world. And let us assume for the sake of argument that I was wrong in saying that a major reason why Evangelicals have such a positive attitude toward Jews, the Jewish people, and the Jewish state is because they take seriously the promise that God made to Abraham when he said, "Those who bless you shall be blessed and those who curse you shall be cursed" (Genesis 12:3). Let us assume that I am wrong — even way off base! Let us assume the Christian Evangelicals are not as good as I have made them out to be. Still, let me ask you these questions. Are they as *bad* as Abraham Foxman and Rabbi Yoffie make them out to be? Are they an enemy that should be demonized? Might we by our rejection be creating another Amalek?

After all, what are the Christian Evangelists being accused of? According to Mr. Foxman, they have "built infrastructures throughout the country intending to Christianize all aspects of American life." "Built infrastructures throughout the country?" Is that not reminiscent of accusations made against the Jews since time immemorial, that we have secret cabals in which we hatch plans to take over the world? And what are these "infrastructures" doing? According to Mr. Foxman they are trying to impose their perspective on "judicial nominees, stem cell research, same-sex marriage, abortion restrictions and faith-based initiative." That might sound pretty scary, except for the fact that Jewish organizations have done the exact same thing! In the words of Hillel Halkin in an insightful column in the *Jerusalem Post*,

> There is not one of these issues on which major Jewish organizations have not again and again fought for politically liberal positions. The Reform Movement, for example, has officially supported legislation furthering same-sex marriage for years. The American Jewish Committee, the American Jewish Congress, the Federation of Reconstructionist Congregations, the National Council of Jewish Women, the Union of American Hebrew Congregations, and the United Synagogue for Conservative Judaism have all endorsed legalized abortion. Hadassah has joined other American organizations in calling on President Bush to revise restrictive federal policies on stem cell research.

Indeed at the very same convention at which Rabbi Yoffie spoke, the Reform Movement came out against Supreme Court nominee Samuel Alito.

So let me ask you: When Jewish organizations took positions on all these issues, did anyone accuse us of trying to "Judaize America?" And how would we have felt if they did? So why, when Evangelicals take positions on these very same issues, do we accuse them of trying to "Christianize America?" How do you think that makes them feel? How do you think they feel when their policies are said to be reminiscent of those of Hitler? When others have used Nazi analogies in regard to Jews — accusing Israel of "Nazi war crimes," of building concentration camps with its security wall, of Ariel Sharon being a Nazi — we have always cried out in protest, saying, "You can criticize us, but don't make any analogies to the Nazis." We Jews have made it an article of faith that the Holocaust was unique and nothing should be compared to it. If we do not like these comparisons when applied to us, why should we apply them to others?

In addition, are we as Jews really under attack and feeling besieged here in America by Christian Evangelicals? Do we feel our rights as Jews are being denied? The Christian Evangelicals have had an extremely supportive president and Congress, favorable to their viewpoints. Yet, has anything really changed? Do you feel so threatened that Evangelicals have to be attacked with such incendiary comments? Does that make sense when we Jews represent just 2 percent of the American population, in comparison to eighty million Christian Evangelicals? The words of Rabbi Yoffie and Abraham Foxman may have sounded good to their liberal constituency, but how do you think they sounded to Christian America?

Of course, whether as Jews or as liberals or as Americans, we have every right to protest when we disagree with positions held by Evangelicals and when we feel they are too close to crossing over the line separating church and state. Indeed, there is a biblical commandment to rebuke someone whom you think is doing wrong. The Torah tells us in the Book of Leviticus: "*Hochai-ach tochiach et amitecha* — thou shall surely rebuke thy friend" (Leviticus 19:17). Yes, rebuke is appropriate and is sometimes necessary: "Thou shall surely rebuke thy friend." But as the commentators point out, make sure that rebuke is given in a manner so that the person who receives it will still remain your friend. Referring to people as "zealots" and "bigots" and making comparisons to the Nazis only means one has not read Dale Carnegie's *How to Win Friends and Influence People*.

The Talmud tells us exactly how to rebuke others: "Our masters taught the left hand may always repulse, but the right hand should bring near." The left hand — the weaker hand — is the one that rejects, rebukes, repulses. The right hand — the stronger hand — must be the one that, at the same time, draws near, reaches out, and befriends. In a remarkable story that for centuries has been censored from the Talmud, we are told of a rabbi who mixed up his right hand from his left. And you know who he did it with? He did it with a man called Jesus. In Tractate Sanhedrin (107b) we are told:

When King Yannai rose up against the sages to put them to death, Simeon ben Shetah was hidden by his sister, and R. Joshua ben Perahiah (and Jesus) fled to Alexandria of Egypt. When peace came, Simeon ben Shetah wrote to R. Joshua, "From me, Jerusalem the holy city, to you, my sister Alexandria of Egypt: My husband dwells in your midst, and I abide desolate." R. Joshua replied, "I understand. Peace upon you." So he rose up, together with his disciple (Jesus) and came to Jerusalem. He happened to put up at a certain inn (run by a woman) where great honor was accorded him. He remarked, "What a beautiful inn." His disciple replied, "Yes, master, but her eyes are bleary." R. Joshua: "You wicked person! So it is with such matters that you occupy yourself!" At that, he brought forth four hundred rams' horns and (had them sound as he) excommunicated him. Though Jesus came day after day before R. Joshua, pleading, 'Take me back." R. Joshua paid no attention to him. But one day as R. Joshua was reciting the Shema, (Jesus) came and stood before him. (Relenting), R. Joshua decided to take him back and motioned to him with his hand. But Jesus interpreted the gesture as a final repulse. So he went off, set up a brick, and worshiped it.

Now many scholars question whether this story ever took place and whether it really involved Jesus. But fact or fiction, it does not matter! We have here a tradition that an overly harsh rejection of Jesus eventually led to the rise of Christianity.

From Timna to Jesus, the message is clear, the message is the same. Know who your friends are and know who your enemies are, and don't mix up the two! Friends are to be embraced, enemies to be rebuked. But they are to be rebuked in a manner that will bring them closer to friendship. I believe Christian Evangelicals are friends to be embraced. But if they are the threat that Abraham Foxman and Eric Yoffie portray them as being, let that threat be met with expressions of disagreement, but let the expressions be made in a friendly manner.

Christmas is a time that makes many Jews feel uncomfortable here in America. But it need not be that way. This is a time of year when America's concept of democracy and pluralism is exhibited at its best and finest. Yes, the President of the United States lights a national

Christmas tree, but he also has a Chanukah party at the White House. There is plenty of room in America for people from Chassidic Jews to Christian Evangelicals. The truth of the matter is that, despite all cries to the contrary, never have we been closer to each other. Let us learn to disagree without being disagreeable, to walk side by side without seeing eye to eye on every subject. Let there be peace on earth, and let it begin with me.

December 17, 2005

CHURCH AND STATE — AND SYNAGOGUE, TOO!

Saddam Hussein was a thug, a gangster, a man who robbed and killed his own people. His capture and execution evoked a worldwide feeling that perhaps was best expressed by that great philosopher, Moms Mabley. When asked if there was anything good she could say about her dead husband, she replied, "He's dead! Good!"

The real questions facing the people of Iraq today are, "Who and what will follow Saddam Hussein?" "What kind of a country will they have?" "What kind of government?" One of the most critical issues facing not only the people of Iraq but also people in countless countries around the globe is the role that religion should play in the state. In Iraq, Hussein led a secular Baath party, which was responsible for the murders of countless Shiite clerics who represented a majority of the population. Is Iraq now to be ruled by Shiite clerics, or is it to be secular as Hussein had wanted? Or, is there some place in between?

The role that religion plays in the state is an issue that has to be dealt with by more than the Iraqi people. The people of France dealt with this issue by calling for a law banning the public displays of religious symbols in schools. The law is designed primarily to ban the wearing of scarves by Muslim students, but the ban also applies to the wearing of crosses by Christian students and a skullcap by Jewish students. Is that the way the question of religion and state should be answered? Or, is a better answer the Iranian one, where the scarves are not only not banned, but the wearing of them is *required* by the religious police, who prowl the streets looking for violators. Is the answer to come from the Mullahs of Afghanistan who impose their religious beliefs on everyone? Or, is it to come from the former Soviet Union, which denied any religious beliefs? The question of religion and state is also one that very much perplexes the people of Israel — a declared "Jewish" state. But surely Israel deals with this question better than Saudi Arabia, which bans the building of any synagogue or church on its holy soil.

One would have thought that, here in the United States, there would be no questions about religion's role in the state. Our Founding Fathers established the principle of separation of church and state. Yet, time has shown that this principle is easier to express in theory than in practice. In recent years, again and again, questions have been raised regarding the separation of church and state. Just how separated are they? Can one place the Ten Commandments in the courtroom? Should we remove the words, "Under God," from our Pledge of Allegiance? Should there be prayer in public school classrooms, and what about vouchers for parochial schools? The questions go on and on.

At no time of the year are we more sensitive to this conflict than at the close of the year. For a long time, Jews and others have raised questions about the legality of displaying Christmas decorations on public grounds. A while back in Kensington, Maryland, a group of Jews sued authorities because at Kensington's holiday tree-lighting ceremony, there was going to be a Santa Claus, which they considered inappropriate. This led to one teenager being tackled by police after he pulled down a sign someone had erected that said, "If Jews can ban Santa, why can't we ban Jews?"

I thought about this question of the public celebration of Christmas when I was invited to light the menorah in Annapolis for Governor and Mrs. Robert Ehrlich. If a Christmas display does not belong on public property, then maybe I should not be lighting a menorah for the state of Maryland. Yet, I decided to go, and I did so for several reasons. I decided to go because I was going to give the governor a Chanukah gift that he really needs. With all of his budgetary problems, I was going to present him with some Chanukah "gelt." I was also going because, if the Ehrlichs — who are Christians — can celebrate Chanukah, then I thought I ought to tell them a story about a Jewish family who celebrates Christmas.

The story is about a teacher who was very curious about how each of her students celebrated Christmas. She called on young Patrick Murphy. "Tell me, Patrick, what do you do at Christmas time?" she asked. Patrick addressed the class: "Me and my 12 brothers and sisters go to midnight Mass and sing hymns; then we come home and put mince pies by the back door and hang up our stockings. Then we go to bed and wait for Father Christmas to come with toys."

"Very nice, Patrick," the teacher said. "Now, Jimmy Brown, what do you do at Christmas?" "Me and my sister also go to Church with Mom and Dad and we sing carols, and after we get home we put cookies and milk by the chimney and we hang up our stockings. We hardly sleep, waiting for Santa Claus to bring our toys," Jimmy replied. "That's also very nice, Jimmy," she said.

Realizing there was a Jewish boy in the class and not wanting to leave him out of the discussion, she asked Isaac Cohen the same question. "Now Isaac, what do you do at Christmas?" Isaac said, "Well, we go for a ride and we sing a Christmas carol."

Surprised, the teacher questioned further. "Tell us what you sing." "Well, it's the same thing every year. Dad comes home from the office. We all get into the Mercedes, and we drive to his toy factory. When we get inside we look at all the empty shelves and we sing, 'What a friend we have in Jesus.' Then we all go on a cruise to the Bahamas."

I wanted to share all this wisdom with the governor. Besides, Chanukah was the first battle in history for religious freedom, and the state of Maryland was created for the sake of religious freedom. Maryland is famous for the Toleration Act of 1649 that gave everyone the freedom to follow his or her own religion. What many people do not know is that the Toleration Act gave freedom of religion to everyone — everyone except Unitarians and Jews! And now, we are lighting a menorah in the Governor's house. So yes, I went!

But still, the question remains: what should the relationship be between church and state? How should it be defined? How should we Jews look on what is referred to as the "December dilemma?"

Interestingly enough, the answer can be found in the Chanukah story. Under Alexander the Great's leadership, the Greek people conquered a good part of the world, eventually including Palestine. Alexander the Great was steeped in the belief that the Greek way of life was the only suitable one for humankind to follow. He enthusiastically infused the culture and society of the Greeks among the nations he had conquered. And Palestine was no exception. Did the Jews accept Greek culture? They sure did, and we still do! So much of Greek culture has become part of the Jewish tradition, starting with the name Alexander itself, which became — and continues to be — a popular Hebrew name. Rabbinic literature makes many references to Greek culture, stoic philosophy and elements of logic and data from Greek sciences. Maimonides is considered one of the great masters of Aristotelian philosophy. Bahya ibn Paquda's masterpiece, *Chovot Halevavot*, is based on neo-platonic thinking. The Hebrew language is filled with Greek words. Mel Gibson is making his movie, *The Passion*, featuring Jews speaking Latin. Shows you what he knows! More of them were speaking Greek, and some of this Greek became part of the Hebrew language with words like "Sanhedrin" and "prozdor" "sanegor," "apotropos" and the good old "afikoman."

We embraced Greek culture. And we were — and still are — the better for it. But then the Greeks took it one step too far when they brought their idol Zeus into our temple. It is one thing to embrace another culture; it is quite another to embrace another religion. It was one thing for the Greeks to worship Zeus — no problem. It is quite another to make the Jews worship Zeus — big problem! That is where the Maccabees drew the line then — and that is where I believe the line should be drawn today.

Christmas is very much a part of American culture. America is not a Christian country, but an overwhelming majority of Americans are Christian, so why shouldn't Christmas be celebrated across our country? Yet, I say it should not be celebrated because it is a secular holiday. To me, that robs Christians of one of their most sacred days. It should be celebrated in America because 75 percent of Americans are Christians

— and the other 25 percent are not being forced to observe it. You want to get up early on Dec. 25th and go to work? *Gei gesunterheit!* Nobody is stopping you! At the same time, nobody is forcing you to bring a Christmas tree into your home. For years, Jewish defense organizations fought against the postal service issuing a Christmas stamp. Marilyn Monroe — yes! Elvis Presley — yes! But Christmas — no! So what did we accomplish? We antagonized 200 million Christians when no one was forcing us to use their stamp! Christians are entitled to their celebrations by the government just as Jews should be able to celebrate our Sabbath and holidays by the government.

To me, the public celebrations of Christmas and Chanukah represent American diversity at its best. Far better that public celebration than the banning of religious symbols as proposed by the French. The problem that the French are confronting now is the reality that they — and other European countries — did not properly integrate the new Muslim populations in their midst. But is that a reason to ban a woman from wearing a scarf or a Jewish boy from wearing a yarmulke? Why should children be taught to hide their religious identity, rather than take pride in it?

It has been a long-held article of faith in the American Jewish community to oppose any form of prayer in our public schools, and to remind everyone of the horrors Jewish children suffered a generation ago when such prayers were recited. But is the America then the same as America today? Isn't there something in us that says that, at a time when kids come to school worried about guns, rape, and drugs, a moment to contemplate on something spiritual might not be such a bad idea? Do we have to continue thinking that the Christian right is always wrong? Years ago, the New York State Board of Regents proposed that the following prayer be recited in all classrooms:

> Almighty God, we acknowledge our dependence upon Thee and we beg Thine blessings upon us, our parents, our teachers and our country.

Was that so bad? Was it such a threat to the Jewish community? When 75 percent of the citizens of the United States are in favor of such a prayer, should we continue to spend our money fighting it, as we spent our money fighting against Christmas postal stamps?

Similarly, what every Jewish organization now recognizes is that one of the keys to Jewish survival in America is the Jewish day school. Why should the collective Jewish community continue to fight against vouchers for parochial schools? No one is forcing your child to attend one. But why shouldn't you have the choice if you want it? And why shouldn't the government support — not the religious — but your child's secular education as it does for public school? Why should that support be denied just because a child is also getting a religious education?

This issue of state and religion is not an easy one to resolve. The fact that it has not been fully resolved here in America speaks of America's strength and not its weakness. It was the Greeks who introduced to the world the concept of democracy and citizenship. Yet, their concept of liberty was very limited. The Greeks had no regard for religious beliefs other than their own. They felt the state should impose religious beliefs. The American concept of democracy and citizenship is much different. Our concept of liberty allows for ongoing discussions and debate regarding religious beliefs and its place in society.

So yes, let us Jews put the "ch" back into Chanukah while Christians put "Christ" back into Christmas. Together, let there be "peace on earth and good will to all mankind."

December 20, 2003

BILAAM'S BLIND EYE — AND THE REPUBLICANS

Unfortunately, here in America, Orthodox and non-Orthodox rabbis rarely have an opportunity to share ideas with each other. We each have our own separate rabbinic organizations, rabbinic leaders, and rabbinic journals. That is unfortunate, because there is much that we could learn from each other. Let me prove it to you! I want to show you how one Orthodox rabbi wrote a book in which he raised a fascinating question regarding this morning's Torah portion. Yet, fifty years earlier a Conservative rabbi wrote a book that provided the answer to the very question the Orthodox rabbi raised. I have a feeling that each of them never knew that the other existed — and that is a loss for all of us. Because the question the Orthodox rabbi raised and the answer the Conservative rabbi gave are important for all of us as Jews to consider in the world in which we live.

During the Intifada, more than 500 Israelis were killed — a staggering amount in a small country like Israel! That was sad — very sad. Yet, what made matters even worse was the realization that, outside of the United States, just about everybody else blamed Israel for the situation. A poll was taken in France, Italy, Germany, and Britain, where 1,000 people in each country were asked this question: "In the dispute between Israel and the Palestinians, which side do you sympathize with more?" In each and every one of these countries, more people sided with the Palestinians than with the Israelis. And when you look at the United Nations, the situation was even worse. Every country there sided with the Palestinians!

Of course, much of this support for the Palestinians could be dismissed and explained as simply being the opinions of uneducated masses, of people who really do not know better, or because there are one billion Muslims in this world compared to only fourteen million Jews. There are all sorts of explanations, but none explains one very puzzling and painful aspect of this opposition to Israel. Often, criticism of Israel comes from people whom you would think should know better; it comes from highly intelligent and respected people. For example, Desmond Tutu, the former archbishop of Cape Town, South Africa, recently said, "People are scared in this country (the U.S.) to say wrong is wrong because the Jewish lobby is powerful — very powerful. Well, so what? The apartheid government was very powerful, but today it no longer exists. Hitler, Mussolini, Stalin, Pinochet, Milosevic and Idi Amin were all powerful, but in the end they bit the dust." Desmond Tutu is a Nobel Prize winner, and he puts Israel in the same category as Hitler and Mussolini and Stalin? He says that people in the United States do not criticize Israel because of the power of the "Jewish lobby?" This, from a Nobel Prize winner?

Let me tell you about another Nobel Prize winner. In 1998, Jose Saramago, a Portuguese novelist, won the Nobel Prize in Literature. This year, Saramago was part of an international group of writers who traveled to Ramallah to observe the Israeli siege of Yassir Arafat's compound. His impression? The situation in Ramallah, he said, was "a crime comparable to Auschwitz." In response to an Israeli journalist who asked him where the gas chambers were, Saramago said, "Not yet here." This, from a brilliant, world-renowned Nobel Prize writer — comparing us to the Nazis! How is that possible? How is it possible that the BBC, one of the most widely respected means of communication in this world, is continuously anti-Israel? How is it possible that Ted Turner, founder of CNN and presently vice president of AOL Time Warner, said Israel is just as guilty of terrorism as are the Arabs. Really? Have you heard of Israel blowing up any Palestinian civilian buses lately? Or targeting and killing a mother and her three children as the Palestinians did so recently?

An Israeli spokesman labeled Ted Turner's remarks as "stupid." But how is it possible that so many seemingly "smart" people turn "stupid" when it comes to Israel? How is it possible that respected, educated, intellectual people who know the facts —that the Arabs have been sworn to Israel's destruction ever since its creation; that, after the Six-Day War, when Israel offered peace the Arabs replied with the famous three no's: no recognition, no negotiation, no peace; and that at Camp David when Ehud Barak offered the Palestinians just about everything they ever dreamt of, they responded with an Intifada — fail to see those facts! How can seemingly brilliant minds be so warped when it comes to our people?

Interestingly enough, Rabbi Yissocher Frand, in one of his books, raises this same question, not in relation to Tutu and Saramago and the BBC, but in relation to a man named Bilaam. Rabbi Frand is an outstanding *Rosh Yeshivah* at Baltimore's renowned Ner Israel Rabbinical Seminary. In the Book of Numbers, we read how Balak, the king of Moab, called on Bilaam to curse the Jewish people and destroy them. Bilaam, according to our sages, was no ordinary man. As Rabbi Frand puts it, "He was a famous wizard, a man who wielded extraordinary power with his tongue. Those he blessed were blessed, and those he cursed were cursed. He did not command armies and navies, but he was more powerful than generals and admirals." Indeed, our sages tell us that Bilaam was the greatest prophet and the most outstanding sage of all the Gentile nations of his day. He was as exalted in the non-Jewish world as Moses was among the Jews. So, wonders Rabbi Frand, how could such a great person, such a brilliant man, attempt to destroy the Jewish people, especially when it was clear to him that he should know better?

As Bilaam was traveling to the place where he would curse the Jews, his donkey stopped, refusing to take another step. Bilaam struck the donkey, and suddenly, miraculously, the donkey opened its mouth and spoke, telling Bilaam not to curse the Jews. You would imagine that Bilaam, being as wise as he is, would then have had second thoughts about this trip he was taking. His donkey was telling him not to go! As Rabbi Frand puts it,

> Imagine yourself driving on the highway and suddenly your car stopped. You pump the gas pedal and the car says to you,

"Enough already! Can't you see I don't want to go there?" What would you do? Would you keep trying to get the car moving, or would you sit back and reconsider your trip? There is little doubt that all of us would be shaken to our very roots in such a situation. But Bilaam, the wise and extraordinary Bilaam, the famous wizard Bilaam — was nonchalant about it ... for all his skill and wisdom, he missed the clearest of all messages.

He continued on his mission to destroy the Jews. How can you explain it?

Unbeknownst to Rabbi Frand, in 1943, Rabbi Israel Leventhal, a giant in the Conservative rabbinate, wrote a book of sermons, one of which provides a marvelous explanation of this puzzle.

Rabbi Leventhal was bothered by something that our sages tell us about Bilaam. According to our sages, "*Bilaam suma b'achat m'eynav haya* — Bilaam was blind in one eye." To Rabbi Leventhal, this is a very strange statement. Writes Rabbi Leventhal, "I could understand if our sages told us that Bilaam was blind in both eyes. That's telling us something that makes a difference, that's important to know. But that he was blind in one eye? Why bother telling us that? What difference does it make? Why should the sages emphasize that he was blind in only one eye?"

Rabbi Leventhal provides a brilliant answer: in telling us that Bilaam was blind in one eye, our sages are telling us more than just something about Bilaam's physical condition. They are telling us not simply about his sight but, more importantly, about his insight. How could such a renowned and brilliant man have his heart set on destroying the Jewish people? If he was so smart, how could he be so foolish when it came to the Jews? Rabbi Leventhal explains it this way: when Bilaam scanned the lives of the peoples of the other nations and prophesized about their fate, he looked clearly with his seeing eye. Thus, he deservedly won a reputation as his people's greatest seer. It was only when he studied the Jews' lives and tried to look into their future that he used his blind eye. The rest of the world he saw clearly. When it came to the Jewish people, he had a blind spot!

And that is the way it has been with our people ever since. Voltaire and Martin Luther and Arnold Toynbee and Henry Ford and Charles DeGaulle — giants in history, brilliant minds — but, when it came to the Jews, they had a "blind spot." And that is the way it is today with the Tutus and Turners and Saramagos and all the others. When they judge and analyze most everything else, they do it with their good eye. But when it comes to the Jewish people, they are blinded by their bias and their internal prejudices.

We as Jews must make sure that we do not make the same mistake. We Jews pride ourselves on being fair, open-minded, unprejudiced, and willing to live by the dictate of our tradition to "judge every person on a scale of merit." Yet, the reality is that we do not act that way with "every" person. For some reason, we, too, have developed blind spots when it comes to certain groups and individuals. We find it difficult to view them with our good eye. Whom do I have in mind? Let me just say two words, and you tell me what is your immediate gut reaction to them: Conservative Republicans.

Do you know that some of our friends are conservatives? We pride ourselves on our liberal tradition — and we should! There are many aspects of the conservative agenda with which we as Jews disagree. Yet, we dare not be blinded to the fact that, when we pick up a newspaper or turn on the television here in America, the most pro-Israel commentators are conservatives — not liberals. They are people like George Will and Alan Keyes and William Kristol and William Bennett and Bill O'Reilly. That is a reality!

Let me tell you another reality that many Jews do not want to admit to themselves. Some of the most vocal and outspoken supporters of Israel on Capitol Hill have been Republicans. Not that we have no friends among the Democrats, but when you read some of the statements made by Republican congressional leaders like Tom DeLay and Richard Armey, you would have every reason to believe that the words were written by Menachem Begin or Ariel Sharon. We Jews have a long record of voting for Democrats. Usually more than 80 percent of our votes goes to Democrats. Yet, Ronald Lauder, former chair of the Conference of Presidents of Major Jewish Organizations, wrote an op-ed article in the *Wall Street Journal* entitled "Jewish Republican Isn't an Oxymoron." Does this mean that I am telling you the next time you are in the ballot booth you should vote Republican? No — I enjoy my job way too much to make such a statement. But I am saying that we should not allow a blind spot to block our vision from seeing where our friends are coming from.

So let us all learn from Bilaam. Let us learn not to be blinded by our preconceived notions, personal prejudices, and hang-ups. Let us see the world with both our eyes wide open. Indeed, let Orthodox Jews not be blinded to what they can learn from non-Orthodox Jews, and let non-Orthodox Jews not be blinded to what they can learn from Orthodox Jews. Let us remember the lesson we learned about Bilaam from Rabbi Frand and Rabbi Leventhal.

And let us remember the lesson of Bilaam, because even Bilaam, with his one blind eye, was able to learn about his blind spot. He came to the Jews' camp to curse them. Before that, his perception of the Jews only came from that one blind eye of his, but when he stood over the camp of Israel, when he actually saw the Jews before him, he was able to view them differently. And he then proclaimed those immortal words: "*Mah tovu ohalecha Yaakov mishkenotecha Yisroel* — how goodly are thy tents, O Jacob, your habitations, O Israel" (Numbers 24:5). It is these very words that we Jews recite every day on entering a synagogue. Amazing! There are so many beautiful verses from the Torah or from the Book of Psalms that we as Jews could recite as an opening, daily prayer, and yet the first words we say come not from a Jew, but from a non-Jew — a non-Jew who was able to overcome his blind spot. The lesson is crystal clear: let us open our eyes and see clearly with both eyes wide open.

June 22, 2002

Part III:
Contemporary Life through a Jewish Lens

ORIOLES VS. YANKEES?

Solomon Schechter, a founding father of the Conservative Movement, used to tell his rabbinical students that in America it was more important for a rabbi to know baseball than to know Talmud. I know a little Talmud, but I know a lot about baseball — so much so that as a child my father used to tell me that if I paid as much attention to studying Talmud as I did to watching baseball, I could have grown to be the next Vilna Gaon. And I used to silently think to myself: I wonder if the Vilna Gaon batted righty or lefty!

I like to focus at times on baseball because it sometimes contains lessons in life. One such time occurred in 1996. Then, one game in the Baltimore Oriole–New York Yankee American League Champion Series became not only a baseball game but also a morality play that provided keen insight into human nature. In fact, it provided me with the opportunity to discover the answer to this all-important question in my life: Am I a New Yorker or am I a Baltimorean? The answer is not so simple. It is not a matter of whether I root for the Yankees or the Orioles. Knowledgeable people would know that, for someone like me who grew up in Brooklyn and was raised as a Brooklyn Dodger fan, you never root for the Yankees. Do you know the Hebrew word for Yankees for people who grew up in Brooklyn? "Amalek — May their memory be blotted out." No, the question runs deeper than which team you root for.

Do you consider me a New Yorker or a Baltimorean? The first 23 years of my life I lived in New York but then I was a rabbi in Massachusetts for 2 1/2 years, and after that, 7 years in Washington, and now, thank God, many years in Baltimore. For more than half my life, I have lived in the Baltimore/Washington area, so how many of you consider me a New Yorker? How many of you consider me a Baltimorean? And how many of you, because of my Boston accent, consider me a New Englander?

I know you might think that it really does not matter, but it does. There was a wonderful article in the *Baltimore Sun* written by Arthur Hirsh in which he writes, "New York City may be in the same time zone as Baltimore but when it comes to the people, the demeanor, and the smell, the two might as well be on different planets." There is a world of difference between being a New Yorker and a Baltimorean. There is a big difference when you walk out of Penn Station in Baltimore and Penn Station in New York. There is a world of difference between driving on Baltimore's light rail and New York's D train. Baltimore Oriole fans are considered the most polite; New York Yankee fans the most rude. Hirsh expresses the difference in mindset between Baltimoreans and New Yorkers in response to this question: How many New Yorkers does it take to change a light bulb? Answer: None of your business. How many Baltimoreans does it take to change a light bulb? Answer: All of them. One to change the bulb, and the rest to talk about how much better things were with the old bulb. The truth of the matter is that Saks is in the center of Fifth Avenue in New York and could not make it in Baltimore, Maryland.

So along comes the 1996 American League Championship Series between Baltimore and New York, which provides the opportunity once and for all to decide whether one is a New Yorker or a Baltimorean — based on how one feels about two people: Roberto Alomar and Jeff Maier.

For more than a week, the stories of these two captured the attention of the American people. During that time, your opinion about Alomar and Maier was much more important than your opinion about presidential candidates. Roberto Alomar, the Baltimore Orioles second baseman, had spit in the face of an umpire. Jeffrey Maier was the twelve-year-old New Yorker who stuck his glove over the right field wall, in clear violation of the rules, nabbing a homerun ball and robbing the Orioles of a victory. Everybody had an opinion about these two, but the opinions differed, depending on whether one was a New Yorker or a Baltimorean. In New York, Alomar was booed mercilessly by the fans. They accused him of having committed an unpardonable sin, a brutal breach of baseball ethics. But when Alomar came to Camden Yards, the fans applauded him. After all, he had apologized, perhaps the umpire had provoked him, and he was going to be punished. The attitude here was let's stop picking on him — everyone makes mistakes.

In regard to Jeff Maier, it was just the opposite. New Yorkers applauded him. He was the toast of the town, appearing on the front pages of the *New York Times* and *Daily News* and *Post*. A deli named a sandwich for him. He appeared on the David Letterman and Rosie O'Donnell shows. He was on *Live with Regis and Kathy Lee*, and you cannot do better than that! He was dubbed "the angel of Manhattan." That was in New York. Here in Baltimore, he was no hero. He was a bratty Jewish kid who had cut school to go to the game, had committed an unpardonable crime, and to top it off, he even dropped the ball! One Baltimorean was quoted in the *New York Times* as saying, "I don't think he is a hero. He ain't no little boy. He's twelve years old. He knows the difference. He cheated. I think he should have been smacked by the glove that should have caught the ball."

So there you have it. Roberto Alomar and Jeff Maier — how do you feel about them? Where do you stand? It will tell you much about whether you are a New Yorker or a Baltimorean. As for me, based on my feelings about these two, I find that I am a Philadelphian. Neither of them is a hero; both deserve to be punished. And while Jeff Maier's crime pales in comparison to what Roberto Alomar did, it sends a bad message to our children when we glorify someone who robbed a baseball team of a victory. And while it is true that everyone makes a mistake, it sends a bad message to our children when a Roberto Alomar spits in the face of an umpire one day and is still playing ball the next.

Yet, the worst message we can send to our children is that our opinions on these and other issues depend on where we live and where we come from. Right and wrong should not depend on whether you are living in Baltimore or New York. There has to be one standard at all times, under all circumstances. Otherwise, all behavior can become acceptable and rationalized, depending on one's own perspective. In fact, it was because of just such an attitude that Adam and Eve were banished from Paradise.

Adam and Eve were banished from Paradise for eating from the tree of knowledge of good and evil. Have you ever wondered what was so terrible about eating from this tree? Should not a human being want to acquire knowledge? Maimonides asks this question in his *Guide to the Perplexed*. It is a perplexing question, but he provides an all-important answer when he points out that there are two kinds of knowledge. There is good and evil, and there is truth and falsehood. Truth and falsehood are clear and absolute. Two plus two equals four. That is not a matter of good or evil. That is just true — absolute. Yet, the knowledge of good and evil is very subjective. What you might consider good, I might consider bad and vice versa. On all questions of morals and ethics, what is good and what is bad are frequently in the eyes of the beholder. Adam and Eve traded in the knowledge of truth and falsehood for a knowledge based on good and evil, and nothing has ever been the same.

For ever since, humanity has had the tendency of making judgment calls based not on absolutes, not on truths, but on the circumstances and the situations and on one's perspective and on whether you live in Baltimore or in New York. It is very dangerous for a society to operate like that because then just about any behavior can be justified. "Thou shalt not kill?" What about a Dr. Kevorkian? "Thou shalt not steal?" What if you are unemployed and society has a bias against you? "Thou shalt not lie?" What about just a small white one to keep your job? True and false never vary. Good and evil are in the eye of the beholder. And that is dangerous, very dangerous.

So after all is said and done, Baltimorean or New Yorker? It really should not matter. It really does not matter. Whether it is a twelve-year-old kid or a Major League baseball player should not matter and it does not matter. They were both wrong. They both did the wrong thing. And we are wrong if we judge them from our own personal bias and perspective.

Having said all this, there is one area in which one's personal bias and perspective do play a role in Jewish law. In fact, one's bias is expected to play a part in Jewish law, and a mechanism to deal with it is built into Jewish law. Jewish law tells us, "*Karov pasul l'eidut* — A relative is prohibited from testifying." You are not allowed to come to a Jewish court and testify on behalf of a relative of yours because it is felt that your testimony cannot be fully trusted. You are naturally going to have a bias based on where you are coming from; in this case, the same family. We see an example of this bias at the conclusion of this morning's Torah portion in regard to Abraham and his brother. And we saw an example of this in regard to Roberto Alomar and his brother.

A famous legend tells us that a man named Terach had three sons — Abram, Nachor, and Haran. Terach ran an interesting business to support his family. He made a living selling idols, and one day his son Abram came into the store and smashed all of them. When his father saw the smashed idols, Abram told him that the idols had had a fight and had broken each other. This was his attempt to show his father how foolish it was to believe in idols. His father did not take Abram's actions lightly. According to the legend, Terach took his son Abram to court and sued him for vandalism for the damage he had caused to his merchandise. He was brought up on trial in the court of Nimrod, and Nimrod said, "Let us test Abram. We will throw him into the fire. If nothing happens to him, there must be a God in Heaven. If he gets burned, then there is no God." So they threw Abram into the furnace. Nothing happened — God saved him. Nimrod and all of his followers were shaken.

Then Nimrod turned to Haran and asked him, "Where do you stand — with your brother or with me?" Haran replied, "I am with Abram." He said this knowing full well that he was risking his life. If he stood with Nimrod, he would be rewarded by all the people. If he sided with Abram he, too, would be thrown into the fire, and who knows what might happen. But Haran just could not help himself — Abram was his flesh and blood, and he naturally stood with him. So Haran was thrown into the fire. And do you know what? He burned to death.

Standing with your brother does not always have a happy ending. But it is, after all is said and done, the natural thing to do.

I thought about this after Roberto Alomar hit a home run in the twelfth inning, leading the Orioles to their victory over the Cleveland Indians in the playoff game. There was an article on the front page of the *Sun* the next day with this headline: "Alomar Answers in the End." And these were the first two paragraphs of the story:

Roberto Alomar stood in the middle of the champagne-soaked Orioles clubhouse conducting a live radio interview. He had hit the game-tieing single and the game-winning homer to put the Orioles in the American League Championship Series. He had answered question after question, made apology after apology, kept his composure amid the booing, the umpires' protests, the unrelenting media storm. And then he saw his brother, Sandy Alomar, Jr., the catcher for the opposing Cleveland Indians, whom he had just brought down in defeat. His brother headed straight to Robbie in the clubhouse, embracing his playoff opponent briefly but firmly. Not a word was spoken, but Roberto Alomar burst into tears.

Here was a man who had been booed and criticized all over the country — except in Baltimore. A man who knew he had done the wrong thing but it was too late to do anything about it. A man who had to keep all of his emotions under control after what he had done. It was nice when, after all was said and done, he had a brother on whose shoulders he could cry. A brother who even though he played on the opposing team, was still, after all is said and done, his brother.

We can all learn lessons from the game of baseball in regard to the game of life. We can learn to judge honestly, not based on personal biases, but based on what is true and what is not. And that should never vary except when it comes to your own flesh and blood. For them, we can always be there to give them the benefit of the doubt, the support and the love they so badly need at crucial times in life.

Let us always keep in mind those immortal words of Grandland Rice: "When the one great scorer comes to write against your name,

He marks not that you won or lost, but how you played the game." Let us always play in a true spirit of brotherhood. Let us play fair, honest, and true, in keeping with the words of our prayers: "Let us purify our hearts to serve God and humanity in truth."

October 19, 1996

Cell Phones, Stem Cells, Circumcision, and Christopher Reeve

Jews have been waiting 2,000 years for the arrival of the Messiah, but at least now, finally, we know why he has not come. Why? Because of cell phones! That's right! That is what Rabbi Shmuel Halevy Wosner, a leader in Israel's ultra-Orthodox community, proclaimed in a sermon. According to this rabbi, cell phones are corrupting our youth, who are wasting their time on the phone and downloading promiscuous pictures. In Rabbi Wosner's words,

> The reason we are not winning complete redemption is because of the persecutor; that is, the cellular instrument. It pursues and oppresses the individual and gives him no rest at any time or at any hour. And today it has already become seeing and broadcasting impure pictures and abominable news and every man and woman, bachelor and maiden, groom and bride, boy and girl, is fingering this terrible instrument.

I read this in *Hamodia*, an ultra-Orthodox newspaper. In the same issue of the newspaper, there was a full page ad proclaiming, "You may be shocked but it is true — countless people have been ruined by the Internet."

Now there can be no question that cell phones and the Internet have their downsides and potentially can cause harm. There are dangers in their use, and we must guard against them. Yet, there is also no question that cell phones and the Internet provide marvelous opportunities as well, and we should understand them and make productive use of them.

We are living during a revolution in communication technology. Rabbi Jonathan Sacks, Chief Rabbi of the British Empire, has pointed out that an earlier revolution in communication technology occurred right at the dawn of civilization with the invention of hieroglyphics. For the first time, knowledge could be passed from one generation to the next not simply by memory but in writing.

And then with the invention of the alphabet came the next revolution in communication. Hieroglyphics involved too many characters, and too few people could write or read it. The alphabet opened up knowledge to the masses. We do not know for sure who invented the alphabet; however, what we do know is that the word "alphabet" itself comes from the first two letters of Hebrew script: *aleph* and *bet*. There can be no doubt that our Jewish ancestors were the first to fully understand the radical implications of this new communication technology. Jewish society was the first one in which every human individual was able to reach his or her true potential through direct access to knowledge.

That is what bothered me about Rabbi Wosner's — and other rabbis' — prohibitions on the use of cell phones and the Internet. To me, they seem so un-Jewish! We Jews have always been at the forefront of all the communication revolutions. We have been the beneficiaries of those revolutions as well. What is wrong with the People of the Book also becoming the People of the Computer?

What is wrong is found in the mindset of certain people — Jews and non-Jews alike — who think that every change, every new discovery, every technical revolution, is an assault on God. Rabbi Benjamin Blech has pointed out that every major scientific step forward has been met with religious opposition based on this principle.

- When the Wright brothers created the first airplane, many considered it an act of heresy; as they put it, "If God meant for man to fly, He would have created him with wings."

• A man by the name of Tagliacci was the first to discover the great potential of plastic surgery. Did you know that his bones were disinterred from a Christian cemetery by religious fundamentalists who said this man had no right to a Christian burial because he had tampered with God's creation? If God wanted humans to look different, He would have created them that way — how dare Tagliacci interfere in God's creation. [Just imagine the shock waves in the Jewish community if this way of thinking about plastic surgery had become the accepted norm!]

• This opposition occurs not only in the scientific arena. When the Panama Canal was built, creating a waterway between North and South America, religious groups held mass rallies in protest of what they considered an act of blasphemy: "What God hath put together, let no man cast asunder," they cried.

• The discovery of the first umbrella was castigated on religious grounds: "If it's raining, obviously God wants us to get wet."

• Politically, when there were tyrants in the past and revolutionaries called for their overthrow, many came to the defense of those tyrants by claiming that there is a divine right of kings. Thomas Jefferson was considered a radical when he advocated that the seal of the United States bear this inscription: "Rebellion against tyrants is obedience to God." That was considered a radical concept by those who believed that the kings and queens of England were chosen by God — and if God chose them, it was meant to be.

• Regarding medicine, the Christian Science movement teaches that we have to accept the reality of sickness as being God's will, and it must be left to the same God who causes illness to bring the cure as well. In fact, during the first decades of the twentieth century, several influential Jews became attracted to the Christian Science movement. In the year 1922, a graduate of the Hebrew Union College, Morris Lichtenstein, founded a similar movement with the imitative name of "Jewish Science," which he claimed was fully in accord with Jewish tradition.

Is it? Jewish tradition teaches, "*Hakol bidei shamayim chutz miyirat shamayim* — everything is in God's hands except for reverence for God." Would Jewish tradition view advances in technology and communication as assaults on God?

This question is so important that Judaism finds its response in the very first commandment given to the Jewish people — a commandment that is among the most widely observed and least understood in all the Torah.

At the age of ninety-seven, the first Jew — Abraham — was introduced to the concept of circumcision when God commanded him, "*Himol lachem kol zachar* — every man among you shall be circumcised" (Genesis 17:10). This concept of *brit* — of a physical covenant between man and God — is a most puzzling one, and it gave rise to the very same question we have been discussing. The Talmud tells us that Rabbi Akiva was asked by a Roman, "How can you Jews go and alter God's creation through circumcision? It's as if you were given a beautiful bouquet of flowers and the first thing you do is cut off one of the flowers because you didn't like the way it was arranged, the way it looks. How dare you tamper with the work of God? If God wanted man circumcised, He would have created him that way."

The response that Rabbi Akiva gave to this question about circumcision represents the essence of the Jewish way of thinking. Rabbi Akiva replied in this way: in reality, circumcision brings the body closer to completion and perfection. Why was not man born circumcised? Because God created man and his world incomplete — imperfect — so that man could then complete the process of creation, making himself complete and perfect. Each human being is supposed to be a "*shutof b'maaseh bereshit* — a co-partner with his Creator in the act of creation."

Indeed, this is this very message that God taught to Abraham when He presented him with this mitzvah of brit — of circumcision. For what does the Torah tell us? "And the Lord said to Abraham: "*Ani el Shaddai* — I am the God of Shaddai." Our rabbis read this phrase as the "God *sheomar dai*" — the God who created the world and said, "Enough, I have done enough for creation. Now it is for you to complete my work." "*Hithalech l'fanai ... v'heyeh tamin* — walk before me and make yourself complete and perfect" (Genesis 17:1). I," says God, "have left the world undone so that you — man — may continue and complete my work."

As our sages beautifully point out, after God created the world in seven days, on the eighth day, God gave humans fire, the symbol and potential for creativity. Unlike the Romans who believed that human beings had to steal fire from the gods, Jewish tradition tells us that humans were *given* the gift of fire from God. God created the world in seven days, and on the eighth day He gave us fire so that we could continue the act of creation. The *brit* itself takes place on the eighth day because on the eighth day, we humans must take over from God and begin our own acts of creation. In fact, the very word that we use for circumcision — *brit* — tells the whole story. What does it mean? It means a covenant, and a covenant means two partners. It means that I have a job and you have a job. I will do my share, said God; now, you — humans — do yours.

And we Jews have always done our share — more than our share! Look at the Nobel Prize winners in 2004. Five out of the six winners in science were Jewish. Five out of six! For every 1,000 people in this world, 998 are not Jewish. Yet, five out of the six scientific Nobel Prize winners were Jewish! Our people have brought so much progress to humankind and relief from illness because we have been co-partners with God in the act of creation.

So, our people should not have a problem with cell phones; neither should we have a problem with stem cell research. Soon after Rabbi Wosner's sermon, Superman died when Christopher Reeve passed away. Christopher Reeve had played Superman in three movies. He was a most popular actor, and then, after a tragic accident, he found himself a quadriplegic. He considered suicide. I was struck by a quote of his I read in one of his obituaries. In 1983 when he was concerned that Hollywood not typecast him just as Superman, he said, "Look, I've flown, I've become evil, stopped and turned the world backward. I faced my peers, I befriended children and small animals and I've rescued cats from trees. What else is there left for Superman to do that hasn't been done?"

Well, Christopher Reeve discovered what else there is for Superman to do when everything else had been done. Christopher Reeve became a "super man" when he was no longer able to be Superman. He became a symbol of courage throughout the world, and he became a leading advocate for stem cell research — which the Jewish religion encourages. Do you know where he found stem cell research at its most advanced? When he visited Israel! Yes, Carl and Rob Reiner have not been able to get themselves to Israel, but Christopher Reeve visited there. He went there because he was so impressed with the work that Israeli scientists were doing on stem cell research.

We Jews can be proud of our superpeople — the men and women who, down through the ages, have acted as God's co-partners should act. God created a world with drugs and medicines and endowed humankind with the intelligence necessary to discover their medicinal properties. We are obliged to use them in warding off illness and disease. God provided the materials and technology that make possible catheters and intravenous infusions and respirators and transplants — and we are obligated to use them to save and prolong life.

This is true not only in regard to illness and medicine and science, but in all areas of our lives. I hear people pray that their businesses should prosper. I hear people pray that their children should follow the proper path in life. These are legitimate prayers, but they are meaningless unless we are willing to do our share to make them come true. It is said that modern individuals have no faith. That is not true. Sometimes they have too much faith and leave it all to God.

Soon there will be another World Series, and I look back to an incident that took place one year when the Baltimore Orioles played in the Series. I know it is hard for some of the younger people in our synagogue to remember that there was a time when the Orioles were in the Series, but it is true! That year, after the first game, newspapers reported that the late Edward Bennett Williams — then the owner of the Orioles — and several of his friends were trapped in an elevator at Memorial Stadium, of blessed memory. What did Mr. Williams do? He prayed, "Dear Lord, we're now in a highly dangerous situation and with each moment it gets more grave and we ask you to please get us out of here, because we don't know how much longer we can last." Lo and behold, the stuck elevator doors promptly opened, and that was great. Thank God for that! Praying to God certainly helps, but I want you to know — and I tell you this as a rabbi who has deep faith in God

— if I were trapped in an elevator, I would not be content to pray to God and leave it all to Him. Jewish tradition would say: if you're stuck in an elevator, yes, whisper a prayer to God, but at the same time scream at the top of your lungs for the elevator repairman to get you out of there! We have got to do our share; we cannot leave it all to God.

I remember when I lived in Brooklyn and it seemed like every year the World Series involved the Brooklyn Dodgers — whom I loved — and the New York Amaleks — whom I hated — and every year the Dodgers lost. It was heartbreaking. One year before the World Series, all the churches in Brooklyn had a prayer recited on behalf of the Brooklyn Dodgers. What happened? They lost! Why? Because what the Dodgers were lacking was not God's grace; what the Dodgers were lacking was a good left fielder! God can't do it all — people must be His "*shutof* — His co-partner."

So, Rabbi Wosner, I understand the dangers of the cell phone and the Internet. Yet, I also know that because of the cell phone, it makes it much easier for me to speak to my mother every day. I also know that, because of the Internet, I can access words of Torah that I never would have known before. These are God's gifts, and we have to be taught how to use them wisely. We cannot all be Nobel Prize winners, but we can all be noble people — co-partners with God in making our society, community, and our homes better places in which to live by performing our own acts of creation and bringing our world closer to perfection.

October 23, 2004

MOTHER TERESA OR RABBI OVADIAH YOSEF: FAITH AND DOUBT

There is an old Yiddish expression that says, *"Az mir lebt delebt min"* —if you live long enough, you'll live to see everything. I thought of these words when it was revealed, in her letters that are now published in a book, that Mother Teresa had spent the last fifty years of her life without feeling God's presence. From a religious perspective, I do not remember ever being as surprised, as shocked, as I was by this revelation. She was considered one of the most remarkable human beings of our time. Now, reading her words — she "found darkness and coldness and emptiness so great that nothing touches my soul," and she referred to God as the "Absent One" — we discover that, except for five weeks in 1959, for most of her life she questioned her beliefs, she had difficulty praying, and she had an almost complete lack of feeling of God's presence. What is one to say?

Well, people have had a lot to say on the subject, ranging from her defenders who condemned the publication of these letters, saying that they were private and that she herself had asked that they be burned, to those who say she must have been clinically depressed, to others who claimed we will never understand what was going through her mind, and to still others who say, "What's the difference what she believed; what is important is what she did." And there are the critics like Christopher Hitchens, who refers to her as a "troubled and miserable lady," and writes, "In doubting God she had secretly discovered the truth."

I also have an opinion, and it is very different from those I just mentioned. I think of how Mother Teresa spent her days. People were dying all around her: children were starving from malnutrition, and young people were dying from AIDS. She was surrounded by such pain, such anguish. I read her book and I could feel her pain and anguish, which started when she began trying to minister to the people in the streets of Calcutta. She describes her first day in these words:

> Children are all over the place — and what dirt and misery — what poverty and suffering.... I just did some washing of sores and dressings, gave medicine to some — the old man lying on the street — not wanted — all alone just sick and dying.... There is a poor woman dying I think of starvation more than TB. What poverty! What actual suffering! I gave her something which will help put her to sleep — but the woman's longing to have some care.... I felt my own poverty there too — for I had nothing to give that poor woman.

Can anyone blame her for questioning God? I cannot! Because in my own, very small way, I have experienced what she had experienced. When I go to a hospital and I see an infant malformed or I see an older person who really, excuse me for saying it, is not much more than a vegetable, I see so much pain. I see young people dying, old people suffering. Don't you think I question a God who is supposed to be "just and merciful?" Going to visit children's wards is particularly painful for me. I find myself asking, "God, what are you thinking?" You don't think I have my doubts? You don't think I'm human?

I want you to know — and it might seem strange — but this Catholic nun had feelings that are very understandable from a Jewish perspective. Judaism was custom-made for people like her. Rabbi Norman Lamm, Chancellor of Yeshiva University, wrote a book entitled *Faith and Doubt*. In Judaism there are always both! Rabbi Soloveitchik, one of the truly great Jewish thinkers of the twentieth century and a man who was religious and observant in every way, once said, "Everyone is allowed to be unsure about God. We all have times when things about God are unclear to us." Rabbi Benjamin Blech put it this way:

Doubt is often defined as a challenge to God. Yet it is not. Doubt only describes the reality of the human being. When one has doubt, when one questions, one is making a statement not about God but about oneself. Human beings do not have perfect knowledge; human beings do not know everything; human beings can be wrong — human beings not only have a potential to grow but a need to grow. Doubt, self-questioning, is thus a necessary attribute of the human being for it is only thereby that the human being can grow.

These are very important words, and I wish some of our rabbis and their followers would take them to heart. Rabbi Ovadiah Yosef, the leading Sephardic rabbi in Israel, in one of his speeches broadcast by satellite to thousands of his followers, said, "Should it come as a surprise if, God forbid, soldiers are killed in war (he was referring to the 119 solders killed in the second Lebanon war)? When they do not adhere to the laws of Shabbat, they do not keep the Torah, they do not pray, they do not put on tefillin every day.... God have mercy on them and make them repent. Then they will all live a good life in peace." People in Israel were in an uproar over his statement that soldiers were dying because they were not religiously observant. One of those who cried out the loudest was Shosh Klein, the mother of Maj. Roi Klein, an observant soldier who flung himself on a hand grenade, thus sacrificing his life to save his fellow soldiers. This courageous soldier shouted out the *Shema* just before the explosion that took his life. How could any rabbi say that any soldier died because he was not religiously observant?

Rabbi Yosef's words hurt me, as they should any thinking human being. Yet, what concerned me even more was how quickly his followers jumped to his defense. The most dangerous statement came from Eli Yishai, a Sephardic cabinet minister who is one of the best known of Rabbi Yosef's followers; Yishai said, "My rabbi does not err. Everything he says is the word of God."

What a dangerous statement to make! The sheer stupidity of it is reflected in the fact that the day after he made this statement, Rabbi Yosef backtracked from what he had said, claiming that his words did not relate to soldiers in modern times, only in ancient days.

CNN had a series of three programs entitled *God's Warriors* that profiled Jews, Christians, and Muslims who believed that they were following the word of God when committing unspeakable acts. The programs featured Christians blowing up abortion clinics, Muslim suicide bombers, and Jewish extremists who have taken the law into their own hands in killing Arabs and in desiring to blow up the Mosque of Omar atop the Temple Mount. The programs were terrible, and Jewish organizations rightfully claimed that they were not balanced. Whereas there are millions of Christian and Muslims who are "God's Warriors," among the Jews there are just a few hundred, and they are condemned by every mainstream Jewish organization. Yet, what is true is that all these Jewish "Warriors" believe that they hear God and are following the word of God, or at least that their teachers "hear" the word of God and they are following His orders. The most despicable crimes committed by Jews in recent memory were all done in God's name. Boruch Goldstein, when he massacred Arabs in Hebron, felt he was following God's word. Yigal Amir assassinated Yitzchak Rabin because he was taught that was what God mandated.

In the book of Kohelet, King Solomon writes, "Do not be overly righteous or excessively wise.... Be not overly wicked nor a fool" (Ecclesiastes 1:16). These verses raise an obvious question. One can understand King Solomon's admonition that one not be "overly wicked" or "be a fool." It is bad enough to be wicked; one certainly should not be "*overly*" wicked and act like a fool. But what about the first verse, the one that tells us "do not be overly righteous" or "excessively wise?" Sure, too much of anything is no good. But when it comes to piety, more would certainly seem better than less. And "*excessively wise*" — is that really possible? Is that such a terrible thing?

Yes it is, and you do not have to take my word for it. Take the word of one of the great sages of the twentieth century, Rabbi Jacob Ruderman, the founder and for many years the leader of the Ner Israel Rabbinical College here in Baltimore — a school that many identify as being "right wing" or "ultra." In one of his classes, this great Torah giant, whose love of Judaism and the Jewish people was total and complete, who was uncompromising in his dedication to Judaism, said that being "overly righteous" and "excessively smart" is even worse than being "overly wicked" and acting like a "fool." He went on to explain that, if a person is overly wicked, at least there is the possibility that one day he or she will realize that and will repent and change. However, people who are overly righteous or excessively smart will think they are always right. There is no chance of their ever seeing when they are wrong, when they are overdoing things. There is no chance of their ever believing that anyone else could be right.

We can all learn a good lesson from a man named Noah. The Torah tells us something about Noah that our rabbis interpret in a rather mind-boggling way. The Torah says that Noach and his sons and his wife and his son's wives went into the ark "*mipney mey hamabul.*" They entered the ark "on account of" or literally "in the face of" the waters of the flood. Rashi asks why the verse is worded this way. He explains that Noah and his family did not enter the ark until the storm actually came. According to Rashi, Noah did not really believe that there would be a flood. God said that there would be, and maybe there would be, but somehow Noah was not completely convinced. So he stayed outside the ark, and when the first rains came, he still did not move. Only when it really began to pour, only then did he and his family enter the ark.

Our rabbis here are depicting Noah as a man with doubts about God. In Rashi's words, "*Noah miktanei emunah haya* — Noah was a man of little faith." "*He-emin v'lo he-emin* — he believed and didn't believe" both at the same time. He had faith in God and did not have faith in God, both at the same time. And how did God feel about this man Noah? It says it right there in the Torah: "*v'Noach matza chein b'einei Hashem* — Noah found grace in the eyes of God.... *Noach ish tzadik tamim haya b'dorotov* — Noah was a righteous man, perfect in his generations" (Genesis 6:9). Not bad as a testament to a man our sages tell us had doubts about his faith.

We are all created "*b'tzelem Elokim* — in the image of God." Let us all do our share, *l'takein olam b'malchut Shaddai* — to bring the world closer to perfection. That is what Noah did. That is what Mother Teresa did. With all her doubts, she continued to do God's work here on earth. And we must do the same. Let us do our share and then we can hope that God will do His.

October 13, 2007

AN ORTHODOX PERSPECTIVE ON REFORM

It's an old and lousy joke. I repeat it because, in light of recent events, it is possible that we will never have to hear it again. It's the one about the Jew who goes to an Orthodox rabbi and asks him, What *bracha* do you make on Halloween? The rabbi responds, "What's Halloween?" So the Jew goes to a Reform rabbi and asks the same question, and the rabbi responds, "What's a *bracha*?" The joke was never a good one, but I think now it has lost all meaning in light of recent changes in the Reform movement.

At the 1999 convention of the Central Conference of American Rabbis, which represents the Reform rabbinate in America, the rabbis sat down and did something that Conservative and Orthodox rabbis rarely have the courage to do. They took a look at themselves and at their own movement, and they admitted to themselves that something was wrong, and changes would have to be made. After much discussion and debate among the rabbis and their congregants, the Reform movement issued a new "Statement of Principles," which *Time* magazine headlined as being "back to the yarmulke." Well, it was not quite that, but the new Statement of Principles was a rather radical change in the thinking and actions of Reform Jews and Judaism. Among other things, the document does the following:

• affirms the importance of studying Hebrew

• promotes lifelong Jewish learning

• encourages aliyah to Israel

• urges observance in some form of Shabbat and holidays

• calls for observance of mitzvot "that address us as individuals and as a community"

This turn toward tradition by the Reform movement did not come easily or happen overnight. The Statement of Principles went through six drafts and thirty amendments, and some within the Reform movement are terribly upset about it. For example, Ronald Sobel, the senior rabbi at Temple Emanuel, New York City's largest Reform synagogue, has been quoted as stating that the guidelines constitute a "distortion of the uniqueness of Reform Judaism." Yet, the question is not simply how Reform Jews are going to react to these principles; it is also how Orthodox and Conservative Jews are going to react. When a change like this occurs within the Jewish world, it does not simply relate to Reform Jews, it affects all of us.

First, on a mystical level! In the famous 32nd chapter of one of the classic works of Jewish thought, the Tanya — the great work of the first Lubavitcher rebbe — the Rebbe sets out the idea that all Jews are united. Their bodies are separate, but their souls are one. They share, as it were, a single, collective spiritual substance. Yes, Orthodox, Conservative, or Reform — it does not matter — everyone is connected. What one does inevitably affects the other. This is most certainly true on a practical level as well. Reform Judaism is the largest movement of Jews in our country. What they do cannot be isolated from us. So how are we to react?

Based on the comments I read from some Orthodox colleagues of mine, the changes in the Reform movement have not at all changed the Orthodox view of Reform Judaism. Israel's Chief Rabbi Israel Lau said the changes really do not mean much of anything. In his words: "It's very nice to have a yarmulke in synagogue and to separate cold cuts from cheese, but it doesn't make them partners in the Bible as it was given on Mt. Sinai." He went on to say that there is still no reason for him, as a Chief Rabbi, to even meet and negotiate with Reform leaders.

Other Orthodox rabbis, while taking note of the positive change in the Statement of Principles by the Reform movement, felt that the changes did not go far enough. The Reform movement's attitude toward conversion and endorsement of patrilineal descent presented too great a gap to cross. In addition, earlier drafts of the Statement of Principles had called for observing Kashrut, immersing oneself in a mikvah, and wearing tallit and tefillin, and all this was cut in the final draft. So, after all is said and done, as Ecclesiastes put it, "*Ein kol chadash tachat hashamesh* — there's nothing new under the sun" (Ecclesiastes 1:9).

As a Modern Orthodox rabbi, I can only say that my fellow Orthodox colleagues are entitled to their opinions, and I certainly recognize and accept their concerns and reservations. At the same time, I must say that, based on their overall attitude, had they been alive thousands of years ago, they would have been among those who might never have been able to enter the Land of Israel.

Let us go back in time several thousand years. The Jewish people, having been redeemed from 200 years of slavery in Egypt, are now standing on the borders of the Promised Land of their dreams. However, they are nervous and afraid, and they lack faith in their ability to conquer the land of Israel. And so they send twelve spies to see the land and its inhabitants and report back to the Jewish people. The spies return after forty days with a majority and minority report. The minority of two is ready to lead the Jews into the Promised Land, but the majority of ten say all hope is lost: the inhabitants of the land are too strong to conquer.

If you study the text in the Torah describing the report of the spies, you will note that both the majority and the minority saw both good and bad in the land. As in most of life, the situation was neither all good nor all bad — but a mixture of the two. The major difference between the minority and majority rested not in what they reported, but rather in the way they made their report, in the order in which they gave it. The ten spies who form the majority give their report starting with the good news as they proclaim, "*banu el ha'haretz asher shlachtanu* — we came unto the land where you sent us. And surely it is a land that flows with milk and honey" (Numbers 13:27). But then they immediately erased the good news with one word *efes* — "but": "*efes ki az ha-am hayoshev ba-aretz* — but the people who dwell in the land are fierce and the cities are fortified." We are not going to make it! Their report started off good, but then along came that one word, *efes—* but. In Hebrew, *efes* also means "zero." What followed after that "but" zeroed out all of the previous good news. The good news was negated, and the bad news became the bottom line. And for that the Jews were condemned to wander in the wilderness for another forty years, until a new generation arose. A generation that would understand that, yes, there is bad news and there is good news, but you cannot allow the bad to negate the good. The positive must always take precedence over the negative.

Sure, to a traditional-minded Orthodox or Conservative Jew there is much lacking in the Reform's Statement of Principles. There is so much in it that still divides us, and the divisions are very real and very dangerous. But that must not cause us to negate all of the good that has come from the Reform's Statement of Principles. And so much of it is for the good.

Consider the following changes.

• Where a Reform service was once almost entirely conducted in English, the new call for studying Hebrew is an important step in uniting our people by sharing in a common language.

• The call for lifelong Jewish learning is no small matter. All Jews could share in such a call.

• Encouraging observance of the Shabbat comes a long way from the times when some Reform Jews looked on Sunday as being their day of rest.

• The encouragement to consider aliyah to Israel is coming from a Reform movement whose early German reformers used to proclaim, "Berlin is our Jerusalem, Germany our homeland."

• And the call for observance of mitzvot comes from a movement whose original declaration of principles rejected "all such Mosaic and Rabbinical laws which regulate diet, priestly purity and dress." No, I do not expect Reform Jews to now start eating glatt kosher and cholov Yisroel, but then again, neither do I!

And no, despite what *Time* magazine headlined, the Reform movement has not gone "back to the yarmulke." But at recent graduations of Reform rabbis, it is reported that most of the graduates were wearing yarmulkes. In more and more Reform synagogues there are kippot and tallitot, and that is a far cry from the story I once read by William Braude, a prominent Reform rabbi in Rhode Island. He told how, at the time of the Holocaust, a special commemorative service was held in his synagogue on Kristallnacht. One of those who came to the service was a man who had been living in Germany and survived the horrors of the "night of the broken glass." He sat down at that service in a Reform temple, and doing what came naturally to him when in a synagogue, he was wearing a yarmulke. An usher approached him and told him that that was not allowed in the synagogue. When he refused to take his yarmulke off, he was asked to leave. Just imagine that a survivor of Hitler's Germany was asked to leave a Holocaust memorial service in a synagogue in Rhode Island for wearing a yarmulke! It is hard to imagine that happening anymore!

Sure, Reform has a long way to go. But so do we! We Orthodox and Conservative Jews have not even stopped to look at ourselves. And until we do, let us continue to insist that the Reform movement change its policies on patrilineal descent and divorce and conversion, policies that have caused a terrible rift among the Jewish people. Yet, at the same time, let us not allow these differences to negate the positive developments in the Reform movement that move them closer to us. Let us remember that famous line of Abba Eban: the Jews are a people who can't take yes for an answer. We should celebrate Reform's turn toward tradition and not make petty, snide criticisms or fail to notice the enormity of the change.

Let us not make the same mistakes as the spies. Let us not allow the bad to negate the good. And this is true in all of life! Ask someone how she liked the wedding? "It was nice. But they sat me too close to the band." How did you like Israel? "It was beautiful, but the waiter was abrasive." How's it going with the job? The family? "Fine, but."

That "but," that *efes*, usually means "zero." It zeroes out all the good that precedes it. There is always going to be good and bad, but we cannot allow the bad to negate the good — not in our own lives and not in our lives as Jews in regard to our Reform brethren. If they still have a long way to go in their ritual behavior, we as Orthodox Jews can start looking at ourselves and recognize that we have a long way to go in our ethical behavior. Proper ethics would tell us that, rather than negate and criticize what Reform Jews do not do, we could use this as an opportunity to affirm and applaud what they have chosen to do.

And they need that praise from us! A colleague of mine points out that one of the reasons why the two spies, Joshua and Kalev, were able to stand up to the ten others was because they had each other. Had either one of them been alone, I do not know if they would have been able to stand up to the argument of the negative ten. Those who fight for a return to tradition in the Reform movement should not have to struggle alone. Orthodox and Conservative rabbis and Jews should be there to encourage them and to strengthen them.

The Reform movement has changed, and it is a change for the better. Sure, they have not turned Orthodox, and I suspect they never will. That is not where they want to be! But if they are not here, at least now they are not way out there! And for this, we should do what the Reform rabbis did when the resolution for change passed. They joined in proclaiming in Hebrew the words, *"Shehechiyanu v'kiymanu v'higianu lazman hazeh* — thank you God for bringing us to this day."

June 12, 1999

ARE JEWS TOO POWERFUL?
THE *VANITY FAIR* PERSPECTIVE

The October 2007 issue of *Vanity Fair* had three articles that may be dangerous to your health as a Jew — or maybe not!

One is entitled "The 2007 New Establishment," and it lists those whom *Vanity Fair* considers to be the 100 most powerful, influential people in American society. I think it was Joseph Aaron in the *Chicago Jewish News* who first took note of a rather remarkable feature of this list. We Jews represent about 2.5 percent of the American people. So one could naturally expect that, of the 100 most influential people in America, there would be listed two or three Jews. How many Jews do you think were on the list? You are going to find this hard to believe, but according to Mr. Aaron's calculation, 51 of the 100 are Jewish! Now, keep in mind that this is not a list of *shleppers* — among the 100 are people with names like Warren Buffet, Bill Clinton, and Oprah Winfrey. Yet, right alongside of them are people with names like Schwartzman and Spielberg and Bloomberg and Geffen and Perelman and Lauder and Wasserstein and Cohen and Weinstein and Weintraub and Friedman and Silver. Not bad, my friends! Not bad when one considers that there are more people born in China every year than there are Jews in the whole world!

As if all this is not enough, on page 306 in the same issue of the magazine, there is another list. This one, which is called "The Next

Establishment," lists younger people that *Vanity Fair* believes will eventually make it to the "big list." There are 26 people on that list, of whom 15 are Jews. Again, over 50 percent!

Then, just in case you still do not get it, on page 308 of *Vanity Fair* there is a list of people who made the "New Establishment" list in the past and are not on this year, but whom the editors believe will be back in the future. There are nine names on this list, and eight are Jews! This is absolutely unbelievable! This is absolutely incredible! In response, the only question is that age-old question, Is it good for the Jews? Is it good to present so many Jews out front in the public, in positions of power, drawing attention to us? Or is it bad, feeding the hatred of the anti-Semites who accuse us of being too powerful and too controlling?

It is not easy to give a correct answer to this question because I believe Jewish tradition provides two contradictory responses. Toward the end of Genesis where Jacob speaks to his children as they are about to go down to Egypt, the Midrash describes the conversation this way: "Jacob requested of them: do not go out with bread in your hands and do not all enter through one gate.... Do not go out with bread in your hands in order not to arouse ill feeling and do not all enter through one gate for fear of the eye." There was a famine in Egypt, and Jacob is telling his children that when they go down to Egypt, they should not let the people see that they have bread. They should not come marching in together as one, because people will be afraid of them, people will envy them, people will give them the "evil eye." With this in mind, one cannot help but think that the articles in *Vanity Fair* are not doing us any favors. It would be better if not so much attention was drawn to our success.

On the other hand, in the Book of Exodus, in the description of the garment made for the High Priest to wear in the Temple, we are told that the hem of his robe had bells on it so that people would know that he was coming. The Lubavitcher Rebbe saw this as a lesson that a Jew should go out into this world proud and confident, trying to spread the message of Judaism. That is just what Lubavitcher Chasidim do these days, with their "Mitzvah Mobiles" and the big Chanukah menorahs they put up in public squares throughout our country. So, from the perspective of the Lubavitcher Rebbe you could say — although he never would have put it this way — "If you've got it, flaunt it!"

What do you think? Lay low or flaunt it? Is *Vanity Fair* good for the Jews or not? I venture to say that your answer will depend on how old you are. Alan Dershowitz put it so well in his book, appropriately entitled *Chutzpah*, when he pointed out, "We are at a generational crossroads. The Jews who were the American pioneers — our first generations of immigrants — were indeed guests in other people's land." Yes, many of our fathers and mothers and certainly our grandfathers and grandmothers felt that they were guests in America. And so they made sure that they did nothing to "rock the boat." They did as little as possible to draw attention to themselves. They had a *sha-shtil* philosophy — lay low and they won't come after us with an ax. And so, Betty Perske changed her name to Lauren Bacall, and Joseph Gottlieb to Joey Bishop, and Issur Danielovich Demsky to Kirk Douglas, and Sidney Liebowitz to Steve Lawrence.

Yet, as Jews grew more successful in America, they also grew to feel at home in America. Suddenly Jews were asserting their rights as Jews. When Jews moved to the suburbs in the 1950s and '60s, many synagogues across the country built their parking lot in the front and the synagogue in the back so as not to upset their neighbors. Then, all of a sudden, in the 1970s, the slogan, "Freedom for Soviet Jewry," was emblazoned on billboards in front of every synagogue, and Jews started demanding their rights and asserting their interests. Sure, it led the Jimmy Carters and the Walts and the Mearsheimers to claim that the Jewish lobby was too powerful. But just one generation ago there was no Jewish lobby! And there was no Israeli Air Force! And by the time others had fought our battle, six million Jews had gone up in smoke!

It was God who told Abraham, "*V'e-escha l'goy gadol* — and I will make of thee a great nation and I will bless thee and make thy name great and be thou a blessing" (Genesis 12:2). As you know, the Jewish people have never been great in numbers, and yet there are people who think that we rule the world! It's unbelievable! There are three-quarters of a billion Hindus in this world. There are more than 300 million Buddhists. There are more Mormons in the world than there are Jews! But who rules the world? Not them! Who rules? Me and you — and our "*mishpocho*" over at *Vanity Fair*. There are lots of people who think that is true! And you know what? I am glad they do! It's very important for our survival.

My teacher, Rabbi Joseph Soloveitchik, of blessed memory, once pointed out an interesting fact about Abraham. Abraham found respect from the outside world only in the aftermath of one particular incident. As we are told in our Torah portion this morning, "Malkizedek, king of Salem, brought forth bread and wine." He went so far as to make a kiddush — "And he blessed him and said: Blessed be Abraham of God most high, maker of heaven and earth." What prompted this profusion of compliments? Why was a Jew suddenly thrust into the role of universal hero? Pointed out Rabbi Soleveitchik, this reception was never accorded Abraham when he fulfilled his characteristic of *chesed*, showing kindness to strangers and hospitality to wayfarers. Helping others won Abraham no worldly praise. It was only now — now that Abraham has pursued the terrorists who held his nephew Lot captive and, in the words of the Torah, "Smote them and pursued them," only then did the world show respect. For what impresses the world is not saintliness as much as strength, not character as much as courage, not piety as much as power.

Let our enemies think that we are all-powerful. As Akiva Eldar once put it in the *Haaretz* newspaper,

> The Arab belief that the Jews rule the world has become one of Israel's most important deterrent factors, no less than its military strength. The lunatic idea that 6 million Jews dictate the policies of a superpower with 280 million inhabitants has contributed greatly to the decisions by Arab and Palestinian leaders, and even to that of the Arab League, to accept — albeit with gritted teeth — the existence of the Jewish state. When Anwar Sadat and King Hussein came to Jerusalem, they had at least one eye fixed on Washington.

Yes, let the Arab world think that we are all-powerful. That is the only way they may come to the realization that they are going to have to learn how to live with us.

And here in America? I am sure there are some people who, when they read *Vanity Fair*, had an upset stomach. But do you think they would learn to love us if we were less successful? Should we be less successful just to please them? The Jews living in the shtetls of Eastern Europe were not successful, had no power. Yet, that did not stop the Cossacks and others from destroying their homes and killing their families! Dov Burt Levy, writing in the *Forward* newspaper, described sitting in a café in London on February 28, 2001, reading the *International Herald Tribune*. He could not get over the fact, in turning to the editorial page, that five of the six columns were written by Jews: Richard Cohen, Stephen Rosenfeld, Robert Caplan, Ellen Goodman, and Thomas Friedman. The sixth column was written by a South Korean by the name of Prof. Han Sung-Joo. Five Jews and a Joo! It is true that having so many Jewish names in positions of prominence drives our enemies crazy. Yet, do you know what? It makes many of our friends feel good!

And we Jews have many friends here in America. Many of them believe that the Bible is the word of God, and they take seriously — very seriously — the words of God's promise to Abraham when He said, "V'avorcha m'vorechecha u'mkalelcha a-or — and I will bless them that bless thee and him that curseth thee I will curse" (Genesis 12:3). Those are very important words in God's promise to Abraham: those who support the Jews will be blessed and those who curse us will be cursed. It is this promise that forms the basis of much of the Evangelical Christian support for the State of Israel. Type in the words of this promise on an Internet search engine; type in Genesis 12:3 and you will see how many Christian Web sites pop up. If you are our friend, you'll be blessed; if you are against us, you'll be cursed. This is one of the facts of history. We speak of the "glory that was Greece and the grandeur that was Rome." But that glory and grandeur soon departed after the Greeks and Romans turned against us. Similarly, soon after Spain expelled its Jews, the sun began to set on the Spanish Empire. In modern times, the Iron Curtain of Communism first began to fall when the Jews sought their freedom. So let people think we are blessed. They just might be right — and they just might be blessed as well. "I will bless them that bless thee and him that curseth thee I will curse."

On a majestic night nearly 4,000 years ago, God promised our forefather Abraham that his people would be made into a "great nation." That pledge by the Almighty was repeated to our forefathers and remains a solemn oath. *Vanity Fair* seems to indicate that the pledge is being fulfilled in our day. We are the most blessed generation in the last 2,000 years of our people. We should thank God for being that privileged generation that has witnessed an Israeli Air Force knocking out Iraq's nuclear reactor and Syria's as well. We should thank God for living in this great country, the good old U.S. of A. where a majority of the members of the New Establishment are Jewish. "*Hashem oz l'amo yitain.* Hashem yevorech et amo bashalom —The Lord has given strength to His people. May He now bless us with peace."

October 20, 2007

JEW VS. JEW

Do you know the old joke about the maid who works for a Jewish family?

> One day she is talking with her friend, and she says, "I have to tell you, I don't understand these Jewish people...
>
> They have a holiday called Shabbos during which they eat in the dining room and smoke in the bathroom.
>
> And then they have a holiday called Tisha b'Av, where they smoke in the dining room, and eat in the bathroom.
>
> And then they have a holiday called Yom Kippur where they both eat and smoke in the bathroom.

The point of that story is that we Jews would rather feast than fast, and yet, I want to make a proposal about fasting. I do not expect this proposal to be accepted by many, but I want to make it just the same. My proposal is that we observe, not one, but two fast days before the festival of Purim.

The first fast before Purim is Taanit Esther, the Fast of Esther, which occurs on the 13th of Adar. Most people know about this fast day, even if they do not observe it. It goes back to the Megillah, in which

Mordecai tries to persuade Esther to go to the king to tell him about Haman's plot, and she is understandably afraid to go. It is dangerous to try to tell the king what to do, but finally she agrees to do so, saying "*Lech k'nos et kol hayehudim*" (Esther 4:16): gather all the Jews, and tell them to pray for me, and to fast for me, and if they do, then with their support, I will muster up my courage and I will go. That is the origin of Taanit Esther.

I have not made any scientific studies, but I suspect that not all of the Jews in our synagogue fast on Taanit Esther. Yet, I know many Jews who ought to consider fasting on an additional day in the week before Purim: they should fast not only on the 13th of Adar but also on the 9th of Adar. According to Jewish legend, the 9th of Adar was the day when the school of Shamai and the school of Hillel had their first disagreement. And even though theirs is the paradigmatic example of a *machloket l'shem shamayim*, of a disagreement that was for the sake of heaven; and even though the school of Shamai and the school of Hillel disagreed with each other respectfully and sincerely, and with no evil intent; and even though the meaning of the Torah was enhanced and was clarified by means of their disagreements, nevertheless, the day when they began to disagree was decreed by some of the sages to be a fast day. That is because even the best disagreement —even a disagreement as sincere, as respectful, and as reverent as theirs was — is still a disagreement, and for a people as beleaguered as the Jewish people, any disagreement is a risk.

This is why the sages declared the day when Shamai and Hillel began their disagreements with each other to be a fast day. Now consider that the Talmud says that, even though adherents to the school of Shamai and to the school of Hillel disagreed on many issues, there was never any personal rivalry or any rancor between them. In fact, the Talmud says that even though they disagreed on many issues, the men from the school of Hillel could still marry women from the school of Shamai, and vice versa, and the people from the school of Shamai and the people from the school of Hillel could still eat at each other's tables. That is because they understood that neither of them had a monopoly on the truth, and, therefore, they never questioned each other's legitimacy. And yet the sages declared the day when they began to disagree with each other a fast day. That shows how precious and how indispensable Jewish unity was in their eyes.

If Jewish unity is that precious, then I think that there are a lot of Jews, both in Israel and in the United States, who should consider fasting on the 9th of Adar, for we are now living at a moment when divisiveness within the Jewish people is a luxury that we simply cannot afford. In fact, it is one that we simply cannot tolerate.

Let me give you examples of what I mean. First, let us consider Israel. It used to be that, as divided as some Jews might be, they stood united when faced with a common enemy. That is no longer the case. Today the Jews of Israel are threatened by Hamas, Hezbollah, and the possibility of a nuclear Iran. Israel has never experienced a day free of conflict— whether from all-out wars or airplane hijackings or suicide bombings or rocket attacks. And yet, through it all, Israelis stand divided — not simply hawks vs. doves, Likud vs. Labor vs. Kadima, but also Ashkenazim vs. Sefardim, ultra-Orthodox vs. secular, Russians vs. Ethiopians, and settlers vs. the government.

How sad and how tragic this situation is, for if there is one lesson we Jews should have learned from our history, it is that we are most vulnerable to a threat from without when we are divided from within. Look in the Purim Megillah where we are told that Haman came before the King and said of the Jews, "*Yeshno am echad m'fuzor u'mforad* — there is one people divided and scattered" (Esther 3:8). What is Haman saying? Explains the Talmud, Haman was pointing out to the King what the problem of Jewish life was then and still is today! "*Yeshno am echad* — there is this people, the Jews, who are supposed to be an 'Am Echad — united as one,' for just as God is one, His children are meant to be one. But look, this people who are meant to be one are scattered and divided." So what happens? "*Vayovo Haman*" — Haman comes to destroy the Jews! Haman realized that the Jewish people are weakest and most vulnerable when they are divided, when they are quarreling among themselves.

In light of the bickering and the bullying that take place on a daily basis among Israelis, I think that the Knesset should bring back the fast on the 9th of Adar! Let them declare an emergency fast on this day, from sunrise till sunset, so that Israelis may regain their perspective and so come to realize that what is good for the country is much more important than what is good for their party or for their ego. And if they do not understand why, then fast on the 9th of Adar.

And in America? I know lots of people in America who ought to be fasting on the 9th of Adar. How about people like the members of the Orthodox rabbinic organization that, before the High Holidays, would place ads in American Jewish newspapers that "warn Jews not to pray in Reform or Conservative Temples." Was there anyone anywhere who stayed home because of those ads? The only thing the ads accomplished was to publicly slap the faces of Reform and Conservative Jews and their rabbis. The fact of the matter is many Reform and Conservative Jews do so much good on behalf of the Jewish community and the people of Israel. Many are deeply involved in perpetuating Jewish life. Why repudiate them and their form of Judaism in so insulting a manner?

Similarly, those Conservative and Reform rabbis and leaders who refer to ultra-Orthodox Jews and rabbis as being "Ayatollahs" and "cave-dwellers" are just as divisive. Is that language really necessary? Does speaking that way about your fellow Jews serve any constructive purpose? At a time when Jewish life in America is in serious crisis, at a time when all the movements are in distress, at a time when the fastest growing group in Jewish life according to every questionnaire is not Orthodox, and not Conservative and not Reform but "other," do we really need this kind of language? Is it really good for the Jews to have this name calling and this denigrating language?

I do not think so. At a time like this, we do not need and we cannot afford vicious backbiting between the groups. Instead, we need to join hands — Orthodox, Conservative, and Reform together — and we need to learn from each other, and listen to each other, and help each other.

You know who I think ought to fast on the 9th of Adar? The Association of Orthodox Day School Principals of the metropolitan region of New York for what they did in 2001. The Yeshiva high schools of greater New York have a basketball league consisting of twenty-eight high schools. It was formed so that observant high-school students who do not play basketball on Shabbos could still play basketball competitively. But at a meeting at which only eleven of the twenty-eight schools were represented because of a snow storm, the heads of these day schools voted in a closed ballot by 7 to 4 NOT to allow the students of the Solomon Schechter High Schools into their league — not to allow Conservative kids to participate together with Orthodox kids in basketball games. One of the principals, who was interviewed by the *New York Jewish Week*, said off the record, "The Schechter schools are not Jewish schools; they are schools with Jewish students...since their Judaic curriculum is inauthentic." In basketball, I think that that is what you call an intentional flagrant foul!

To their great credit, let it be noted that Rabbi Haskell Lookstein, the head of the Ramaz School in Manhattan, and six other principals made a statement that if the Conservative students are not allowed to play, then they will withdraw their schools from the league. Yet, did not those principals who wanted to bar the Solomon Schechter schools send a horrible message not only to Conservative Jews but also to their own students and to their own parents? The message that we believe that we have the only correct way of understanding the Torah and that we will not play ball, literally, we will not play basketball with Jewish high-school students who do not agree with us? What those principals did was a blot on Orthodoxy. The only suggestion that I can give to these principals (who are not interested in hearing suggestions from me anyway) is to fast on the 9th of Adar — because, if the sages said that we need to fast because the schools of Hillel and Shamai disagreed, how much more so should we fast, over this sin, of principals daring to say, "Your kids can't play with our kids because they don't understand the Torah the same way we do."

We are living at a difficult time here in America when an enormous number of Jewish young people are marrying out. At this difficult time, shouldn't we be looking for as many ways as we can possibly find for Jewish kids to meet each other, across all the denominational lines that now separate them? Doesn't that make sense? And yet, instead, USY, the organization of Conservative teenagers, has its programs; and NFTY, the organization of Reform Jewish teenagers has its programs; and NCSY, the organization of Orthodox teenagers, has its programs, and never the three do meet. And nobody seems to understand that if we do not provide our children with the opportunity to meet each other, how are they ever going to fall in love and marry each other?

When the German government recently invited rabbis to visit Germany, it did not make a difference to them whether the rabbis were Orthodox, Conservative or Reform. And if it did not matter to them, why must it matter to us? Little more than a half-century ago, in that very same Germany, the government issued orders to round up all the Jews to achieve the "final solution to the Jewish problem." They killed six million of us, and it did not matter to them whether they were Orthodox, Conservative or Reform, so why does it have to matter to us?

How sad it is, how dangerous it is, how tragic it is, and how unnecessary it is that, at such a critical time in Jewish life, both here and in Israel, Jews are wasting their strength bashing and denigrating and de-legitimizing each other, instead of listening to each other, learning from each other, and working with each other, for the good of the whole Jewish people.

May we not be guilty of this sin of divisiveness, and may we not have to fast on the 9th of Adar. Instead, let us unite together as one as the Jews did in the Purim story, and then one may hope that we will see the fulfillment of the words of the Megillah: "La'Yehudim hayta orah v'simcha sasson viy'kar — and the Jews had light and gladness, rejoicing and festivities" (Esther 8:16).

March 3, 2001

Madonna and Kabbalah

I am going to teach you the meaning of one word. It is a Hebrew word that I am sure all of you have used or heard, but, I suspect, very few of you can really define it. The word? KABBALAH! What is Kabbalah?

If you ask most Jews to tell you something about Maimonides, they will have very little to say. But if you ask most Jews to tell you something about Madonna, suddenly they have a wealth of knowledge. Let me show you! What is Madonna's Hebrew name? You see — you know! It is Esther! Now, what is Maimonides' Hebrew name? You are not so sure. Madonna has put Kabbalah on the map. And that, in and of itself, says it all. Kabbalah has become the "hit" of Hollywood. You do not have to be Jewish to love Kabbalah. Mick Jagger, Rosie O'Donnell, Marla Maples, Gwyneth Paltrow, Demi Moore, Guy Ritchie, Courtney Love, and of course those great mystics, Britney Spears and Mike Tyson — they and so many others have been attracted to Kabbalah by attending Kabbalah Centers, which are now located in more than fifty cities around the world.

In my quest to find the answer to "What is Kabbalah?," I went to the Kabbalah Center in New York. What I found there is everything that Kabbalah is *not*.

• In the line for the information table, the person in front of me was a teenager with a large tattoo on his arm, asking for a copy of the Zohar, the Book of Mysticism. The Zohar is written in Aramaic and its English translation is incomprehensible. Kabbalah is not for teenagers with tattoos — or without!

• For sale at the Kabbalah Centre was Kabbalah Mountain Spring Water. It is the only water Madonna will drink. The bottle says the water cleanses the soul. This reminded me of another bottle of water I had seen in Israel. That bottle was under the supervision of not one, not two, but three rabbinic authorities — which only goes to show that you can be a *gonif* under rabbinic supervision. Kabbalah is not holy water.

• The Centre also sold a red string, which Madonna, Britney Spears, and many others now wear. At the Centre, a little red string sells for $26. You want a bargain? Go to Wal Mart — it sells for $1.79! And it is just as effective! Does the red string, as claimed, ward off the Evil Eye? Look at Britney Spears — she wears it and got married twice in one year! So much *nachas* from one child! Do Jews believe in the Evil Eye? Many do. But that is not kabbalistic; you will find that in the Talmud. Indeed, you can find it in our own language with the expression: "If looks could kill ..." Does wearing red ward off the Evil Eye? Some Jews believe that, but that too is not kabbalistic. It is hard to really find a basis for this tradition. Some say it comes from the Book of Joshua, where a prostitute named Rachav used a red bow as a sign to the Israelites to protect her after she had helped them. Others say it comes from the Tabernacle of old, where red dye from a worm was the color of one of the ritual items. Thus, the red is to remind us that we are to hold ourselves as lowly as a worm, so as not to draw too much attention to ourselves, so as not to arouse the envy of others. When Britney Spears appeared on the cover of *Entertainment Weekly* wearing little but a red string, was she really not looking to draw attention to herself? Kabbalah is NOT a red string.

Kabbalah has become big business. There are now not only Kabbalah water and Kabbalah strings but also Kabbalah candles, Kabbalah white powder to cleanse your house (try Ajax — it is better), Kabbalah perfume, and Kabbalah tee-shirts. Madonna wears one during her performances that has emblazoned on it these words: KABBALISTS DO IT BETTER. Now, of course, as Bill Clinton would say, "It depends on what the word 'it' refers to."

One of the greatest medieval halachic scholars, the Ran, immortalized by his commentary on the Talmud, wrote, "I do not force my way into the study of Kabbalah, since I did not receive the knowledge from a wise master." The Ran did not know anyone wise enough to teach Kabbalah, but Phil Berg and his wife can? And Madonna — their best-known mystical disciple — is the woman who became famous by simulating sex in front of teenagers on MTV and whose vulgar displays include kissing Britney Spears on stage and going naked in her films. She does not have a clue about what Kabbalah is, if she could say — as she has — "I think Kabbalah is very punk rock." No, it's *not*!

So what is Kabbalah? Kabbalah is based on a work called the Zohar, which means "the splendor." The Zohar is a commentary on the Torah. So if you do not know the Torah, you cannot study Kabbalah. In the 1200s, Moses deLeon, a Spanish Jew, discovered the Zohar, which we believe Rabbi Shimon bar Yochai and talmudic sages gathered, wisdom that even preceded Sinai. It was given by fallen angels to Enoch, who transmitted it orally. Kabbalah means "to receive." It is to receive a revelation of truth that has been passed down by teacher to student, generation after generation.

The Torah teaches us what a human being should do; it gives us 613 mitzvot and tells us how to act. But it still leaves us with the question of what does it all mean. Marlon Brando did not realize that he was raising the ultimate kabbalistic question when he said that as people draw closer to death they look back at life and ask, "What was that all about?" The Kabbalists tried to answer the same question, but then again, so do philosophers — with one important difference. Philosophy is based on logic — Kabbalah has no logic. In Hebrew, philosophy is called *Chakirah*, which means "to investigate," to understand what I can grasp. Kabbalah, meaning "to receive," means to receive from a higher source. The wisdom of Kabbalah cannot be proven scientifically. It does not have to be proven. for it tries to understand that which cannot be seen — the spiritual, not the physical.

In some ways its spiritual focus, in and of itself, explains why Kabbalah has become so popular in Hollywood. Hollywood stresses the physical; it houses the rich and famous in their grand mansions and huge cars and beautiful yachts. And yet, so many of them know that something is missing in their lives. So they are always searching "out there" for fulfillment, turning to everything and everyone from Maharishi Mahesh Yogi to Tibetan Buddhism, to Deepak Chopra, to Wayne Dyer to Hare Krishna, to crystals, to New Age, to Scientology — and to the Rev. Sister Faye! Now, it is Judaism's turn. What we are seeing, in some ways, is a reflection of the old story of the elderly Jewish woman who gets off a plane in India and says that she must be taken to the Supreme Yogi. She embarks on a challenging and difficult trek by donkey, camel, and elephant to the top of the highest mountain. When she reaches the peak, she is ushered into the magnificent temple and taken before the Supreme Leader with his long beard, turban, and flowing robes. To him she proclaims, "Sidney, it's time to come home."

Now the search for "meaning" has struck home. The truth is that many of us Jews are like the Hollywood crowd. As much as we have, we feel — we know — that something is missing. As much as we may have in the bank, we still feel an inner impoverishment. As much as we eat, we still feel an inner void. As much honor as we receive, we still feel a lack of self-worth. As much as we travel, we still feel a sense of boredom. We feel tense, ravished with inner self-doubt, empty on the inside. That is why "spirituality" has become such a buzzword in the Jewish community. As Jews we have made it! We have made it physically but not spiritually. Spirituality is the process through which the individual strives to meet God. How do we make that connection? The Torah and Talmud teach us how to serve God. Kabbalah shows us how to become one with God.

The Kabbalah is based on the idea that God is the *Ein Sof*, which means "without boundaries." As the *Ein Sof*, God is inaccessible and unknowable. However, God does make the Divine Self known through a series of ten *Sefirot*, or emanations from His Divine light. It is through these spheres that the individual can make contact with God. And then God gave us a repository for His Divine light. That is called our soul. *That* comes from God. We say it in our prayers: "*Ha-neshama lach* — O Lord the soul is yours. *V'ha-guf pa-alach* — and the body is your work."

Originally, according to the Kabbalists, Adam and Eve were all "soul," no body. That was the way it was meant to be. But after they sinned, the Torah tells us that God made "garments of skin" for them. What were the garments? Their bodies. God helps form the body, but the body comes from the earth and that is where it returns. But the soul? The soul came from God, and it returns to God. The next world — the World to Come — is referred to as being the *Olam Haneshamot* — the world of souls. So much of Jewish tradition is based on this concept.

Let me give you an example. Many Jews light a candle to commemorate the memory of their parents. Many do this before every recitation of Yizkor. Still more do it on the Yahrzeit of their parents, and still more light a candle as they sit shiva at the house of mourning. Why a candle? In the Book of Proverbs (20:27), we are told, "*Ki ner Hashem nishmat ha-adam* — the soul of a human is a candle unto the Lord." But in what way is a candle representative of a human being's soul? Science teaches that what goes up must come down. Kabbalah teaches that what goes down — must come up! The soul of a human being that came down to earth must go back up, just as a flame defies gravity by climbing higher and higher.

Can Kabbalah prove this? No. It does not have to. Can I prove to you that you have a soul? No. I do not think I have to! There is something in all of us that tells us there is more to us than just flesh and blood. There is something in us that yearns for more than the physical. There is something in us that makes us want to constantly raise ourselves to a higher place. And that is our soul! Our soul is constantly yearning to reconnect itself to its Divine source.

The soul wants to return to its original home, but God has placed it here in our bodies and sentenced it to life. Sometimes a little of our soul escapes from the body. Do you know when that happens? When we sleep! When we are asleep, our body loses much of its control, and so the soul has an opportunity to roam a little bit. According to the Kabbalists, this explains our dreams. As Rabbi Benjamin Blech points out, Freud said dreams release the id. The Kabbalists say dreams release the Yid! When we dream about something taking place in China, according to the Kabbalists, there is some reality to that dream. Every dream has some morsel of truth; do you know why? According to the Kabbalists, while you are sleeping here in Baltimore, your soul took a little trip to Beijing to see what is going on there.   Thank God, your soul comes back — otherwise you would be dead! And that is why every morning the first thing a Jew says is, "*Modeh ani lefanecha melech chai v'kayam* — I am thankful to you, O living and eternal King," "*Sh-hechezarta bi nishmati* — for you have returned my soul within me." I know a portion of it left, but thank God, it is back and I can continue to live.

And then every morning we continue our prayers by saying "*Elokai neshama shenatata bi tehorah hi* — O God, the soul you placed within me is pure. You created it, you fashioned it, you breathed it into me, you safeguard it within me, and eventually you will take it from me." Yes, God made it, fashioned it, and put it into us, and that soul He gave us was pure — which raises the question for the Kabbalists of how do we keep it that way. They respond that, just as the body needs nourishment, so does the soul need nourishment. Yes, chicken soup for the soul! And just as the body's nourishment must be physical, the soul's nourishment must be something spiritual.

How do we feed our soul? How do we keep it pure? How do we draw ourselves closer to God? Well, according to the Kabbalists, there are lots of ways. Some say through study, others through prayer. Some say through rituals, other through meditation.

Let me just draw your attention to one more way the Kabbalists see us feeding and purifying our souls. It is by something we Jews often speak of: it is called *Tikkun Olam*. We usually take Tikkun Olam to mean "good deeds," but its literal translation is "repairing the world." What is it that needs to be repaired? Explain the Kabbalists — and this is a significant Kabalistic concept — before the universe was created, God was light and the light was everywhere. In order to make room for the universe, God withdrew some of the light by shrinking himself (a process called *tzimtzum*). This light was stored in great vessels under God's thrones of Justice and Mercy, and this made space for the world to be created. However, the vessels were not strong enough to contain God's light, and so they were shattered (*shvirat hakeilim*). As the vessels broke apart, they formed shells (*klipot*) around each spark of God's light. These shells are all around us, and whenever a person performs a mitzvah, somewhere in the universe one of these shells opens up and a spark of light flies back to God. This teaches us that every single act of goodness we perform helps restore God to wholeness. Every single act of goodness we perform has cosmic consequences.

Rabbi Jack Riemer points out that a scientist named Dr. Jack Demirgian took dollar bills from a number of different cities, put them under a microscope, and did a study of what they can teach us. He found that dollar bills from Iowa or Idaho have almost no residue of cocaine on them. But 12 percent of the dollar bills that came from Miami had traces of cocaine on them. When asked if this means that 12 percent of the people in Miami are involved in drug dealing, the doctor said no — but you have to understand that once a dollar gets into your wallet, it rubs against the dollar next to it and that is how the tiny amount of cocaine gets transferred. Kabbalah teaches that what is true of dollars is true of us: whether we realize it or not, every person whom we rub shoulders with, every person we come in contact with — whether we know it or not, whether they know it or not — is affected by the encounter. A smile we give someone may brighten her day. A nasty look may depress him. A kind word may lift someone's spirits and start a chain reaction of cheerfulness. Or, as the first person teaches in Mitch Albom's best-selling book, *Five People You Meet in Heaven*, "There are no random acts ... you can no more separate one life from another than you can separate a breeze from the wind." Each of us, say the Kabbalists, in our own little way, can make our contribution to "repairing the world." And in so doing, we purify our soul.

So, yes, our tradition provides us with many different paths to follow to keep our souls pure. But even the best of us cannot do it all. All of us fall sometimes and sin, rendering a part of our soul impure. Those impurities come to light when we pass from this world to the next world. It is then that our souls have to be judged and go through a cleansing process. If your soul is never nourished during the course of its lifetime, if your soul has become very dark and impure, then it must go through a severe cleansing; all the impurities must be removed. Do you know what that process is called? That, according to the Kabbalists, is what hell is. As Rabbi Adin Steinsalz puts it, "The deeper the transgression, the more deeply it is ingrained within the soul. The greater the pain of cleansing, the deeper the level of hell."

Hell is not a place; it is an experience and it does not last forever. For the worst sinner, for the one with the most blemished soul, the cleansing process can last a maximum of twelve months. This is the reason why Kaddish is recited for eleven months — if we said it the full twelve months, we would seem to be implying that our loved one was so wicked that he or she required the maximum amount of time for purification! Once the purification process is completed, the soul survives in the "presence of God," drawing ever closer to the Almighty — sometimes staying forever in the "world of souls" and other times, according to the Kabbalists, being reincarnated into a new body to give it another chance for purification.

There is one day of the year that is supposed to remind us of all that I have spoken about today, and that day is Yom Kippur. There is a verse in the Book of Psalms, "The days were formed and one of them is His." Which day is "His?" Say our sages, that day refers to Yom Kippur. Every day of the year we see the world from our perspective. But there is one day — God's day — when we get a glimpse of the way the world looks from *His* perspective. While Shabbos and other holidays speak to our bodies *and* souls, Yom Kippur speaks to our soul — only to our souls. Indeed, on Yom Kippur we deny ourselves all bodily pleasures so that we can concentrate on our souls. Yom Kippur is the day in this world that is the closest to all the days in the next world — a day of no physical pleasures, only spiritual ones. So if you like Yom Kippur, you are going to love the next world! But if Yom Kippur has no meaning to you, if the spiritual just does not "speak" to you, then what is going to happen when you go to a world with no Broadway shows, no country clubs, no fine restaurants — a world of study and prayer and meditation. What will you do all day?

So let Yom Kippur be a time for you to reflect on this question. Go home tonight and speak to your family; speak to them as you always do on Kol Nidre night — speak to them about food. But this year do not talk to them about physical food, but of spiritual nourishment. All year long you are so concerned about your bodies; for the next twenty-four hours give some thought to your soul. If Madonna can, so can you! At a time when so many — Jews and non-Jews alike — are finding meaning in Jewish rituals and traditions, isn't it time for many of you to ask yourselves, How come it has so little meaning for me? Others are meditating with our prayers; shouldn't you ask yourselves, How come I'm not — how come I can't? When surveys show that 50 percent of all those who will vote in this year's election attend religious services once a week, shouldn't you be asking yourselves, Why not me? Am I missing out on something? When everything Jewish is "in" in America, isn't it time to confront why your Judaism is not "in" in you? They are studying Kabbalah all over the world. Isn't it time for you to set aside some time to study what being Jewish is all about? Isn't it time for you to come to appreciate your heritage as a Jew as much as Madonna seems to appreciate it as a Christian? What does she know that you don't know?

When you really think about it, I — as a rabbi — should not ridicule Madonna. After all, she, a Catholic, is proud of her Hebrew name, observes the Sabbath, is interested in Jewish sources, and went to Israel for Rosh Hashana. Not bad for someone who was known as "the Material Girl!" Now, Madonna is telling us, "Let's get spiritual." Don't take her word for it, or Phil Berg's. It is God's word, and God's world — here and there! Let's get spiritual so that we can experience the meaning of the words of our prayer: "*Kol zeman sh'haneshama b'kirbi modeh ani l'fonecha* — as long as my soul is within me, I gratefully thank you, O Lord."

Kol Nidre, September 24, 2004

DAYENU FOR A POPE

No matter how distant some Jews may have moved from their religious moorings, there is one song found in the Haggadah that still plays on for them. Everyone knows this song, perhaps because it has such a peppy melody or because it has such a simple refrain. It has become so popular that it is no longer restricted to the Pesach Seder. You might hear it at a wedding or Bar Mitzvah reception, or even in the elevator! This is the song whose refrain has one word: *Dayenu!* For whatever reason, Dayenu is known and loved and looked forward to by all of us — straights and gays, vegetarians and *chazir fressers*. Next to "Hava Nagilah," we Jews have made "Dayenu" our most popular song.

I think it is important for all of us to understand that "Dayenu" is more than just a catchy melody, more than just a children's song. "Dayenu" contains a point of view on life that is either absurd or profound and either way is so different from how we usually look at life that it is worth thinking about.

Listen to what we proclaim to God in the words of "Dayenu": "If you had just taken us out of Egypt and not led us safely through the desert — Dayenu — it would have been enough for us." Would that really have been enough? "If you had just led us through the desert and not brought us to Mt. Sinai, it would have been enough." "If you had given us the Shabbat and not given us the Torah — it would have been enough." Is this true? If God had not given us the Torah, or if God had not brought us to the Land of Israel, or if God had not given us the Shabbos, would that really have been enough? If God had started the task of making us His people and then left us in the middle, would that really have been enough? Does that make sense?

I think it does! What "Dayenu" is saying is, If God gives you half a favor, don't knock it! If God does part of a good deed for you, that is no small thing. Don't be like those who say, "If He gives me everything I want and need, then I will be grateful. But if He starts on the way and gets me partway there, then I'll complain and feel frustrated and angry." Very simply, what I am suggesting to you is that "Dayenu" teaches us to be grateful for partial favors, because partial favors are as much as any of us ever get in this life. You have to be grateful for what you get and not be warped by what you don't.

This message takes on heightened meaning for us this Pesach as we continue to reflect on the historic visit to Israel by Pope John Paul II. Reflect on who this man was. Perhaps it was best expressed in these words from the *Jerusalem Report*:

> No individual has done more to foster reconciliation between Christians and Jews than this Polish Pope. He is the first Pontiff to speak about the right of the Jews to return to their land, the first to describe anti-Semitism as a sin against God, the first to explicitly insist on the enduring validity of God's covenant with the Jewish people, the first to visit a synagogue, the first to describe the Jewish people as Christianity's "elder brother," the first to bring Holocaust commemoration to the Vatican, the first to routinely incorporate meeting with Jewish leaders in his pilgrimages around the world.

And the first to instruct the Vatican to establish diplomatic relations with the state of Israel, overriding protests from Vatican diplomats who feared an anti-Christian backlash in the Muslim world. Dayenu? Is that not enough?

Not for some Jews! No matter what the Pope said or did, it was not enough because they continue to focus on what he had not said or what he had not done, while being unable to appreciate what he had said and done. Both here in America and in Israel, some Jews continue to harp on those issues that divide Jews from Catholics, such as the behavior of Pope Pius and the Church during the Holocaust, Edith Stein, and Kurt Waldheim. Some Jews even complained that, during the Pope's visit, his Mass caused some Sabbath desecration. Are we going to be blind to what this man did during his visit? The last Pope who visited Israel refused to refer to Israel by name. He refused to meet with the chief rabbis or other dignitaries. This Pope came, met with the prime minister, with the president, and with the chief rabbi, and he visited Yad Vashem. Who will ever forget the picture of this man with a crucifix dangling from his neck visiting the Western Wall and putting a kvitel into the crevices between the stones, as Jews have done for centuries? It was one of the most incredible photos I have seen during the course of my entire lifetime! And then to read the message he wrote on that kvitel: "God of our fathers, we are deeply saddened by the behavior of those who in the course of history have caused these children of yours to suffer and ask you for forgiveness. We wish to commit ourselves to genuine brotherhood with the people of the covenant." Dayenu? Was that not enough?

No, not for some Jews who complained that the Pope should not have worn a crucifix at the Wall. Are they aware of the fact that the Pope is not Jewish? Do they realize what his visit to the Wall — the last remnant of our Temple — really meant? Are they aware of what his visit to Israel said? The simple truth is that the creation of the State of Israel in 1948 was a body blow to Christian theology. The Jews were not supposed to be there. The script called for them to be scattered and persecuted until the end of time, to suffer until they accepted Jesus. But we had the audacity to rewrite the script, and last month, right before our very eyes, the Prince of the Catholic Church showed that he accepted it. It could not have been easy. When you remember the words that Popes have used to describe the Jewish people down through the ages, it could not have been easy for Pope John Paul to refer to us as "elder brothers in the faith." He first said this on a Good Friday, the same day that for centuries Catholics had recited in their churches "a prayer for the conversion of the perfidious Jews." And now a Pope is saying, "It must be understood that Jews who for 2,000 years were dispersed among the nations of the world, had decided to return to the land of their ancestors. This is their right." Dayenu? Is that not enough?

No, not for some Jews. Not for those who criticized the Pope for not apologizing for the Holocaust and denouncing Pope Pius's silence during the war. I do know that the church was guilty of much that took place during the Holocaust, but I also know that one infallible Pope does not get up and say that another infallible Pope was wrong. I also know that a Pope who is the leader of a church does not get up and criticize a church that Catholic theology teaches is composed of the body of Jesus. Popes just don't do that!

But let me tell you what Pope John Paul did do! During his visit to Yad Vashem, he came face to face with Edith Tzirer, a Holocaust survivor. This is her story. In a small town near Cracow, Poland, in 1945 — on Liberation Day — Mrs. Tzirer was fourteen years old then, painfully thin, with tuberculosis, and she was all alone. She had just been released from a labor camp. Wearing her camp uniform, she was riding a train to Cracow where she had lost contact with her family at the beginning of the war in 1939. The train ran out of fuel and stopped in a small town. While the other passengers ate and drank, Mrs. Tzirer sat off in a corner. "I don't know to this day how he saw me," she said. "He moved some people aside and came to me and asked me why I was sitting there like that." 'Did you eat? Did you drink?' he asked. I said, I hadn't in a number of days. He went and brought me my first cup of tea, the first cup in three years. He was a seminary student," she said, "young, tall and handsome with blue eyes. To tell you the truth, I thought it was God himself who had showed up."

Mrs. Tzirer said the man told her to come with him and board another train, a cattle car, bound for Cracow. She told him she was too weak to walk, "He picked me up. He took me on his back and carried me. We walked for three, four kilometers — I'm not sure — through the snow." The man told her that his name was Karol Wojtyla and that he was from the town of Wadowice.

Now, he was Pope John Paul II, and she had waited fifty-four years to thank him in person for saving her life. When she came face to face with him at Yad Vashem, she broke down and cried. She could only get one sentence out of her throat. It is a sentence from the Talmud,

"*Kol ham'kayem nefesh achat b'yisroel . . . . k'ilu kiyaim olam molay* — He who saves one life in Israel is as if he saved an entire world." Dayenu? Not for some Jews. I am beginning to think that for these people, if the Pope decided to convert to Judaism and became a Belzer Chasid and went and spit on the grave of Pope Pius, these people would say, "Too little, too late!"

The fact is that these Jews are reacting just the way their ancestors did during the first Pesach. After the Jews left Egypt they traveled for a week. Then they came to that awesome moment and event in time: the Egyptian army behind them in pursuit, the swirling waters of the Red Sea in front of them ready to envelop them. Lo and behold, what happened? You saw it in the movie! The waters parted! "*V'hamayim lahem chomah* — the waters parted and became like a wall," allowing the Jewish people to walk through to safety. Can you just imagine how the Jews must have felt when they saw this unfold before their very eyes? Our rabbis in the Talmud cannot contain themselves in the words they use to describe the awesomeness of this event, going as far as to tell us, "*Ra-ata shifchah al ha-yam mah shelo ra-ah Yechezkel b'nevuato* — a simple handmaiden saw wonders at the Red Sea that the prophet Ezekiel never could have even imagined in his prophecies." It was unbelievable!

Yet, do you know what happened next? Do you know what our rabbis tell us the Jews did as they walked through the parted waters? They complained? That is right! They complained! What was the complaint? They complained that the sea bed was muddy. In the words of the rabbis at the Red Sea, one Jew said to the other, "*B'Mitzraym b'chomer u'bilvanim u'vayam chomer mayim rabim* — in Egypt we had mud and bricks and now more mud." While one of the truly great wonders and miracles of history unfolded, the Jews complained! They weren't satisfied — enough was never enough.

Yes, that is the way some Jews felt then, and that is the way some Jews feel today. And they feel that way not just in terms of a Pope but also in terms of life itself. That is when this attitude really becomes problematic, for each of us is involved in a desperate search for the key to happiness and contentment. Every one of us is burdened with problems, anxieties, tensions, and dissatisfactions. How many among us can truthfully say, "I'm absolutely happy, perfectly content." No, like the Jews after the miracle of the Red Sea, we all come to recognize that in life's journey one problem is solved only to have another arise. There is always a new obstacle lying in the way: concerns about our children, our jobs, our health, our age. How desperately we need to find the ability to say Dayenu for what we do have now, for the good that does exist in our lives. Yet, for so many it is so hard to say that. How often do we say, "If only I could buy a larger home, I would be so happy!" "If only I had three cars! "If only I could join the country club!" "If only our children were more successful." "If only I had a better job!" "If only I could earn the respect of the community!" "If only I had time for more leisure!" "If only, if only . . . I would be so happy and never again complain about anything." But when our hopes have been realized, how soon we forget all these yearnings and how swiftly we again become discontented! If only we knew how to say Dayenu!

Is it not true that much of the unhappiness found in married life today is due to the inability of husband and wife to say Dayenu once in a while? We have become so expert at being critical of what our spouses do not do for us that we have forgotten the importance of expressing our gratitude for what they *do* do for us! If we are only going to say Dayenu when our mates are perfect, then we are never going to say it!

Let me tell you about a famous debate in the Talmud between the school of Shamai and the school of Hillel over what are considered appropriate grounds for divorce. The school of Shamai says that only marital infidelity is reason for a *get*. The school of Hillel disagrees. The school of Hillel said that if your wife overcooks your dinner, that too is grounds for a *get*. Now generally speaking, the school of Hillel was known to be the more moderate, the more sensitive one. How come it seems so harsh in this case? My father, of blessed memory, used to explain that it was not being harsh; it was just being sensitive to the wife. If you have a husband for whom you do so much, and all he can do is complain that the meat is too well done — get rid of him! Who wants to live with someone like that! Better a little Dayenu! Instead of "burtching" about what is wrong, we deserve a little recognition of what is right.

Parents and children set such unreasonable expectations for each other. I sometimes think that the waiting rooms of psychiatrists are filled with people who never learned to say Dayenu for what their parents did for them. So many are bitter and crushed by the wrongs their parents did them, never once being able to appreciate all that was right that their parents brought into their lives.

And how difficult it is for parents to say Dayenu! Instead of rearing well-adjusted, fulfilled, self-confident young people, how many emotional hang-ups we pass on when we throw up to them idealized goals, always comparing them and pushing them, never being content with who they are and what they are. Never stopping to say to God: Dayenu — I'm satisfied.

These words take on great importance in dealing with the death of a loved one. Death rarely comes at the right time or in the right way. We are always left with pain and anguish, grief and questions. But are we going to allow the pain to overwhelm us, or are we to conquer our grief? As one congregant said to me after the passing of her husband, "His death may not have had dignity, but I'm going to maintain mine. I didn't have him for as long as I would have liked — not nearly as long as I would have liked — but I'm grateful for the years that I did have him. I'm grateful for the partial favor I received." If you are able to say Dayenu when you have to and not let the partial favors that you get become spoiled by the fact that they are not total favors, then you are a wise person.

Let us learn to say Dayenu — thank you God for bringing marvelous, loving human beings into our lives, for all that they did, and for all that they were. Dayenu — we offer our eternal gratitude.

Pesach, April 27, 2000

EARRINGS FOR MEN?

Ten years ago, nobody spoke about it. But today it is an issue that causes friction in many homes, has to be dealt with in almost every school, and requires once and for all a Jewish perspective on the matter. What is that issue? Men wearing earrings.

The fact is that earrings for men are "in" these days. When you walk down the street it is not unusual to see men wearing earrings, sometimes in one ear, sometimes in both. It is not yet as common to see earrings on men as it is on women, but it is becoming more and more common, although I am not sure why. What is your reaction when you pass by a man wearing an earring or two? Does it make you uncomfortable? And if it does, why? Or, to put the question in terms that our grandparents and great-grandparents would understand, "Are earrings for men good for the Jews?"

Interestingly enough, the Torah provides us with an insight on this subject, and it comes from one of the darkest moments in the history of our people. Moses is atop Mt. Sinai receiving the Tablets of the Law, but the Jews lose patience and tell Aaron that they want to build an idol. They want to make a golden calf. And what does Aaron say to them? "Remove the rings of gold that are in the ears of your wives, sons, and daughters and bring them to me. *Vayisparku kol ha-am et nizmei hazahav asher b'oznaihem* — and the entire people removed the gold rings that were in their ears and brought them to Aaron" (Exodus 32:2). The entire people! The men and the women, their sons, and their daughters were all wearing earrings, which were used to make the golden calf. It thus seems obvious that the Jewish perspective on earrings in general and on men wearing them in particular is a rather negative one. Wearing earrings led to trouble and idolatry. The lesson is clear.

Yet, the lesson is not so clear because there is one other reference to men wearing earrings in the Torah that has a very different message. This reference is in connection with our forefather Jacob, when God told him to return to Bethel, the place where he saw the ladder connecting Heaven and earth. The first thing that Jacob does after he hears this command of God is to tell his family to give up their foreign gods and to purify themselves. So what does his family do in response? Says the Torah, "They gave to Jacob all the alien gods that were in their possession. *V'et ha-nizamim asher b'oznaihem* — as well as the rings that were in their ears" (Genesis 35:4). Both the women and the men were wearing earrings! But here the earrings seem to have a very different connotation. At the scene of the golden calf, the earrings were used to create an idol; here, they symbolized the rejection of idols and a positive connection to God.

So what is the real story? Are earrings — both for women and for men — good or bad? And the answer is, Both! What we see here illustrates an important Jewish perspective on the world around us. Things, in and of themselves, are neither good nor bad. What matters is how they are used.

We see the same Jewish perspective on mirrors, for example.

When it came time to build the tabernacle in the wilderness, the Midrash tells us that the women asked to have a share in its building. Moses wondered what could they give, and so they told him something like this: "We have no silver and no gold and we are not craftsmen or carpenters. We had jewelry but we already gave it away for the making of the golden calf. The only things we have are mirrors — can we give you our mirrors? And would you make something sacred for the sanctuary out of them?"

Moses was shocked at the idea. Mirrors? Mirrors are the instruments of vanity. How can you use them in a holy temple? It's out of the question. But God said to Moses, "*Kiblum ki heym chavivim allai* — Accept them and use them for they are very precious in my sight." For, if it were not for those mirrors, there might not be a Jewish people.

Why? Because when the Israelites were slaves in Egypt, they had to do backbreaking work from morning to evening. They worked like animals, they were treated like beasts, and when they came home at night they were exhausted. They felt degraded and demoralized and barely human. Yet, the women, who were waiting for them, had beautified themselves in preparation. They were the only bit of beauty that these men saw in the midst of all that evil. By fussing over their appearance, by caring about how they looked, they kept their men's morale up; they gave them hope and dignity and trust in the future. And so the men would make love to them, and that is how children were born in the midst of all that suffering. That is why God said, "Accept these mirrors and use them to make one of the holy objects in the sanctuary." For if it were not for those mirrors, the Jewish people would have died out in Egypt. And so, according to this Midrash, there is a time when fussing over your appearance, caring about what you look like, is not a sin but is a mitzvah instead.

So the Jewish perspective seems clear, whether in regard to earrings or mirrors or whatever object: nothing is all good or all bad. It depends on the circumstances; it depends on what the object is used for. Let me suggest to you this morning that this is not only true of things but of people as well.

I thought about this when I walked through the streets of Berlin, as part of a delegation from the North American Boards of Rabbis, meeting with both members of the Jewish community and officials of the Berlin and German governments. Despite the fact that I had once vowed that I would never visit Germany, this was my second visit to Berlin. As soon as you arrive in Berlin, you are overwhelmed by the city, by how it has been rebuilt and reborn. Once again it is the capital of Germany, and soon it is going to be the center of the European continent. But when you are a Jew coming to Berlin, you find yourself noticing things that you do not notice in other cities: the blonde hair and blue eyes, the harsh sound of the German language. All the people

I saw I tried to figure out their age, and I wondered whether they were alive *then*. What were they doing during the war? Every corner I passed, I wondered to myself, "How many Jews were gathered up on that corner, spit at, kicked, separated, exiled, and even executed?" At the hotel where we were staying, the Kempinski, you walk up to the door and see a plaque in German that informs you that the Kempinskis were a well-known Jewish family whose restaurant, on that very spot, was a Berlin landmark and flourished until the Nazis came to power and "Aryanized" the place in 1937.

I looked at these people in the hotel, on the streets, in lobbies, and in nightclubs, and I thought, "Their fathers were the Nazis; their fathers were the murderers who shot babies, raped women, and gassed Jews." And I thought of the words of Winston Churchill who once described Germany by saying, "If you turn Germany over, you would find stamped on it the words 'Made in hell.'"

Yet, I looked at these people a second time, and I had to accept the fact that it was their *fathers* who had committed the atrocities and not them. Sure, some of the Nazis are still around, but this is a new generation — they did not do it! Would they do it if they could? I would have to ask that same question of the people who walk the streets of France and Austria and so many other European countries as well.

I am supposed to hate these Germans, but I just cannot get myself to do so! Not when I read these words in the *New York Times*: "Germany has become Israel's most important ally outside of the United States, providing critical support in the military intelligence, political, and economic fields." Germany is now one of Israel's best friends. Did you know that the first Israeli passports issued after the state's creation in 1948 declared themselves valid, "For all states except Germany?" But today Germany is one of Israel's major trade partners, Israeli and German intelligence services have a very deep and close relationship, and Germany sends more tourists to Israel than any country except America. Sure, there has been a rise in anti-Semitic, skinhead incidents in Germany, but at the same time Germany has a higher rate of immigration of Jews from the former Soviet Union than any other European country.

So, you ask me, are the German people good or bad? And I will answer, "It depends. It depends on whether it is the father or the son." One day we visit the Sachsenhausen concentration camp, a place where tens of thousands of Jews were forced to leave Germany either by going up in smoke or by transport to Auschwitz. The next day we meet with the German Foreign Minister, Joschka Fisher, and when asked what message we should bring back to American Jews, he replies, "Come to Germany!" Indeed, in Berlin, the seat of the Third Reich, where the Catholic Church was silent during the Holocaust, now the Cardinal of Berlin warmly greets us and calls for closer relations! There *is* a difference between the fathers and sons!

And there is a difference among the sons themselves. Wherever we went in Berlin we felt comfortable enough to wear our yarmulkes. At the same time, our bus was constantly being guarded by security agents. While we were in Germany, one of Berlin's many Holocaust memorials was desecrated. Yet, at the same time, we met with German high school students who told us of their great shame regarding Germany's past and how they consider themselves fortunate to have been born after the war! Similarly, while some elements of German industry still resist payment of restitution for the slave labor they used during the Holocaust, every German official we met — the Foreign Minister, the Speaker and the President of the Bundestag, and the President of Germany — went out of their way to assure us that they and the government were dedicated to making the restitution available as quickly as possible while Holocaust survivors are still alive.

The German leaders and church officials treated the American rabbis as dignitaries! It is important for us to keep in mind that not all *Germans* are bad! Neither are all *Arabs* bad! Because in light of the recent revelations of President Bill Clinton's pardon of Mark Rich and Pincus Green and four Chassidim — all of whom were accused of robbing millions of dollars from the U.S. government — there are certainly some people in America saying that all *Jews* act like that! We know that, among our people, there are some good ones and some bad ones, and we must recognize the same is true of other people as well.

Let me just add: this is true not just in regard to "people" but to each person as well. It is important to remember this truth at the Pesach Seder. Frequently there are battles over who should be invited to the seder, because invariably, in every family, there is one relative who is despised by some other member of the family. I remember once reading an article that had a fabulous title: "When Bitter Herb Is Your Brother-in-Law — How to Survive the Sedarim with Family." At holidays when families gather together, it is important for every family member to remember that even though there is someone in the family who has hurt you, who has done something spiteful to you, that person is not all bad. Believe me, he's got his own problems! No one is all good, and no one is all bad. Very often it depends on circumstances. We have to keep this in mind when we relate to the other members of our family.

It was the sainted Maharal who once wrote, "If the thing is impure, it is impossible that it will not have some purity within it. Likewise, if the thing is pure, it is impossible that it will not have within it some impurity. And man is like this as well — it is impossible that all human thought will follow one path." Yes, there is some purity and some impurity in each and every one of us. And yes, each of us sees things differently, and it is not a matter of good and bad. It is like earrings and mirrors — and just about everything else in this world.

March 17, 2001

Part IV:
What Judaism Teaches Us about Human Nature

IT IS WHAT IT IS

I want to begin by thanking all of the people who, this year and every year, send me beautiful New Year cards with New Year wishes. But, I do not know who to thank for one Rosh Hashana card I received because it was unsigned. It read: (cover) "On Rosh Hashana wishing you a wonderful holiday, a fantastic year and most of all ... (inside) a short sermon!" Well, I guess all of you have to settle for a wonderful holiday and a fantastic year ... two out of three ain't bad! Maybe we will do better with our Yom Kippur cards. That's right, there are now cards to be sent for Yom Kippur. I found them while surfing the Web, cards which say: "Wishing you a happy Yom Kippur." One card has a man in a blue suit wearing a tallis and kippa, rocking back and forth to the tune of "That's What Friends are For," alongside an open Torah wishing you a "Happy Yom Kippur." Another website offers to send your friends and loved ones Yom Kippur fruit and gourmet baskets!

Happy Yom Kippur! It seems to be an oxymoron, but surprisingly we find these words in the Mishnah which informs us, "There were no days as happy for the Jewish people as the 15th day of Av and Yom Kippur." Yom Kippur — the happiest day of the year according to our rabbis! Historically, Yom Kippur was happy because when it ended, there was a sort of a Sadie Hawkins party where Jewish singles would meet. But it runs deeper than that. Yom Kippur is a day when we are supposed to reconcile ourselves with our family and friends, with our God and with ourselves. And there is nothing that can make us happier than that. So, today I want to speak to you about happiness.

W. H. Auden referred to the 20th century as "the age of anxiety." It looks like the 21st century may turn into "the age of dissatisfaction." I am thinking of the many people I know, many of the people you know, many of the people in the synagogue this morning who are unhappy and dissatisfied; people having a hard time coping. They just feel down. Try as they might, life just hasn't turned out the way they had hoped. There is disappointment, frustration, anxiety ... at times things just seem out of control. And it's taking a terrible toll. All of us have our moments; it is just that for some the moments seem like a lifetime. We all have our moments when we feel down and when we feel we just cannot get it together, when we are uptight or we are just feeling blue. Little wonder then that the pursuit of happiness has become a major growth industry. In the last year or so there have been nearly a dozen books written on happiness and the most popular class taught at Harvard University is on the subject of happiness ... and it is taught by an Israeli!

And so in these moments before Yizkor I want to discuss with you the Jewish perspective on how to achieve a measure of happiness. And while it is found in ancient texts, the wisdom can be incorporated into two very contemporary phrases that all of you have heard, and all of you have said, phrases that have almost become a mantra of modern times. The first is five words that we have heard from people ranging from Donald Rumsfeld and Al Gore to Alex Rodriguez and Angelina Jolie. The five words? IT IS WHAT IT IS. Al Gore said it when it was declared that he had lost the 2000 Presidential election. Angelina Jolie said it when asked if she minded being branded the other woman in the Brad Pitt–Jennifer Aniston split. Donald Rumsfeld said it before the U.S. attack on Baghdad. Alex Rodriguez said it after making a costly error in a playoff game. IT IS WHAT IT IS. The words seem simplistic, indeed one could ask: What is the "it" that it is? But the reality is that these words form an important stepping stone to happiness. They represent an all–important mind set which tells us that there are certain things in life that are beyond our control. And if you ever hope to achieve some measure of happiness in life, you are just going to have to accept that. Our sages put it in these terms when they taught us: "Children, life and sustenance do not depend upon merit; they depend upon mazel." This word "mazel" can be translated as fate, the constellations, or just plain luck. Yes, so much in this world depends upon luck. And some people have more than others. And you can complain all you want — it will make you miserable. But it will not make a difference! Why? Because IT IS WHAT IT IS!

On this year's fifth anniversary of the 9/11 tragedy, the New York Times had reporters interview about 30 families who had suffered the loss of a loved one in the Twin Towers. They wrote a few paragraphs describing how each of the families was dealing with their loss. The family of Michael Roberts caught my attention; a young man, a firefighter, cut down in the prime of life. His mother attends Little League dinners to present the same award for character that her son had once won to make sure that his memory is kept alive. In her garden, she planted Irish roses she sees every day. The garden patch has nine sides and is eleven panels high. There is one rose — an orange one — which represents Michael, which she looks at first thing in the morning, and often it causes her to cry. The story concluded with her husband having once told her to stop crying. "Honey," he said, "It is what it is." That night she took a piece of oak tag paper and wrote: IT IS WHAT IT IS. "That was a turning point," Mrs. Roberts said, "When I can't deal, that paper is what I hold on to."

I know a lot of people who might be better equipped to go on with their lives if they had that piece of paper as well. The reality is that so much in life cannot be controlled — and the sooner we accept that the happier we will be. We cannot control *who* our neighbors are and we cannot control *what* they have ... and what we do not have! Our neighbors may be the Joneses, and you know you are going to be miserable if you spend all your life trying to keep up with the Joneses. And that is what so many try to do. And it is such a waste ... a waste of time, a waste of emotional stability. It makes us blind to what we have while forcing us to focus on what we do not have. If we would stop to think about it, I think most of us would realize that we have a lot more than our parents had; a lot more than we ever dreamt we would have. But we are not happy because our next door neighbor has more. So many people in our community are unable to accept that no matter how big our house, there is going to be a neighbor with a bigger house! No matter how much money we make, someone is going to make more! No matter how much Botox we pump into our cheeks, someone is going to be prettier! That's the way it goes in life. We have no control over it. What is "it?" "IT IS WHAT IT IS!" And the sooner we accept that, the happier we will be.

You know something we cannot control? We cannot control getting old. This summer I read two new best-selling popular books about getting old, Norah Ephron's "*I Feel Bad About My Neck*" and Philip Roth's "*Everyman.*" (I do not know why I was so interested in reading about "aging." Perhaps it was because, while in Ocean City, I took my grandchildren to the Jolly Roger Water Park and I saw that there was a reduced entry fee for seniors. I asked how old one had to be to be considered a senior and this young whippersnapper responds, "Fifty-five." And I thought to myself that I would rather pay the full price than be labeled a senior.) Anyway, both Norah Ephron's and Philip Roth's books focused on the aging process. Norah Ephron focused on one part of her body. In her words: "Every so often I read a book about age and whoever wrote it says that it's great to be old. It's great to be wise and age and mellow; it's great to be at the point where you understand just what matters in life. I can't stand people who say things like this! What can they be thinking? Don't they have necks?" Philip Roth's book was much darker, focusing as it does on the surgeries and bypasses, the pains and debilitation that are inevitably part of the aging process for Everyman and Everywoman as well. Sure, we can have plastic surgery. We can watch what we eat. We can exercise, but there is just so much we can do! It is like the person who said, "I feel like my body has gotten totally out of shape, so I got my doctor's permission to join a fitness club and start exercising. I decided to take an aerobics class for seniors. I bent, twisted, gyrated, jumped up and down and perspired for an hour. But by the time I got my leotards on, the class was over!" Yes, eventually the class is over and we are going to get old ... if we are lucky ... lucky enough to live long enough to get cancer or Alzheimer's or Parkinson's disease.

I recently visited with one of our members who has a degenerative illness. It seemed like only yesterday he was one of the vibrant and successful members of our community ... strong-willed and independent. Now he is very dependent ... dependent on the kindness of others. He is sitting at the kitchen table, being fed — just as he was fed some 80 years ago when he was a baby. But now he is being fed not by his mother — but by his wife. And sometimes, like a baby, he turns his head away and his wife, like his mother once did, tries to get the spoon into his mouth. He is still a handsome man, he tries to button his shirt by using his two thumbs, but he needs someone to shave him and comb his hair. He has golf trophies in his living room, but now someone has to take him to the bathroom. He still has much to say, but spends most of his time trying to chew his food.

I see scenes like this all the time — in homes and in nursing homes. I have come to see that, for the most part, when a family puts a loved one in a nursing home it is not because the family did not *want* to take care of their loved one ... it is because they *could no longer* take care of them. And now that I am a senior, I have to confront the reality that my senior moments are someday going to turn into senior years. And I cannot help but wonder: will someone one day have to feed me? Or some day will I have to feed someone?

A friend recently told me that it would be nice if his parents were able to grow old together at the same time. He sees how unhappy his mother is, having to take care of his father. Yes, it would be nice if we could control when and how we are going to grow old. But you know what? IT IS WHAT IT IS! For the most part, it depends on our genes and it depends on mazel. And not everybody has such luck. That is the reality of life. And now I find myself wondering when I look at a bride and groom standing under the chuppah, exchanging rings and promising each other undying love, "In sickness and in health," do they really know what that means? Do they really know what they are getting into? Do they really know what it is going to be like? Whether it is standing under the chuppah holding the hand of your spouse or standing in the Intensive Care Unit holding the hand of your spouse ... IT IS WHAT IT IS! That's life! That is love!

And you know what? Many are not prepared to make that commitment; to live up to that commitment. It is not easy staying married. The truth of the matter is, as much as we share in common, all husbands and wives are different; we all come from different homes and different backgrounds. From birth, by nature and by nurture we are different. And oftentimes those very differences are what attracted us toward each other. A more laid-back person might have been attracted to a more outgoing person for excitement. And a more outgoing person to a more timid person for stability. But while they say that opposites attract, what they do not tell you is that after a while they may fight like cats and dogs, who are also opposites that attract. And so words of "I love you" and "I need you" can very quickly change in a marriage to words of "Why don't you?" or "Why can't you?" or "Why aren't you?" We are looking to change that person and comparing them to others who seem to get it.

There is a story about a man who walks into the street and manages to flag a taxi. He gets into the taxi and the cabbie says, "Perfect timing. You are just like Moishe." The passenger says, "Who?" The cabbie answers, "Moishe Glickman. There's a guy who did everything right. Like my coming along when you needed a cab. It would have happened like that to Moishe every single time." The passenger says, "There are always a few clouds over everybody." But the cabbie responds, "Not Moishe. He was a great athlete. He could have gone on the pro tour in tennis. He could golf with the pros. He sang like an opera baritone and danced like a Broadway star and you should have heard him play the piano!" Passenger says, "Wow, some guy!" Cabbie says, "You ain't heard nothing yet! Moishe knew how to treat a woman and make her feel good and never answer her back even if she was in the wrong. His clothing was always immaculate and his shoes were always polished." The passenger says, "An amazing fellow. How did you meet him?" And the cabbie replies, "Well, I never actually met Moishe." So the passenger asks, "Then how do you know so much about him?" Says the cabbie, "I married his widow!"

Yes, we always look bad when we are compared to others; indeed, when our spouses compare us to the person they *thought* they married. But we *are* the person they married! For better or for worse, we are who we are! And telling a worrier not to worry is expecting too much. Telling a person who is hard of hearing to turn down the TV may be asking too much. And thinking that you are always right, you must admit, is a bit much. There are too many things that do not lend themselves to compromise, that do not lend themselves to change. And expecting and insisting on your spouse being who they are not is asking for trouble. Not everything is worth fighting over because, Lord knows, there is so much to fight about ... just when we go to bed! A new book, "Two In Bed," describes the warfare that can take place when husband and wife go to bed ... What should the temperature be in the room? ... Should the TV be on or off? ... What about reading in bed? ... And eating? Who is taking up too much of the blanket? ... Where is the alarm clock and what time should it be set for? ... Should the children – or pets – be allowed in the room? ... Right side or left? All this *before* the snoring and hot flashes start! There are some issues that can best be solved only by saying: IT IS WHAT IT IS!

That is where marriage counseling is headed these days. In its fancy name it is called "Integrative Couples Therapy." But what it basically means is that instead of trying to help couples *change* each other, they are now focusing on helping couples *accept* each other. Sure, certain behavior like physical and psychological abuse should never be accepted. But certain behavior must be tolerated because not everything is worth fighting over. Sometimes you just have to accept that IT IS WHAT IT IS! And you know what? Miracle of miracles ... sometimes in accepting those differences, something remarkable happens. Your spouse begins to think of you as being sensitive and sensible; the kind of person who "gets it." What is "it?" IT IS WHAT IT IS!

And you know what else? Some people must come to accept that their marriage was not meant to be. They made a mistake – and that is no reflection on either of them. IT IS WHAT IT IS! But need that be the cause of hate? For revenge? For making each other and your children miserable for the rest of your life? Some years ago I told you a story. It was a composite of several stories that have happened many times over. It was a story about a young man's Bar Mitzvah and the incredible tension that came with it; with the mother telling me she didn't want her ex-husband up there at the bimah. How the day of his Bar Mitzvah the boy was a nervous wreck; sweating from the tension that is going on in the front row, waving to his father, but quickly looking to see if his mother was watching.

I told you this some years ago. But now the years have passed and I have a new chapter to add to the story. Now I am coming across these same parents again when their children are getting married

... and they still hate each other! They are still throwing daggers at each other! They are still destroying their children's simcha! They still haven't accepted that IT IS WHAT IT IS! Now the arguments are no longer about aliyot. Now it has to do with who is walking down the aisle ... with the divorced parents, without the divorced parents, together or apart ... and what about the second husband or wife? And who is going to stand under the chuppah? Suddenly the wedding aisle is being turned into a military zone! What should have been a Six Day War has turned into the 100 Years War, putting their children in the position of being the monkey in the middle; being torn, tugged and played from both sides. And it does not end at the wedding! It continues on ... when their kids become parents the fights become over things as meaningless as what the second spouse is going to be called. Please, do not do that to your kids. In the crazy, mixed up world in which we live there is so much pressure and stress in a marriage. Do not add to it! If your marriage did not work out, you, more than anyone else, should understand and accept that it is not your children's fault. What is it? IT IS WHAT IT IS!

Indeed, in the best of homes, in the most stable of homes, many of our children are just not going to turn out to be exactly what we want them to be. And some parents just cannot accept that. And so, instead of *guiding* their children, they attempt to *control* their children. While there are still many parents who are not sufficiently involved with their children, today there are a good number of parents who are overly involved with their children. It starts in pre-school and it continues in university ... parents telling teachers how to best educate their children, parents text-messaging their children in school, using the cell phone like an umbilical cord which they never want to cut. The newest cell phones enable you to know where your children are every minute of the day. That is not letting children *grow* up; that is *dragging* them up. That is not allowing children to learn from their mistakes. It is forcing children to learn from *your* mistakes. That is not allowing children to some day be independent adults. That is just going to make children — when they are adults — be dependent like children. Sure, some behavior cannot and should not be accepted ...the drinking and drugs and the sex. But some behavior — some of the rebellion and desire to do things their way — is part of growing up and you have to learn to accept it. IT IS WHAT IT IS!

Our children are not to be loved and appreciated only when they go our way and give us joy. If that is the way we are, we will never be happy because our children are not always going to go our way and give us joy. Of course, there is some behavior that is totally unacceptable. And we have every responsibility as parents to say so. But we have to be careful not to cross the line from being *involved* parents to being *intrusive* parents. And we have to accept the fact that while we must try and guide our children, at some point we cannot control them. When a child makes a college or career choice that we do not like, when a child decides to move to another city, when a child does not get married, when a child informs us that he or she is gay ... we have a choice. We can go and lay guilt trips on them and on ourselves ... we can go and knock our heads against the wall and make ourselves miserable. Or, we can say IT IS WHAT IT IS and go on with our lives.

And one man who is wise enough to have done just that is the Prime Minister of the State of Israel, Ehud Olmert. Mr. Olmert comes from a strong right-wing, nationalistic background, but he is the only one in his household who does. One of his daughters is a Leftist, the other an outspoken lesbian who stands near checkpoints to interfere with the work of Israeli soldiers. He has a son who is a deserter from the Israel Defense Forces and another who never served and who lives in Paris, and his wife is a member of Women in Black; a group that habitually sides with Arabs against Jews. Little wonder that it is well known that the Olmert family table is filled with arguments. And yet, the family retains its unity. Asked to explain how that is, Olmert said, "What's the big deal? They're entitled to have their own opinions. I never questioned their right to be wrong." Smart man, that Mr. Olmert. He may not be a military genius, but he is a smart family man. You know what they say: You can pick your friends, but you can't pick your family! IT IS WHAT IT IS!

The Chasidic master, Reb Nachman of Bratslav taught: "*Mitzvah gedolah l'hiyot b'simcha tamid* ... it is a great mitzvah to always be happy." That is a difficult mitzvah to keep. But one major step forward in fulfilling it is to remember that so much in life is beyond our control. So much in life depends on mazel. So much in life depends upon the hand we are dealt. And rather than complain about it, bemoan it, or even try to change it, when it comes to those who are nearest and dearest to us ... when things don't go our way, the only way to remain happy is by maintaining the attitude of: IT IS WHAT IT IS!

And yet, having told you all this, I have not told you enough. It is not the whole story. IT IS WHAT IT IS — is not the whole story! Because there is another often quoted popular phrase heard these days that tells us of another "it" — another "it" that Judaism tells us is a necessary ingredient for happiness. What is "it?" IT AIN'T OVER TILL IT'S OVER! It was the great "philosopher" Yogi Berra who introduced these words to the world, but they are very much in keeping with Jewish tradition; a tradition which tells us that while it may be difficult, if not impossible, to change our circumstances and to changes our loved ones, we can, in fact, change ourselves. And it is never too late to do so! This is the meaning of this whole High Holiday period as reflected in the story the Talmud tells us of a man named Eliezer ben Durdaya. Eliezer ben Durdaya came from a fine background and a great future was predicted for him. But he became addicted to the allure of lust and passion. He saw his life was being wasted. He prayed for help from others but then he melted in tears and said, "*Ein hadavar talui elah bi* — it all depends on me." With this realization, he became a changed man. And when this incident was reported to Rabbi Judah the Prince, he said, "There are those who obtain immortality in one hour."

Yes, we may not be able to change others. IT IS WHAT IT IS! But we can change ourselves. And it's never too late. Because you know what they say: IT AIN'T OVER TILL IT'S OVER!

Let Mel Gibson learn this, or else he is going to kill us. Kill us because he is an anti-Semite? No, that is not going to kill us. But he better change from being a drunk driver, because they kill a lot of us. Lots of us are doing things that harm ourselves and that harm others. We cannot change others ... but we can change ourselves. Just ask Bill Wilson — the man known to legions of alcoholics as "Bill W." There was a book written about him by Susan Cheever whose father — the noted writer, John Cheever — was an alcoholic who taught his daughter how to mix a martini by the age of 6. Bill Wilson's story is a fascinating one. In 1934 doctors concluded that he was a hopeless drunk and told his wife that there was no cure for him, except for putting him into an asylum. Wilson had checked himself into hospitals three times; all to no avail. As Cheever writes, "The more he decided not to drink, the more irresistible drinks seemed to become." Then a friend told him of the work of the eminent psychiatrist Carl Jung and the American psychiatrist William James, who had both come to the conclusion that only God could give one strength to stop drinking. Wilson never had another drink. One thing led to another ... and Alcoholics Anonymous was started, with countless people's lives having been changed for the better because of it. All because of Bill Wilson!

I found his story interesting, but that is not what fascinated me. What fascinated me was the description of Bill Wilson on his deathbed. A lifelong smoker, he had been fighting emphysema for years, and now he was losing the battle. On his deathbed, Christmas Day of 1970, he wrote a note to his nurse asking for three shots of whiskey. And he was upset when he did not get it. A week later he asked for booze again and then again on Jan. 8, and then on Jan. 14. He had been sober for 34 years and yet he wanted a drink. In fact, he had wanted a drink every day of his life.

Yes, it is not easy to change. Every day it is a battle! Bill Wilson had a propensity to drink. He could not get rid of it, but he was able to control it. All of us have certain propensities and inclinations and desires ... it might be the result of our nature or our nurture ... and it is not easy to change. Not whether you are a drinker or stingy or selfish or an abusive spouse, an absent parent or disrespectful to your parents ... it is a battle every day of your life. But the battle can be won, we can change ... if we want to. None of us are robots or puppets. We are human beings and as such, we are not only shaped by our environment; we shape it. We are not only responsible for our past; we are also capable of changing our future. We can change if we realize: IT AIN'T OVER TILL IT'S OVER!

This summer, in very different ways, I learned how true these words are from two generations of my family ... from my mother and from my granddaughters. Yes, it is true — we are all going to get old. And our bodies are going to break down. IT IS WHAT IT IS! But while that is true of most everything from our necks down ... from our necks up IT AIN'T OVER TILL IT'S OVER! We can still be young in mind and heart. I had thought that becoming a grandfather would make me feel older. After all, close your eyes and picture your grandfather ... he was an old man! But the fact is, I have discovered that spending time with my grandchildren makes me feel younger! In many ways I've returned to my youth; once again building sand castles and going to water parks, going round and round on the merry-go-round, getting painted tattoos, experiencing Disney On Ice and Dora the Explorer and the circus and the zoo and being reminded of the central fact of life: "The wheels on the bus go round and round ... while the people on the bus go yackety, yak, yak." I've never had so much fun! But something in back of my mind keeps asking why did I not do more of this with my children? I guess I was very busy and I thought that later on I would have time. And I was right! Now I have time; the problem is — now they are busy!

Our children are ours for so few years, and every moment is precious, never to be relived. And some of us let it slip through our fingers and then it is gone before you can blink an eye. Even when we spend time with our children, we are not really with our children ... we are with our children and our cell phone ... with our children and our computer ... with our children but thinking about the office. You can change that, you know. When I'm with my grandchildren — and only when I am with my grandchildren — I turn off my cell phone. Why? Because IT AIN'T OVER TILL ITS OVER.

On a very different level, this summer I learned how true these words are from my mother. My mother had a very difficult spring and summer, spending four months in hospitals and rehabilitation centers. She fell and broke her hip and the usual happened: the surgery was a success but then there were "complications," complications that almost killed her. As she approached the age of 94, we thought we were losing her. She said that she has no complaints to God; she had lived a wonderful life, was blessed to have a beautiful marriage and real nachas from her family. And then she lay in the Intensive Care Unit of the hospital, hooked up to a ventilator and respirator, day after day hanging on. And eventually, thank God, the tube was removed from her throat and the respirator was disconnected. She opened her eyes and her first words to me and my brothers were: "You can take my apartment off the market." Yes, where there is life, there is hope. Even in an Intensive Care Unit you can have a sense of humor and be grateful to be alive. IT AIN'T OVER TILL IT'S OVER. At 94, we are still learning a lot from my mother. And she is not the only one.

Art Buchwald, the noted humorist and columnist, turned 80 this year and was put in hospice, dying of kidney failure. But after six months they threw him out! He refused to die. And he says he is having the time of his life because all of his friends, thinking he was dying, came and visited and told him how much he meant to them, how much they loved him, how much they were going to miss him. Buchwald says he wishes everyone would have the opportunity to hear their eulogies while they are still alive. Then we would have the chance to tell our spouses and our children that they matter more to us than our jobs, more than anything else. And we could tell our friends how much they mean to us and how much they inspired us. And if we were on the outs with someone, we might never have been able to change them, but there is still time for us to reach out to them.

There are lots of people like my mother and Art Buchwald who we think are dying ... but are living. And there are lots of other people whom we think are living but are, in fact, dying. Now, in these moments before Yizkor, it is our responsibility to reach out and do what we can do, remembering: IT AIN'T OVER TILL IT'S OVER.

And in these moments before Yizkor, I want to pause to reflect on what our parents would want of us before it is over for us. And I hope you will take my words to heart. All of our parents had different hopes, dreams and expectations for us. But I think all they all shared one hope in common. They wanted us to get along with our brothers and sisters. And I know that is not always easy to do. So much of who and what we are is a result of who our siblings are. The fact is that in our most formative years as children we spend more time with our siblings than with friends, parents, teachers, or even by ourselves. But somewhere down the line something goes wrong. We discover that with all of the shared genes, environment, and experiences we and our siblings are not the same. And we do not like the differences. But you know what? IT IS WHAT IT IS! As brothers and sisters we do not have to like everything about each other in order to love each other.

Our forefather, Jacob, had twelve sons, and they had a lot of trouble getting along. They went as far as selling their brother, Joseph, into slavery. But at the end of his days, the Torah tells us: "*Avicha tsiva*" — father Jacob commanded Joseph to forgive his brothers. You see, to Jacob — to any parent — when their children fight it doesn't matter to them who is right or who is wrong. All that matters is that they stick together. That is what our parents command us.

We cannot change *who* and *what* our siblings are. IT IS WHAT IT IS. But as we get older our relationship with our siblings can change. In our mobile society where the concept of lifelong friends rarely exists anymore, it is our siblings whom we can turn to in times of need. It is our siblings who are going to sit shiva for us. I always think back to the brother/sister relationship Shirley MacLaine and Warren Beatty have. They see eye to eye on very little and yet they have a very deep relationship. When Shirley MacLane was asked how to explain it, she replied in two words: "We're blood." I love that! "We're blood." IT IS WHAT IT IS!

So, if your relationship with your sibling is not what it should be — and what it could be — remember: IT'S NOT OVER TILL IT'S OVER. Tonight, when Yom Kippur is over, go home and call or if it is easier, email your sibling. No, you do not have to tell them, "I love you." "I need you." Just wish them a happy New Year, tell them you miss them and ask them to reply. And when they ask you why you reached out, you can simply say to them: "*Avicha tsiva* — our parents commanded us."

And in regard to our parents, the fact of the matter is, there too, you need mazel. Some of us had the mazel of having saintly parents. Some of us were not so fortunate. We have to accept that IT IS WHAT IT IS. And it has nothing to do with us. For our parents it's over. But we still have a life to live. And just as we now come to say Yizkor for our parents, some day our children will come and say Yizkor for us. And how will they remember us? HBO had a special last year featuring Kirk Douglas and his son, Michael. Theirs was not always a good relationship. Kirk Douglas was not always a good father and Michael not always a good son. Since Kirk Douglas suffered a stroke in 1996, he is a different man. Toward the end of the program, Kirk asks Michael, "Was I a good father?" And Michael answered, "You have *ultimately* been a great father." Not all of us have been good at all the roles we have to play, but IT AIN'T OVER TILL IT'S OVER. *Ultimately* we can be remembered as having been great at what we did. I am working on my "ultimately" and I hope you will do the same.

In life there is pain and there is pleasure. There are joys and there are sorrows. There is life and there is death. We have one life to live and we are commanded to live it, to appreciate it and to enjoy it. Even when things are not so enjoyable, IT IS WHAT IT IS. At all times, under all circumstances, *mitzvah gedolah l'hiyot b'simcha tamid* ... it is a great mitzvah to always be happy. And if you have not been happy until now, let this be your mitzvah in the year that lies ahead. At whatever stage we are in life, in a sense, we have only just begun because ... IT AIN'T OVER TILL IT'S OVER. With a full heart, I genuinely wish all of you a Happy Yom Kippur, and happiness all the days of your lives.

Yom Kippur, October 2, 2006

Leap Before You Look

I have not lived in New York for the past forty years, but there are memories of New York that never go away. One, for me, has to do with New York's subway system. Throughout my four years of high school I took a subway every day. And during my college years, I used to take three trains from Brooklyn to Yeshiva University in Washington Heights! Taking the subway was a natural part of life, and it is the way millions of New Yorkers get around every day. But one thing, for me, was not natural — those people who used to stand at the edge of the platform looking to see if the train was coming. Not only would I never do that, but I used to get nervous watching someone else do that! There was a fear that I had — a fear that many had — of what would happen if someone fell on the tracks with a train heading right toward them.

I was reminded of that fear when just such an occurrence took place on the trains of New York on January 2, 2007. Here is the way the *New York Times* described it:

It was every subway rider's nightmare, times two.

Who has ridden along New York's 656 miles of subway lines and not wondered: "What if I fell to the tracks as a train came in? What would I do?"

And who has not thought: "What if someone else fell? Would I jump to the rescue?"

Wesley Autrey, a 50-year-old construction worker and Navy veteran, faced both those questions in a flashing instant yesterday, and got his answers almost as quickly.

Mr. Autrey was waiting for the downtown local at 137th Street and Broadway in Manhattan around 12:45 p.m. He was taking his two daughters, Syshe, 4, and Shuqui, 6, home before work.

Nearby, a man collapsed, his body convulsing. Mr. Autrey and two women rushed to help, he said. The man, Cameron Hollopeter, 20, managed to get up, but then stumbled to the platform edge and fell to the tracks, between the two rails.

The headlights of the No. 1 train appeared. "I had to make a split decision," Mr. Autrey said.

So he made one, and leapt.

Mr. Autrey lay on Mr. Hollopeter, his heart pounding, pressing him down in a space roughly a foot deep. The train's brakes screeched, but it could not stop in time.

Five cars rolled overhead before the train stopped, the cars passing inches from his head, smudging his blue knit cap with grease. Mr. Autrey heard onlookers' screams. "We're O.K. down here," he yelled, "but I've got two daughters up there. Let them know their father's O.K." He heard cries of wonder, and applause.

Power was cut, and workers got them out. Mr. Hollopeter, a student at the New York Film Academy, was taken to St. Luke's–Roosevelt Hospital Center. He had only bumps and bruises, said his grandfather, Jeff Friedman. The police said it appeared that Mr. Hollopeter had suffered a seizure.

Mr. Autrey refused medical help, because, he said, nothing was wrong. He did visit Mr. Hollopeter in the hospital before heading to his night shift. "I don't feel like I did something spectacular; I just saw someone who needed help," Mr. Autrey said. "I did what I felt was right."

The reaction to this extraordinary event was remarkable. New York's Mayor Bloomberg awarded Mr. Autrey the highest medal that the city can give to any civilian. Jay Leno and David Letterman both had him on their programs. Citizens sent him checks and gifts in appreciation for what he did. One person sent him a check for ten thousand dollars. Another sent him money with which to open a college tuition fund for his children. President Bush saluted him. What was most impressive is that in all of his public appearances—at the mayor's ceremony, on television, and in his interviews with the press—Wesley Autrey was modest and self-effacing. All he said was, "I am no hero. I just happened to be in the right place at the right time. Anyone who was in my place would have done the same thing."

Let me ask you a question. Would you have done what Wesley Autrey did? Would you have jumped onto the tracks with that train heading right toward you, putting your own life in danger to save the life of another person? Is it true that Wesley Autrey is not a hero, that he just happened to be in the right place at the right time, and that anyone who was in his place would have done the same thing? The fact of the matter is that there is no way to know for sure! When we are born, there is nothing in our genetic makeup that predisposes us to being a hero or a villain. All of us, as children, picture ourselves as being a 'Superman' or a 'Batman' or a 'Zorro' or "Spiderman,' but there is no way of knowing if we will fulfill that dream until we are finally put to the test. Because let me tell you something about Superman, Batman, Zorro, and Spiderman — they all shared something in common. Before becoming superheroes, they were all ordinary people; there was nothing special about them in their regular lives. Remember Clark Kent? He was a "mild-mannered reporter." Bruce Wayne? He was a wealthy patron of the arts. Similarly, Zorro and Spiderman and the Lone Ranger had nothing special about them in their daily lives. It is just that at some point they were put to the test, and they found out something about themselves that they never could have known before.

Do you know what? You do not have to be "super" to do heroic actions. In an article in the *Journal of Religion and Society* about righteous Gentiles who helped rescue Jews during the Holocaust, the author writes that these Gentiles refused any special praise for the acts they performed. They claimed that they were just ordinary people fulfilling their duty. They said they helped the Jews because they found themselves in situations where they could help and had the ability to see that they were able to help.

That is nice. But you and I know that it ain't necessarily so! Not everyone who was able to help did, in fact, help. When put to the test, all too many failed. And they had to live with that knowledge for the rest of their lives.

That is true not only for those who failed to help during the Holocaust. The famous playwright, David Mamet, once wrote, "On June 6, 1944, thousands of American paratroopers jumped into Normandy. Four men refused to jump. Can anyone imagine the rest of these men's lives? What prodigies of self-excuse, rationale, or repression they must have had to employ. Their lives, in effect, ended the moment they refused to leave the plane; as would the lives of the Jews had they refused to go into the sea." Well, I have bad news for Mr. Mamet. The truth is that most of the Jews refused to go into that sea. When confronted with the kind of situation that Wesley Autrey faced, when challenged whether to jump in a life-or-death situation, the Jews turned out to be quite cowardly.

Soon after the Jews were liberated from Egypt and were on their way to the Promised Land, suddenly they were confronted with the swirling waters of the Red Sea in front of them and the Egyptian army behind them. So they cried out to God, and what does God tell Moses to do? "*Daber el b'nai Yisroel v'yisa-u* — tell the Jewish people to go forward" (Exodus 14:15). But no one moved. Everyone was fearful of drowning. When the Israelites stood at the edge of the Red Sea, none of the leaders had faith in God; none wanted to go in the water. All the leaders suddenly became very polite, each one saying to the other, "After you." Suddenly, out of nowhere, along comes a man named Nachshon ben Aminadav, who, in an act of great faith and courage, plunged into the swirling waters. According to our tradition, because of Nachshon, and Nachshon alone, because of his courage, heroism, and faith in God, the Almighty split the sea, thus saving the entire Jewish people. The Jewish people have remembered Nachshon's name ever since. This is why in modern Israel, the ones in the army who go first, who take the lead in a difficult or dangerous assignment, are called *Nachshonim*.

It is interesting to note that the Torah describes the events at the Red Sea in two different ways. In one verse we are told that the Jews walked "*bayabashah b'toch hayam* — on dry ground through the sea" (Exodus 14:29). In the second verse we are told that the Jews walked "*b'toch hayam bayabashah* — through the sea on dry ground" (Exodus 15:19). A biblical commentator explained that the two versions were necessary because they describe two types of people. One type was like Nachshon, who walked "through the sea on dry ground"; at first they walked in the sea and only after they showed their faith in God were they able to walk on dry ground. The rest of the Jews — the more timid among them, those who lacked faith — waited on the shore; they waited until the waters were already divided. They walked "on dry ground in the midst of the sea."

All of Jewish history was changed for the better because of Nachshon. Yet, the history of those Jews who stood at the banks of the Red Sea and did not jump was also changed, but all for the worse. For the rest of their lives, these Jews would have to live with themselves knowing that Wesley Autrey, the hero of the New York subway, was wrong when he said, "Any one who was in my place would have done the same thing." Not necessarily, Mr. Autrey. And I can prove it to you! I can prove it by what is happening in the Middle East, and I can prove it by what is happening in America.

Look at the Middle East today, and you will find it hard to believe that this was once the center of the civilized world, that these were the countries that gave the world leading thinkers in the fields of medicine and astronomy and philosophy and mathematics. Today the Middle East has turned into the "killing fields." I am not talking about how Muslims are killing Americans or Israelis in the Middle East. I am talking about the way Muslims are killing Muslims in the Middle East. *New York Times* columnist Thomas Friedman writes, "How could it be that the Danish cartoon of Mohammed led to mass violent protests, while unspeakable violence by Muslims against Muslims in Iraq every day evokes about as much reaction in the Arab/Muslim world as the weather report?" Muslims are killing their fellow Muslims in the most barbaric manner, and these murders are happening every day — not by the tens but by the hundreds! The murderers could be Shiites or Sunnis or Kurds or Iranians or Palestinians or Lebanese or Al-Qaeda or Hezbollah or Fatah or Hamas or Baathists or the Mahdi Army. They are killing on Muslim holy days, they are killing in Muslim mosques, and they are killing both the young and the old! And as Thomas Friedman asks, "Where is the Muslim Martin Luther King?" Where is the Muslim leader — religious or political — who is prepared to jump into the waters of the Red Sea, who is prepared to jump onto the tracks of New York, who is prepared to step out from all the rest? And yes, by doing so he is putting his life in danger to cry out against violence because it has to be done. In a world of more than a billion Muslims, there does not seem to be one person who is willing to stand up and stand out as an advocate for peace. Instead, the Muslim world is left to idolize people like Saddam Hussein, Yassir Arafat, and Sheikh Nasrallah.

Here in America we Jews were caught up in the controversy swirling around Jimmy Carter's book, *Palestine: Peace not Apartheid*. Make no mistake about it: the book is very damaging to the cause of Israel. It is written by a past president of the United States and a man who has a following for some of the good works he has done. Mr. Carter is entitled to his opinion on who is at fault in the Arab/Israeli conflict, and he does seem to be of the opinion that it is Israel's fault. Yes, he is entitled to that opinion, but he is not entitled to lie about the facts, which he has done in many instances in his book and in his public appearances. Former President Carter has been taken to task for his lies. Jeffrey Goldberg and Deborah Lipstadt did it in the pages of the *Washington Post*. Ethan Bronner did it in the book review section of the *New York Times*. Alan Dershowitz did it on the *Huffington Post*. Ken Stein did it by resigning his position at the Carter Center in Atlanta. Martin Peretz did it in the *New Republic*. David Makovsky did it in *U.S. News and World Report*. Joshua Muvarchik did it in the lead article in *Commentary* magazine. And Dennis Ross did it in the *New York Times*. They all took President Carter to task! They all jumped into the controversy and said what had to be said when they could have remained silent. That is the good news. So what is the bad news?

Did you notice what all the people I named had in common? Goldberg and Stein and Ross and Lipstadt and Dershowitz and all the others are all Jews. But where were the non-Jewish voices? In fact, fourteen members of the board of the Carter Center resigned because of his book. That is fourteen out of two hundred. All fourteen were Jews. They attempted to get some of the other 186 board members to join them in resigning, but to no avail. Why the silence by the non-Jewish members? Some may argue that this silence by the non-Jews does not matter. Sure it matters! It allows Carter to claim that his only critics are Jews, and it allows Carter to claim that Jews control the media. It feels as if Carter would throw all the Jewish people onto the train tracks and there do not seem to be too many people who would be willing to jump in and help save us. They are afraid of what might happen to them.

Trees — and the whole of the natural world — played an important role in the lives of the ancient Jewish people. Trees continue to play an important role in modern Jewish history as well. The twenty-five million people who have read *The Diary of Anne Frank* know what I mean. In her diary, Anne Frank describes how she would look out from the attic — through the only window that was not covered to prevent anyone from seeing movement in the apartment where the family lived — and there was a tree, a chestnut tree in front of it. Anne writes in her diary,

> Nearly every morning I go to the attic to blow the stuffy air out of my lungs. From my favorite spot on the floor, I look at the blue sky and the bare chestnut tree, on whose branches little raindrops shine, appearing like silver ... and at the seagulls and other birds as they glide on the wind.... As long as this exists, I thought, and I may live to see it, the sunshine, the cloudless skies, while this lasts I cannot be unhappy.

It was that tree that gave Anne Frank hope to carry on. Unfortunately, that tree, which some estimate to be more than 150 years old, developed a disease and had to be cut down. But one person stepped forward and said, "Let's take a sapling from the old tree and replant it." The sapling has the precise same DNA as the tree. It will take many years to match the glory and beauty that Anne Frank's tree possessed, but it keeps alive the memory of Anne Frank and her hope in humanity.

When I read about this tree, I thought of a story in the Talmud that tells of a man who was journeying on the road and saw a man planting a carob tree. He asked the man how long it would take for the tree to bear fruit. The man replied, "Seventy years." The traveler then asked him, "Are you certain that you will live another seventy years?" And the man replied, "I found carob trees in the world. As my forefather planted these for me, so I, too, plant these for my children."

So that is the story in life. There are those who plant trees and replant the saplings, and those who only wait until the tree can give them shade. There are those who are willing to run into the sea through dry land, and others who only wait for the dry land to appear before they are prepared to move. Some who jump in gain much fame, like an Oscar Schindler or a Raoul Wallenberg. Others are just the people you meet every day like Wesley Autrey. It is people like these who fulfill the talmudic dictate: "He who saves one life is as if he saved an entire world."

We all have the ability to do our share to save the world. And if we all did our share, the prophetic dream would be fulfilled of our living "in a world in which none shall hurt, none shall destroy, for the earth shall be filled with the knowledge of the Lord, as the waters cover the sea."

February 3, 2007

ANIMALS AND THE JEWISH TRADITION

People have always had mixed feeling about animals. Some love them and some do not. To some, an animal can be man's best friend. Others say, "You better keep them on a leash!" In the Borough Park neighborhood of Brooklyn in which I grew up, very few people had pets, so sometimes it is hard for me to identify with the attachment some people feel toward their animals. I think back to former President Clinton's dog, Buddy, of blessed memory. Clinton once explained that he had an uncle named Buddy of whom he was very fond, and he honored his uncle by naming the dog after him. It is hard for me to imagine any Jewish family in which the family perpetuates the memory of Bubbe Sarah by naming the house dog Sarah, or naming their dog Shawn, after their Zayde Shloime. It could not happen because we Jews recognize that, no matter how much we love pets, dogs are not human.

But not everybody sees it this way. Germany became the first European nation to vote to guarantee animal rights in its constitution. The Bundestag voted to add "and animals" to a clause that obliges the state to respect and protect the dignity of humans. Newspapers reported that Farley Mowat, a famous Canadian author, labeled the yearly seal hunt in Newfoundland a "holocaust." It seemed as if he was equating the killing of seals with the killing of Jews. Mowat defended himself by saying, "I do not make a distinction between the massive destruction of any kind of animal – whether it is human or non-human."

What does Judaism have to say about this attitude? Where do humans stand in relation to the animal kingdom? What are our responsibilities to animals? And if we personally do not like animals, is it our responsibility as Jews to "save the whales?" What does our tradition tell us about animals that speak to us like humans do?

There is a law in the Torah that provides us with much insight on these questions. It is a law that most all of us rarely, if ever, observe but one that requires little effort and brings great reward. It is the mitzvah of *Shiluach Haken*. If you find a bird's nest in a tree or on the ground and there are young birds in this nest, and the mother bird is sitting in the tree, says the Torah, "Do not take the mother bird and the eggs. First the mother bird must leave and then you may take the eggs or the small birds" (Deuteronomy 22:7–8).

What is fascinating about this mitzvah is that it is considered the easiest of all the 613 commandments in the Torah to observe. All you have to do is wave your hand to shoo the mother bird away – and you have done a mitzvah. Even more fascinating is the fact that this is one of only two commandments in the Torah for which a reward is promised – the reward of length of days. The only other mitzvah in the Torah for which a reward is promised is that of honoring one's parents, the commandment considered the most difficult in the Torah to observe, and there, too, the reward is the same: length of days.

It is important to analyze the purpose of this commandment. Why did the Torah command us to shoo away the mother bird before taking the eggs? The simple answer is that this is an act of compassion, but the answer is not really so simple. The *Sefer Ha-Chinuch* is a book written hundreds of years ago that attempts to give an explanation for each of the 613 commandments in the Torah. For most commandments, the explanation takes a page or two. But surprisingly, on this commandment, the *Sefer Ha-Chinuch* goes on for pages and pages, for its purpose and the reason behind it were matters of great dispute between two of the greatest Torah commentators who ever lived: one, whom we know as Maimonides, and the other, whom we know as Nachmanides.

Maimonides takes the traditional position that most Jews have always held. From Maimonides' perspective, the entire purpose of this commandment is to show compassion for the feelings of the mother bird. In his words, "It is because animals have a great anxiety when they see the suffering of their young, just as human beings do. For the love of a mother for the young is not something dependent on reason; it is rather one of the functions of the mental power that is found in animals, as it is found in man." So, according to Maimonides, while human beings are on the highest rung in the animal kingdom, animals and humans are very alike in their feelings and in their emotions. Therefore, the mother bird has to be sent away so that she should not have to suffer from seeing her child taken from her. That is what Maimonides says.

Nachmanides comes along and says that no, that is not true. In fact, God's concern is not for the sensibilities and sensitivities of an animal. In Nachmanides' words, "God did not have pity on a bird's nest and His compassion did not reach to its young. For God's mercy does not extend over creatures with animal natures ... for if so He would have forbidden the slaughter of animals." No, says Nachmanides, animals are animals — and humans are humans, and never the twain shall meet. God's concern is not for the feelings and sensibilities of an animal. But if that is the case, then why are we, in fact, commanded to shoo away the mother bird? Writes Nachmanides, we do so not for the bird's sake, but for our sake. The purpose of this and so many other commandments is to purge a human being of callousness and cruelty and savagery. How we act will not affect the animal, but it will very much affect us.

A manifestation of Nachmanides' position is found in a responsa written by the greatest Jewish decisor of the last half of the twentieth century, Rabbi Moshe Feinstein — of blessed memory. In one of his books, Rabbi Feinstein responds to this question: if while you are sitting in a Succah, bees come in and make it impossible for you to stay and thus fulfill the mitzvah, are you allowed to kill the bees? Rabbi Feinstein answers yes, but with the following caveat: you should kill the bee not by stamping on it, but by putting a cup over it. Now, the fact of the matter is, if you are a bee, the method of killing really does not make much of a difference — if you've gotta go, you gotta go. In fact, the case could be made that, from the bee's perspective, the quicker, the better. Yet, Rabbi Feinstein's response was not based on the sensibility of the bee, but on the sensibilities of a human. Rabbi Feinstein was trying to assure that a human would not be in the position of directly killing any living creature.

There is an important lesson here that goes way beyond Judaism's attitude toward animals. It goes to the very heart of the Jewish tradition, a tradition that is based on deed, rather than creed. In the words of the *Sefer Ha-Chinuch*, "*Acharei hape-ulot nimshachim ha-levavot* — our heart is moved by our actions and deeds." If we act loving, we feel loving. If we act charitably, we feel charitable. Deeds shape the heart more than the heart shapes the deeds. You do not have to like animals to treat them nicely. You don't have to be a mensch to act like a mensch. What you have to do is act like a mensch, and then, one hopes, you will be a mensch. In the Jewish tradition, what we think is not what counts. It is what we do that counts, because doing the right thing will lead us to thinking the right thing! Former President Jimmy Carter spoke very much from the Christian tradition when he talked of the sin of lusting from the heart. In the Jewish tradition, there is no such sin — as long as the lust stays in your heart and goes no farther!

This represents a basic difference between Judaism and Christianity. As Rabbi Shmuley Boteach points out, both religions begin with the premise that humans must be made better, but whereas Christianity argues that only inner faith and divine grace can change an individual, Judaism maintains that inner transformation comes about through external action. Rather than the heart fashioning hands, hands fashion the heart. In Judaism, it is not the heart — or indeed, even the mind — but the hands that serve as the fundamental religious organ. We do not care *why* someone does the right thing; we just want a person to *do* the right thing! Because eventually, that person will be doing it for the right reasons.

A classic illustration of the difference between the Jewish and Christian approach is found in the respective words each religious group gives for the alms given for the poor. The Christian word for helping the needy is "charity," derived from the Latin word *Caritas*, which means "dear." It is not enough to feed the poor; they must be dear to us as well. In Judaism, the word we use is *tzedakah*, which means "justice." When a man knocks on your door and says he is hungry, you must feed him whether you like it or not, whether you like him or not, or even if you consider him a lazy and irresponsible parasite. You still cannot withhold assistance. That is justice! *Why* you do it does not count — *what* you do is what counts!

It bothers me whenever a person who hears that others have made a large gift to the school or synagogue complain that they are doing it only for the honor or the naming opportunity and not because they are so generous. "Who cares?" says Judaism. Just do right for whatever reason, and eventually it will become habit-forming. Do not question the motives — it is the results that count!

One of the greatest biblical teachers of our time was the late, great Nechama Leibowitz. Her books on biblical studies are considered classics. Most every rabbi — Orthodox, Conservative, or Reform — has them. She never attained the image of a superstar scholar because she was very quiet and modest in her personal life, never seeking honor or glory. A book written about her gives her the honor and glory that she deserves. I found one particular story about her in the book to be most insightful. A rabbi had written to her about a student of his — a girl — who wanted to take a job as a counselor in a coed school. The rabbi had told this girl that if she felt she was "saving souls" he would encourage her to take the job. "But if you're only going there to meet boys, better you should stay home." Nechama Leibowitz very much disagreed with his approach. She wrote back,

> You should do everything in your power to encourage her . . . you say she should scrutinize her motives and see whether she is doing this for the sake of Torah, or in order to meet boys . . . can you be serious? If I began to calculate what pushed me to teach — what percentage of me wanted to promote the study of Torah, and what percentage of me wanted to make a living, and what percentage was egotistical desire for praise, and what percentage was a way of running away from loneliness and an empty house after my husband died — it would be better not to ask at all. Can such a thing be calculated? Would this girl be able to do it? I would not even advise her — absolutely not!

Nechama Leibowitz was so right! It is not for us to question the motivations of our actions or the actions of others, because then we would never do anything. It is for us to act right, and then, one hopes, we will be able to think right.

It is good to remember this teaching by Maimonides: on Rosh Hashana, we should assume that all our deeds are being placed on the scales of judgment before the Almighty, with good deeds on one side and bad on the other, and the scales are exactly even. Even more, says Maimonides, consider that the deeds of the whole world are being weighed and their good and bad deeds are also even. The next deed we do, no matter how small or seemingly insignificant, may either tip the scale of judgment in our favor and in favor of humankind, thereby assuring us a blissful future. Or God forbid, if our next deed is an evil one, it might doom us and the whole world by tipping the scales of judgment against us.

Notice, Maimonides is speaking of the scales being filled with our *deeds* — not with our *thoughts*. What we *think* and what motivates us are not what counts. It is what we *do* that counts. Every little deed, every action, no matter how small or how seemingly insignificant — even as insignificant as shooing away a mother bird — can have a dramatic effect on our lives and the lives of others.

Remember these words in the Ethics of our Fathers: "*V'chol maasecha b'sefer nichtavim* — all deeds are being inscribed in the Book." May all our deeds — regardless of motivation — be good ones.

August 17, 2002

SMILE, YOU'RE ON CANDID CAMERA

I want to tell you a story. It's a true story. Of course, all of my stories are true stories, but some are truer than others. This one actually happened! This one must be considered the truest of all, for it was recorded on videotape.

I officiated at the wedding of the daughter of one of our nicest congregants; they are wonderful people who are genuine friends. A few weeks after the wedding took place, they invited me over to watch the videotape of the ceremony. I sat down in their den, made myself comfortable, saw them press the PLAY button on their VCR, and there, right before my eyes, the wedding procession began. And while the bridesmaids and ushers and the family were marching down the aisle, with the music playing, suddenly I could hear voices on the tape — a few people were engaged in conversation while such a solemn occasion was unfolding. Who could be so crude and insensitive? To make matters worse, their conversation was making fun of the relationship between the *machatonim* (in-laws). Who among the guests — the so-called friends of the families — would be doing such a thing? And then I realized that I recognized those voices — OH MY GOD —IT'S ME, THE CANTOR, AND THE GROOM'S RABBI!!! We had been standing under the chupah and, it being a lengthy procession, we had flipped off the microphone in front of us and started kibbitzing and talking to each other, not realizing that right above us a small microphone had been placed for the video. Every word we were saying was being recorded as the wedding party was marching down the aisle. And there I was, sitting in their den, watching and listening as the bride's mother came down the aisle, and one of my co-officiants — I will not tell you which one — makes a derogatory remark about her dress. Fortunately, I replied that I liked the dress and thought she looked good. But then, as the bride was coming down the aisle, I noticed her uncle in the audience, and I made a comment about him that — well, it would have been more appropriate for PeeWee Herman, not your rabbi! Smile, you're on Candid Camera! How I regretted what I had said. If only I had known that it was all being recorded, how differently I would have acted!

Ours has become the video society. Everything seems to get recorded. At another wedding at which I officiated, the bridal party had come down the aisle, and then the door swung open and the bride started to come down the aisle on the arm of her father. Her face was radiant; her father's eyes were glistening. They got halfway down the aisle, and then the photographer said, "Wait, the camera wasn't working. Back up and let's do that again." And they did!

Watching that reminded me of a story when video cameras first came on the scene. It happened at a Jewish catering hall where a young Jewish couple was getting married. Everyone was having a great time, including the father of the bride who was footing the bill, but still somehow was enjoying himself as much as anyone else. For whatever reason, he had brought with him a large cash payment to pay the caterer after the wedding was concluded. The cash was in his wallet, which was in the inside breast pocket of his jacket. The dancing became more and more frenzied. The bride's father, like some of the guests, removed his jacket and placed it over his seat. The wallet, of course, was inside his jacket. The dancing and music and merriment went on and on. Finally it was time to leave. The father put on his jacket, felt for his wallet — and there was no wallet! Nothing! A thorough search was made, but nothing was found. The caterer, of course, would accept no excuses or explanations. The father had his checkbook, and so he wrote out a check. What else could he do? Most all of the guests had by now departed. Only the bride and groom and their immediate families were still in the hall, along with the videographers who had been filming all evening long. Then, someone, realizing that with the new camcorder being used, you could watch the party instantly, suggested that the wedding party look at the tape. The videographer began to show what he had taped, and there they were – guests, friends, relatives – dancing and celebrating. And there he was, clear as day, the father of the groom, reaching into the jacket pocket of his new in-law, removing the wallet and pocketing it. Mazel Tov!

So now let me ask you, What if we realized, everyone of us, that there was someone out there, videotaping our every action in our places of business, in our offices, in our homes. Would we act differently than we do? Of course we would! Well, let me tell you. Someone is! In a very real sense, all that we do is being videotaped. That is what the High Holidays are all about. God opens our *Sefer Ha-chaim*, our Book of Life, in which, as our sages describe it, "*V'chol ma-asecha b'sefer nichtavim* – All of our deeds are recorded." They are all part of the Divine record. While we are in this world, all of our actions are being videotaped. How true are the words Bette Midler sings: "God is watching us from a distance." And it is all being recorded in our Sefer Ha-chaim – our Book of Life.

But let us be most cognizant of the fact that it is not only God who is watching us and recording our every action. For this phrase, Sefer Ha-chaim, can be translated not only as the Book of Life but it can also mean the Book of the Living. Whether we like it or not, whether we know it or not, everything we do is constantly being recorded in the biographies of those around us. All of our actions are being photographed and tape recorded by others, shaping their lives and leaving an indelible impact.

All of us who are parents should ask ourselves this question: How often do we pause to realize that each and every day we are making indelible entries into our children's Book of Life? And how enduring these influences prove to be. The amount of charity we give, the excuses we offer for not giving, the comments we make behind the backs of friends, the references we make to the color of a person's skin, our business ethics, our moral behavior, how we act at parties, and what we eat and drink and watch on television – all of these and so much more are being inscribed between the covers of our children's Book of Life; they are being videotaped on the camcorder of their souls.

Read the books of the rich and famous. Brooke Hayward, daughter of actress Margaret Sullivan and producer Leland Hayward, tells of a family history of breakdowns and suicide. In *Mommy Dearest*, Christine Crawford depicts her mother, actress Joan Crawford, as a promiscuous lush, given to brutal child abuse. Roxanne Pulitzer writes of how her father was an alcoholic. And then there are the books by the children of the Reagans and Bing Crosby and all the others whom we popularize and idolize — but their children know the truth. The children were there, recording their every action in their hearts. Not just celebrities' children but all of our children record our every action.

A colleague once pointed out an interesting view of a father-son relationship. Charles Francis Adams served for many years as Ambassador from the United States to Great Britain. He was busy with affairs of state and evidently did not have too much time to give his family. His son, Brooks Adams, and he had very interesting notes in their diaries about a day they spent together fishing. The son, Brooks Adams, has the following entry: "Went fishing with my father. The most glorious day in my life." The father, Charles Francis Adams, has this entry in his diary about the very same day: "Went fishing with my son. A day wasted." The father did not realize the impact he was having on his child. No different, I am sure, than did the parents of Alan Dershowitz, who writes of how so much of his love for Judaism and his supporting the underdog came about because of the conversations he heard his parents have at the family Shabbos table.

For better or for worse, all that we say and do is recorded by our children in their Book of Life, and it affects them for the rest of their lives. What kind of conversations are our children hearing from us? What kind of behavior are they recording about us? Holding our child's hand, teaching him how to keep score, or giving her a wink of approval — small, seemingly insignificant gestures like these are no different from a major family upheaval. They all have a profound impact, years and years later, in ways we can never imagine, because our children are watching and recording. It is all being written down in our Book of Life and in theirs as well. The camera is constantly rolling. Our fights, our behavior, our disagreements about the children — for our kids that is all part of their Book of Life and they have to live with it for the rest of their lives. The best day of their lives and the worst day of their lives — we are the ones who make them happen. And unfortunately, all too often, we do not even know it. Perhaps this was best expressed in the following reading:

WHEN YOU THOUGHT I WASN'T LOOKING

When you thought I wasn't looking,
you hung my first painting on the refrigerator, and I wanted to paint another.

When you thought I wasn't looking,
you fed a stray cat, and I thought it was good to be kind to animals.

When you thought I wasn't looking,
you baked a birthday cake just for me, and I knew that little things were special things.

When you thought I wasn't looking,
you said a prayer and I believed there was a God that I could always talk to.

When you thought I wasn't looking,
you kissed me good-night and I felt loved.

When you thought I wasn't looking,
I saw tears come from your eyes and I learned that sometimes things hurt — but that it's alright to cry.

When you thought I wasn't looking,
you smiled and it made me want to look that pretty too.

When you thought I wasn't looking,
you cared and I wanted to be everything I could be.

When you thought I wasn't looking,
I looked ... and wanted to say thanks for all those things you did ... when you thought I wasn't looking.

And it is not just our children who are looking. We are having an impact on the lives of so many people, indeed, even on strangers, without even realizing it. Some years ago our synagogue's Religious

Services Committee passed a historic resolution.   Because of the pandemonium at our Simchas Torah celebrations, it was moved and approved that the rabbi be barred from drinking liquor and throwing candy at the services on that day.   It was a courageous act on the part of our Religious Services Committee, taken while I was out of town on vacation.   When I heard about it, the ban on alcohol did not bother me. Between gout and kidney stones, my drinking days were numbered. But barring the throwing of candy — that really bothered me!   There is something in me that just loves giving out the candy and lollipops to children at services.   I asked myself why I love it so much, and I thought of Mr. Solomon Ryback.   I had not thought about him for maybe close to fifty years.   He was a prominent member of my father's synagogue.   He sat in the front row and was very charitable.   But what made me remember him was the fact that every Shabbos he gave out Hershey chocolate bars to the kids!   He was that shul's "candy man." And I remembered how I and, I suspect, many other children would wake up on Shabbos morning never hesitating to come to shul.   No, not to listen to the cantor or to the rabbi's sermon, but to get that candy bar from Mr. Ryback.   How many children in my father's congregation, in this congregation, in so many other congregations, grew up coming to shul because of the sweet taste left in them by the "candy man."   And now, so many years later, I guess a part of Mr. Ryback lives on in me.

So it is not only singer Bette Midler telling us "God is watching us from a distance," but it is also, as the rock/philosopher Sting tells us, "Every move you make, every breath you take, I'll be watching you." Everything we do is being watched and recorded by all those around us.   "No man is an island entire unto himself," wrote the poet.   We are all having an impact on others.   We are all the product of others — parents and grandparents, brothers and sisters, friends and strangers, those who have bruised us and betrayed us, those who have sustained us and strengthened us.   Everything they did, everything we do, is recorded and remembered.

But do you know what?   It is never too late.   It is never too late to change our record.   Remember that video of the wedding with which I began?   What happened to that video?   Did I and my colleagues ruin it forever so that the bride and groom could never really enjoy watching it?   No, I am sure they and their families have watched it time and again. Do you know why? Because they gave the video back to the videographer, who erased those parts that should not have been there. You can do that with a video recorder. Just use the buttons that say STOP, PLAY, EJECT, PAUSE, FORWARD, and REVERSE.

And while we are here, we have the ability to push the very same buttons with our lives. We still have time to edit the videos of our lives, to go back and repair the damage. We have the ability to give the time, to show the love, to set the example that might have been missing until now. The camera is constantly running, right until the end.

As God inscribes us in the Book of Life, may we use that as an opportunity to make beautiful imprints in the Books of the Living.

Yom Kippur, September 18, 1991

KOBE BRYANT, SCARFACE, AND JEWISH KINGS

Everyone seems to know who Kobe Bryant is. He rose to national fame in 1996 when he became the first guard in NBA history to be drafted out of high school. Twice he was the NBA's leading scorer. Yet, perhaps what made him most famous were the 2003 headlines across the country that informed us that this star had been accused of sexual assault. The charges were eventually dropped, and the two sides settled the matter outside of criminal court. While that chapter in Kobe Bryant's life has been closed, there are still lessons to be learned from it. There are three lessons for Kobe Bryant to consider — actually, for all of us to consider — from the Torah portion of "Judges" in the Book of Deuteronomy.

On a simple level, I have to tell you that if Kobe Bryant was an observant, Orthodox Jew, he would never have gotten into trouble. The Torah teaches, *"Shoftim v'shotrim titein lecha b'chol shearecha"* (Deuteronomy 16:18). The literal translation is "Judges and guards shall thou place at all thy gates"; this is a statement of the need to establish a system of law and order in every community. Our tradition has come to read this verse on a personal level as well, for the rabbis tell us that each and every individual has to place watchdogs at all of his or her "gates": at the eyes, ears, and mouth. We must do whatever we can to protect ourselves from doing wrong. It is in this spirit that observant, Orthodox Jews practice the law of *Yichud*. This means that a single male and single female who are not related to each other are not allowed to be alone with each other. Plain and simple. That is why you often see an ultra-Orthodox couple meeting in the lounge area of one of the hotels downtown. They will only meet and "date" each other in public. In this way, they are placing "judges and guards at their gates." They are not tempting temptation.

Now, I do not know what went on in Kobe Bryant's hotel room, but this I do know: that woman should not have been there. He should not have invited her, and she should not have accepted. They both would have been better off had they placed "judges and guards at their gates."

But they did not. Was Bryant guilty as charged? There is no way of knowing for sure. But one must be suspicious based on previous track records of professional athletes, for he is not the first one to stand accused of a sexual crime. Such crimes have almost become a daily occurrence, and many have gone unpunished. There was a fascinating op-ed column in the *New York Times* by Jeff Benedict, author of the book, *Public Heroes, Private Felons: Athletes and Crimes against Women*. Benedict pointed out that, according to recent Justice Department statistics, whereas for the general population 32 percent of rapes reported to police resulted in an arrest, and more than 54 percent were convicted, when it came to athletes the numbers were almost completely reversed. Of 217 felony rape cases forwarded to police involving athletes, 172 resulted in an arrest, but of the 172, only 53 — 31 percent — resulted in a conviction.

I do not have to tell you that there is something wrong here. And I do not have to tell you that this miscarriage of justice is exactly what the Torah had in mind when it taught in the next verse, "*Lo tateh mishpat lo takir panim* — you shall not pervert judgment, you shall not respect someone's presence" (Deuteronomy 16:19). What does it mean, "You shall not respect someone's presence?" Explains Rashi, "This is an admonition addressed to the judge that he should not be lenient to one and harsh to the other; for example, letting one stand and the other sit. There should be no favoritism shown just because the judge recognizes one because he is more famous or wealthy than the other." The court records would seem to indicate that this lesson is being lost here in

America where athletes are held in such awe and have the money and powerful lawyers and public relations specialists that perhaps lead a jury to give them the benefit of the doubt.

Indeed, it is the awesome popularity of athletes today that brings us to our third lesson from the Torah portion. Athletes have become today's royalty, and they are falling victim to the same issues regarding power that the Torah portion addressed in regard to the royalty of old. We are told, "When you shall come to the land of Israel and settle therein and you will say that you want a king to lead you, thou shall set a king over thee whom the Lord thy God shall choose." Thus, the king, as leader, had such influence and importance that only God could choose him. Then the Torah goes on to tell us that there were to be three restrictions on every monarch. Every king would have three safeguards to limit his power:

- The first is that the king could not have too much money.
- The second is that the king could not have too many horses.
- The third is that the king could not have too many wives.

In fact, it has been pointed out that the Hebrew word for "throne" — the symbol of royalty — is *kisey*, and the three Hebrew letters that make up this word represent the three restrictions on royalty's power.

- The *kof* stands for *kesef*: not too much money.
- The *samach* stands for *soos*: not too many horses.
- The *alef* stands for *ishah*: not too many wives.

Let us look at what these three mean in terms of America's royalty today. Our athletes are not to have too much money? Lebron James, a basketball player, signed a contract with Nike for $90 million! (That is more money than the salaries paid to the rabbis of Beth Tfiloh, Beth El, and Baltimore Hebrew Congregation combined!) What made that contract all the more remarkable was the fact that he had never played a professional basketball game before signing it. In fact, he had never played a *college* basketball game. He had just graduated high school, and he was given $90 million! Many young men, because of their athletic prowess, are having millions of dollars thrown at them, and they are totally unprepared for the responsibilities that come with it.

Do you know what all that money leads them to become? It leads them to become a Mike Tyson. Mike Tyson, professional boxer, filed for bankruptcy. He was bankrupt after having made approximately $400 million in the last twenty years in the boxing ring! In two years he spent $230,000 on pagers and cell phones alone. He owed one limousine service $308,000.

All this money leads to the second warning to the king: that he not have too many horses. The horse in ancient times was a symbol of power. We have given our athletes a power that corrupts not just them, but all of us. The *New York Times* reports that on December 22, 2002, Mike Tyson walked into a Las Vegas jewelry store and picked up a $173,000 gold chain lined with 80 carats in diamonds. He walked out without paying. And it does not look like he is going to pay! The proprietor of the store is quoted as saying, "He had open credit with me. Knowing him for so long, I gave him the merchandise and knew he'd pay later." The name of the proprietor is Mordechai Yerushalmi, which only goes to prove that a Jew can be a dope as well. The Bryants and the Tysons and the James — and all the others are given power that is totally undeserved, all because they know how to shoot a basketball into a hoop or catch a football or hit a baseball. We make them into icons and idols and make them feel all-powerful.

And then do you know what happens? What happens is what Moses told God after the Jews sinned and made the Golden Calf: "Don't blame them! It's your fault! You gave them all the gold when they left Egypt. They weren't ready for it, able to deal or cope with the riches and so they abused it." In memorable words, our sages have Moses saying to God, "*Mashal labein* — it is comparable to a son to whom a father gives money and stands him in front of a house of ill repute. "*Mah yaaseh habein shelo yechteh*" (what a beautiful phrase) — "What do you expect of the kids — that they won't sin?" What do we expect of our athletes? We put them on pedestals when they're kids — throw money at them in the millions — and we are surprised when they fall?

Which leads to our third safeguard placed on the king, in which he is warned not to have too many wives. King Solomon, as you know, violated this restriction. According to tradition he had 750 wives. Wait — in his spare time, he also had 300 concubines! Now that's a king for you! You also might recall that King Solomon got into trouble because of all these women. Really, what does a man need 750 wives for? I can understand 365 — but what motivates a man to have twice that many? Is it not simply a matter of vanity — of ego gratification — the need to be the big man on campus? One of Kobe Bryant's friends, in defending him, said, "Kobe would never do what he's accused of. He doesn't have to. He can have so many women any night without forcing himself on them." I must tell you that I cannot get over the scene when Kobe Bryant appeared in court. People outside cheered him as he left. Now you tell me: what were they cheering — the fact that he *may* have been guilty of sexual assault or the fact that he was *definitely* guilty of committing adultery? That is what we cheer?

Tony Montana, in the movie *Scarface*, got it right just like our sages said when he said, "In this country you gotta make money first. When you get the money, you get the power. Then when you get the power, you get the women." That is the climate we have created in our society — a climate that has made athletes into royalty with money, power, and vanity leading to their own self-destruction and the destruction of the moral fiber of the youth of America.

Was Kobe Bryant innocent or guilty? No one knows for sure. But all of us should know that we are guilty — guilty of contributing to the moral decay in our society. Our guilt is reflected in all of the lessons from today's Torah portion that have somehow fallen by the wayside. We do not put watchdogs at our gates. We all put ourselves in positions where we tempt fate. We ignore the second lesson by our hero worship that puts athletes on pedestals and allows the rich and famous to get away with things for which others would be punished. And we do not heed the third lesson — the lesson of the dangers of money, power, and vanity run amok. We may not be able to change the lives of a Mike Tyson and Kobe Bryant, but we can change the lives of those living in our homes by instilling these lessons in them.

August 30, 2003

What Have You Done for Me Lately?

I do not remember it, but I can tell you the date that my family first recalls my ever coming to shul. As an infant I did not go to shul because in those days there was no *eruv*, and so my mother would not push a baby carriage on Shabbos. In addition, hard as it is to believe, in my youngest years I was a bit rambunctious. I was, in the Yiddish translation, *ah vilder chaya* (a wild animal)! But on that Saturday night, November 29, 1947, as soon as Shabbos was over, my father insisted that my mother bring me to shul. Throughout that Saturday afternoon and evening, the United Nations was debating and voting on a partition plan for a Jewish State in Palestine. At that same time, the Jews in my father's shul in Borough Park in Brooklyn — many of them refugees from the Holocaust — had been reciting *Thillim*, Psalms, with great fervor. Hundreds had remained in synagogue after the evening service as a radio was put on to hear the UN vote. My mother felt that I should be home asleep, but she remembered the words my father said to her that night: "Jews have waited for this day for 2,000 years. I want Moishella to be here to witness it. Maybe the Moshiach is about to come." Sixty years ago, November 29, 1947, was the night the UN voted in favor of a Jewish State in Palestine. I do not remember it, but my family remembers it as the first time I was ever in shul!

That was a great moment in time for the Jewish people. For 2,000 years, we had been in exile; for 2,000 years, ours was a homeless people. And now we had come home. No one who was alive then will ever forget that moment. But now, at the sixtieth anniversary of the UN vote, not that many people are celebrating that momentous occasion.

Today we have a new generation of Jews, and according to a recent survey, more than half of them just do not feel comfortable with the whole idea of a Jewish State. It seems hard to believe but it is true! We are raising an entire generation of Jews who feel no sense of attachment to Israel. If you ask me why they feel this way, I would tell you that they are a part of a generation that has grown up with this mantra: "WHAT HAVE YOU DONE FOR ME LATELY?"

There was a time when Israel made us feel proud and tall as it defended itself against all those who sought to destroy it. But there have not been too many Six-Day Wars lately. Nor have there been too many Entebbes or too many wondrous airlifts of Ethiopian Jews lately. And so more and more Jews are looking at Israel with a shrug, wondering, "WHAT HAVE YOU DONE FOR ME LATELY?"

Not everybody feels that way. Certainly, the people of Israel do not feel that way! I experienced their pride and love in a never-to-be forgotten moment when I was on sabbatical in Israel ten years ago. It was Saturday evening, November 29, 1997. Weeks earlier, Sherry and I had purchased tickets to see the Israeli Philharmonic perform Beethoven's Ninth Symphony that evening. We did not realize it at the time, but November 29, 1997, was the fiftieth anniversary of the UN partition vote. And so, fifty years later, on Saturday evening, November 29, 1997, there were celebrations commemorating that moment in the major cities throughout Israel.

There was also a celebration at the symphony that night. Before the performance, a brief movie was shown that recorded the historic vote that had taken place at the United Nations that same night fifty years earlier. The vote had been 33 in favor and 13 against, with 10 abstentions. After the brief movie, the lights went on in the Mann Auditorium, and the mayor of Tel Aviv came out on stage. Invited to the performance that evening as guests of the State of Israel were the ambassadors from the thirty-three countries that had voted in favor of the creation of Israel fifty years before. As each name was called out and as each ambassador rose, there was a massive outpouring of applause and cheers. It seemed as if everyone was standing, applauding, with tears in their eyes. I stood there and I thought to myself about some of these countries to which Israel was expressing its gratitude – countries like Czechoslovakia, the Dominican Republic, Ecuador, Guatemala, Haiti, Iceland, Liberia, Nicaragua, Panama, Paraguay, Peru, the Philippines, Poland, Uruguay, and Venezuela. Some of these have not cast a favorable vote for Israel since. Most all of the countries have been surpassed by Israel in almost every area of endeavor in just fifty years. And yet, here it was, fifty years later and Israel was still recognizing and thanking them for their vote of support. Certainly, the people of Israel were not asking, "WHAT HAVE YOU DONE FOR ME LATELY?"

There is a lesson here for us to remember, not only as Jews in relation to Israel but for each of us as individuals in relation to those whom we love and care for. So let me tell you about Meyer Kripke, from whom we can all learn a similar lesson. Meyer Kripke is a rabbi, but not just any rabbi. He is a very different kind of rabbi, and his is a very different kind of story. You see, Meyer Kripke is a rabbi who gives money! Meyer Kripke learned a lesson one Thanksgiving that he put into practice.

Meyer Kripke was born in Toledo, Ohio, in 1914, one of seven children. He came to New York in the 1930's to study at the Jewish Theological Seminary. There he met a student from Brooklyn named Dorothy Karp. They were married at the Seminary in 1937, a week after he was ordained. Rabbi Kripke served at several synagogues before coming to the Beth El synagogue in Omaha, Nebraska, in 1946 at a salary of $7,500 a year. His wife helped supplement his income by writing children's books, one of which caught the eye of a woman named Susie Buffett. Mrs. Buffett discovered that Mrs. Kripke lived only two blocks away from her, so she called her, was invited over, and they became close friends. So much so, that when Mrs. Kripke was ill with a brain disorder, Mrs. Buffett drove her new friend to physical therapy once a week.

Eventually, their two husbands, Meyer Kripke and Warren Buffett, a man who was in the investment business, became friendly as well.

Over the years, the Buffetts would invite the Kripkes to Thanksgiving dinner at their house and because the Kripkes kept kosher, the Buffetts served tuna salad for Thanksgiving. It was at one of those dinners that Mrs. Kripke encouraged her husband to ask Mr. Buffett to invest the $65,000 they had managed to save over the years. Rabbi Kripke did not want to bother his friend Warren, who did not usually spend time dealing with clients who were investing only $65,000. But eventually, Rabbi Kripke asked, and Warren Buffett accepted.

As Warren Buffet's reputation continued to grow and as he became one of the wealthiest men in America, Rabbi Kripke's investment continued to grow as well. When the Kripkes celebrated their sixtieth wedding anniversary, his wife's condition had deteriorated, and Rabbi Kripke decided it was time to put his affairs in order. He called the Jewish Theological Seminary and told them that he would like to make a gift — but not just any gift. He made a gift of $8 million from the $25 million his $65,000 investment had turned into. He donated this money to the Jewish Theological Seminary in honor of his wife, adding that it was at the Seminary sixty years before that he had met and married his wife, and besides, the Seminary had never charged anything for the wedding.

The story is a bit different, but it is different not only because it is the rabbi giving the money. It is different because Rabbi Kripke's mindset runs contrary to modern thinking. Rabbi Kripke felt a debt of gratitude for something that had occurred sixty years earlier, while for many today, the more frequently exhibited attitude is "WHAT HAVE YOU DONE FOR ME LATELY?"

Do you know there are lots of men saying those words lately and that they are saying it to their wives? Men like Warren Buffett. You see, the Kripkes and the Buffetts stopped getting together for Thanksgiving, due in large part to the fact that the Buffetts themselves did not get together anymore. They were living their own separate lives. That is happening with lots of couples I know of these days. I know so many husbands and wives, who after years of marriage, pick up and leave, feeling that they have outgrown each other when so much of that growth was made possible by their spouse's sacrifice and support and love and understanding during the early trying years of their marriage. And now, "WHAT HAVE YOU DONE FOR ME LATELY?"

And you and I know of many children who echo these words as well — children whose parents struggled to make ends meet, children whose parents' goal in life was to make sure their children had more and better than they had. But then, as the children grew bigger, they did not grow better. They grew more distant and had other priorities; between working and vacations and golf, there was not much time to call or to bring over the grandkids. And besides, "WHAT HAVE YOU DONE FOR ME LATELY?"

Thanksgiving weekend is a good time for us to take stock of what we have and what we have to be grateful for. We have a glorious Jewish homeland. We have glorious homes. We have so much more than most any of us could have ever dreamt of having when we started off in life. So let us not get caught up in this WHAT HAVE YOU DONE FOR ME LATELY mentality. Rather, let us be grateful for all the good that God has helped bring into our lives — as Americans, as Jews, as parents and children, as husbands and wives — as we echo the words of our daily prayer: "*Modim anachno loch* — we give thanks to Thee, O Lord." "*Al nisecha sh'bchol yom imanu* — for Thy miracles which are always with us and for Thy marvelous goodness toward us at all times."

November 24, 2007

A Beautiful Body — with Wrinkles and Bumps

On the holiday of Succot, we are obligated to fulfill the mitzvah of living — or at least eating — in a *Succah*, a booth commemorating the way our people traveled for forty years on their journey to the Promised Land. The fulfillment of this mitzvah is unique. It has been pointed out that doing most every other mitzvah involves one or another part of the human body. Take, for example, the mitzvah of *Tfillin*, the phylacteries that the male Jew is required to put on in the morning. The mitzvah involves a person's arm and head. Take the mitzvah of *kashrut*. It involves a person's mouth and stomach. To fulfill the mitzvah of *lulav* and *etrog* requires the use of our arms and hands. If you think about all the mitzvot, you will realize that each and every one of them involves a part of, or perhaps several parts, of the Jewish person.

There is only one mitzvah for which this is not true, and that is the mitzvah of Succot. A Jew builds a *Succah* and lives within it. This means that the entire body is involved in observing the mitzvah! When Jews are in the *Succah*, every part of them — their hands, arms, head, feet, heart, and nose — is inside the *Succah*! On Succot, our focus as Jews is on the whole body.

At this time of the year, the focus of the American people is on the body as well. Millions of Americans tune in to the annual Miss

America pageant, in which fifty-one contestants vie for the prize of being crowned Miss America. To win that prize, they are judged on all sorts of qualities: their personality and character, their talent — from twirling batons to classical singing — and on their intelligence as well. One year, Miss New Jersey was a Princeton student; our own Miss Maryland was a Georgetown law student and intern in the State's Attorney's office. All this counts — but you and I know what really counts! In the *Washington Post*, the reporter, evaluating the contestants for the crown that evening, wrote, "Miss Kentucky is the one to watch. Great look, great story, great presence — and a really skimpy swimsuit." And guess what? She won, because that is it! After all is said and done, the Miss America contest focuses on the body. And in so doing it is one of the most dangerous programs on American television. In its own way, it causes more violence than those crime shows riddled with dead bodies.

You see, there is a fatal flaw in the Miss America pageant. What most people tuning in do not realize is that, among the more than 120 million women living in our country, only 51 look like the contestants! Yet, they are the ones who are made into the ideal, and they are the ones whom a whole generation aspires to look like. We have become a nation obsessed with our bodies and with trying to look thin. This quest for the perfect body has become our century's search for the Holy Grail. You hear people all the time saying, "I'm so ashamed of myself. It's a sin what I ate last night." Indeed, there was a cover story on the tabloid *Weekly World News* with the headline, "Holy Scriptures Show You How to Lose Weight Fast. BIBLE PRAYERS TO FLUSH OUT BODY FAT." Well, I can prove to you that prayers do not work that way. If they did, there would not be an empty seat in my synagogue! The Miss America pageant is just the most visible symbol of our country's obsession with body and weight — an obsession that is causing undue harm to countless women and men in our country.

Did you know that, according to *Psychology Today*, 62 percent of teenage girls and 67 percent of all women over the age of thirty are unhappy with their weight? The desire to be thin is so powerful that people would *die* for it! Fifteen percent of women and eleven percent of men surveyed said that they would give up more than five years of their lives to be their desired weight. As one heartbroken woman to find my name mentioned in the *New York Times* crossword puzzle, but in truth, I feel more proud to be included in your rich and insightful teachings. Thank you for looking after the young girls; they desperately need our guidance.

Camryn Manheim understands what true beauty is. For what is beauty? It is interesting to read the biblical commandment regarding the four species used on Succot. In the Book of Leviticus, we are told, *ulkachtem lachem bayom harishon pri etz hadar kapot tmorim va-anaf etz avot v'arvei nachal* – and you shall take for yourself the fruit of a beautiful tree, date palm branches, twigs of the myrtle tree, and brook willows" (Leviticus 23:40). For three out of the four items mentioned the palm branch, the myrtle, and the willow — we know exactly what the Torah had in mind. But what about that first one — the *pri etz hadar*, the fruit of the beautiful tree? What fruit is that? the sages asked. After much analysis, they decided that it was the *etrog*. The *etrog* is what is beautiful?

So what makes one *etrog* more beautiful than any other *etrog*? The Talmud tells us that a truly beautiful *etrog* must possess the following qualities. First, it must be built like a *migdal* – a tower. That is, the upper portion should be narrow, and the bottom should be wide. And second, to be beautiful, the *etrog* should have many *belitot* — many bumps. It should not be smooth like a lemon; it should have wrinkles.

Think about that description for a moment. To be considered beautiful, the *etrog* must possess a small top, a big bottom, bumps, and wrinkles. In American society, a woman built like a beautiful *etrog* would be considered a prime candidate for plastic surgery. So what is going on here? Is the *etrog* some sort of a Jewish joke, possessing as it does almost every negative characteristic in regard to beauty? Yet, it is just this fruit that is chosen to be the "*pri etz hadar* — the fruit of the beautiful tree."

Yet, the *etrog* did not have to be chosen as that fruit! Nowhere does the Torah mention the word "*etrog*." It simply tells us, "Take for yourselves the fruit of a beautiful tree." It is our rabbis who tell us that this verse refers to the *etrog*. But why, of all fruits, to pick just the one that is a prime candidate for Dr. Atkins and Weight Watchers and liposuction? The choice of our rabbis is based on some very strange

put it, "How can you feel good when you are cons
with images of how you should look, but don't?" Sh
a conference entitled, "Facing the Mirror — Confror
Healing the Heart," sponsored by the National Stude
Women and Judaism. You see, there is a significant
this obsession with thinness. Although no firm statis
most people in the field are in agreement that an
proportion of Jewish women suffer from an eating di

Yet, there is something very un-Jewish about this
weight. The description of the ideal, beautiful woma
Songs is one "whose neck is like the Tower of David,
are pillars of marble." This description obviously did n
in mind! A Talmudic reference to two great sages, Yisl
and Elazer ben Shimon, mentions that they had su
protruding stomachs that, as they stood facing each o
stomachs touching, a pair of oxen could pass through
And then the Talmud adds that their wives were even he
"If I Were A Rich Man" fantasy of Golde was "looking lil
wife, with a proper double chin." Indeed, King Solomo
the Book of Proverbs describing the *Eishat Chayil* — the w
— has a lesson for all of us. The *Eishat Chayil* is being p
intelligence, her managerial skills, her lack of vanity, and
She is called "more precious than rubies," and there is not
how she looks.

If I were asked to be a judge at the Miss America co
know whom I would pick? I would pick Camryn Manhe
be a mitzvah for the American people if she were Miss A
is an actress who played the role of Eleanor Fruitt, a la
TV drama, "The Practice." Camryn Manheim weighs mc
pounds, and in an earlier sermon about her, I spoke of how
she had to be to go into the acting business; I said that she s
as a role model for teenage girls who are making themselv
their weight. There is a postscript to the sermon I delivere
Manheim. You see, she heard about the sermon — someor
her — and I received the following note from her:

I only wish that when I was developing my self-estee
self worth that I had a rabbi like you. I used to get so

analysis. Some say it is because the *etrog*, not the apple, was the fruit eaten by Adam and Eve in the Garden of Eden. That is what makes it beautiful? Others say that because the word *"hadar"* is really the Greek work *"hudor,"* which means water, and because the *etrog* tree is often in need of irrigation, the fruit in question must be the *etrog*. That is what makes for beauty? Indeed, to justify the choice of the *etrog* as being the fruit of the beautiful tree, Eleazar of Worms, a great rabbi, showed that the numerical value of the letters of the words *pri etz hadar* is the equivalent of the numerical value of the word *etrogim*. Yet, I would not even dare to offer this explanation to you because it does not work. Figure it out for yourself: *etrogim* adds up to 660, and *pri etz hadar* to 659. It's off by one!

So the questions still remain. Why did our rabbis choose a fruit that has a small top, a big bottom, bumps, and wrinkles as being the beautiful fruit? Obviously, something else is involved here, something that tells us volumes about the Jewish concept of beauty. For our sages and for our tradition, beauty did not refer to the outer appearance. Beauty is not only skin deep but runs much deeper. The accepted explanation for why the *etrog* is considered beautiful, according to many, is not because of its appearance, but more so because of its character and nature. The *etrog* has a unique characteristic: "Ha-dor b'ilano mi-shana l'shana — it is the one fruit that clings to its branch throughout the year." No matter what the weather or season, the *etrog* is always there. The *etrog* is beautiful because it always remains loyal. It always remains attached and close to its roots. In the Jewish tradition, beauty is descriptive of the heart — not the body. It speaks of the spiritual, not the material.

It matters not how you are built physically. You can look like an *etrog* — with bumps and wrinkles and fat in the wrong places — but to paraphrase the words of the Hallel: "Me-et Hashem hayta zot — you are God's gift to us ... Hi niflot b'eineinu — and you are beautiful in our eyes."

Succot, September 25, 1999

THOSE WERE THE DAYS?

I have always been struck by a strange phenomenon relating to sleepaway summer camps. Invariably, the camps that we Jews send our children to have Indian names like Camp Running Bear or Camp Cayuga. I have wondered whether Indian parents in turn send their children to camps that have Jewish names, like Camp Hava Nagilah. I wonder! I am beginning to see a similar phenomenon when it comes to the food served at Jewish wedding receptions. It used to be that the biggest line was for the lamb chops. The last couple of years I have noticed that at Jewish weddings the biggest line is at the sushi bar! Do you think at Japanese weddings people run to the gefilte fish? Where do we Jews come to sushi? Perhaps it goes all the way back to biblical days, to days described in the Torah.

As the Jewish people traveled on their way to the Promised Land, what do we find them doing? They are doing what seems to come naturally to them: they are complaining! It seems as if, from the moment they left the land of Egypt, the Jews never stopped complaining — it was always something! When the Red Sea split and the Jews walked through, their lives saved, do you know what they did? They complained that the sea bed was muddy. Then they complained that they were hungry, and then they complained that they were thirsty, and then they complained about the leadership. In the Torah portion of B'haalotcha, the complaint is about the food — not that they had no food, but about the kind of food.

Now, Jews complaining about food is almost cultural. You know the story of the Jewish couple who were finishing their meal in a fancy restaurant and their waiter comes over to them and asks, "Was *anything* okay?" So Jews complaining about food comes as no surprise. What is surprising was the basis of their complaint, when they cried out, "*Zacharnu et ha-dagah* — we remember the fish we used to eat free in Egypt. Now we have nothing but this manna to look forward to." Now tell me, do you really think the Egyptians served the Jewish people fish during our 210 years of slavery? Is that how you picture the Egyptians treating our ancestors — serving them spicy salmon roll, or yellow tail, or tuna with scallion? The description that we have of what the Jews ate in Egypt was *matzoh*, the *lechem oni* — the poor people's bread. What fish? How do you explain the people's complaint of missing the delicious fish they were served in Egypt?

It seems to me that our ancestors fell victim to a syndrome that many of us experience to this very day. It is called the syndrome of "the good old days." Many people have a tendency to always picture the past as having been much better than it really was. Whatever is wrong today, they think was much better in "the good old days," somehow forgetting the fact that the "good old days" weren't really that good. It is this syndrome that perhaps gave rise to one of the most popular and most dangerous songs that we all know: "Those were the days, my friends. We thought they'd never end." It is a great song, but it is dangerous! It leads us to the misconception that *now* we have problems, but back then — "Those were the days, my friends."

I thought about this when I read an article recently about the Lower East Side of New York. The whole area is undergoing an urban renewal — there are now tours showing some of what is left of the "good old days" that we Jews so nostalgically recall about the Lower East Side. Mention the Lower East Side and what immediately comes to mind was a golden age for the Jewish people: Yiddish theatres and synagogues and knishes and pushcarts, and "*bei mir bist du shain,*" and children running in the streets, and families celebrating holidays together. "Those were the days, my friends."

But allow me to let you in on a little secret: it wasn't quite like that. There is a wonderful book called *A Bintel Brief*, a collection of sixty years of letters to the Yiddish newspaper, the *Jewish Daily Forward*, from Jews who lived on the Lower East Side. The *Jewish Daily Forward* was *the* newspaper for the Jews on the Lower East Side at the turn of the century, and "*A Bintel Brief*" was one of its most popular columns. It was our people's version of "Dear Abby," with people writing in and asking advice in regard to all areas of their lives. Read those letters, and you will get a clear picture of the "good old days." There are letters written about poverty, unemployment and starvation; about young people in the sweatshops developing tuberculosis; and about young girls lured into brothels. Many are pathetic, touching letters from despairing women whose husbands had deserted them and their children, leaving them with no means of support. "Those were the days, my friends." The number of men who left their families became so great at one point that the *Forward*, with the help of the National Desertion Bureau, created a special column just to trace them. Men "not getting it" is not a new phenomenon!

Bill Clinton's immorality in the White House was worthy of the condemnation that it received. He did bring shame on himself, his family, and his country. Yet, all those commentators who wrote that Clinton personified the low level of leadership in our country today were falling victim to the "good old days" syndrome. You really think it was so much better back then? Among the presidents whom historians believe were involved in extramarital relations are not just the usual suspects like Kennedy and Johnson but also Eisenhower and Harding and Washington and Jefferson and Lincoln and Wilson and Roosevelt. While running for president, Grover Cleveland was forced to acknowledge that he had fathered a child out of wedlock. He then went on to win two terms as president. When his political opponents tried to destroy him with chants of "Ma — Ma — where's my Pa?" his supporters successfully countered with, "Gone to the White House, ha ha ha!" "Those were the days, my friends." I'm told that in the movie, *Pearl Harbor*, there is a scene after the attack showing the crippled FDR struggling to his feet to impress his Cabinet with the need for courage in the face of adversity. Of course, it never happened, but that does not stop us from picturing yesterday's leaders as being on a much higher level than those of today.

And what of our children?   Rabbi Norman Lamm points out this description given by a member of our own people:

There is yet one other evil disease regarding raising children that is not practiced by other peoples. A child sits at the table with his father and mother, and he is the first to stretch forth his hand to partake of the food. He thus grows up arrogant, without fear or culture or refinement, acting as if his father and mother were his friends or siblings. By the time he is eight or nine years old and his parents wish to correct their earlier mistakes, they no longer are able to, for childish habit has already become second nature ...

Another bad and bitter practice: parents take a child to school and, in front of the child, warn the teacher not to punish him. When the child hears this, he no longer pays attention to his school work and his disobedience grows worse. This was not the practice of our ancestors. In their days, if a child came crying to his father and mother and told of being punished by a teacher, they would send with him a gift to the teacher, and congratulate the teacher ...

This report comes to us from Rabbi Mosheh Hagiz, and it was written more than 250 years ago! "Those were the days, my friends." We make a big mistake when we depict our children of today as all being potential "Columbine murderers," undisciplined, unrestrained, immoral, and spoiled. Need I remind you, that in the "good old days," Cain killed Abel, Esau tried to kill Jacob, and Joseph's brothers threw him in a pit. "Those were the days, my friends." Kids today are no better or worse than before. They are what kids have always been: bearers of unlimited potential, with a natural striving for the good and the holy. To think of them as being anything else, to think that things used to be better, robs us of much joy and hopes for the future.

Unfortunately, most American Jews are doing just that when it comes to the State of Israel. I tell people that I am going to Israel, and they look at me as if I have said that I am going to Northern Ireland! Except there is one big difference: the Irish keep going to Northern Ireland, but we Jews have stopped going to Israel. Certainly, the situation there is not a good one. There is the danger of war, the ever-present concern for safety.   Forgive me for being the one to tell you, but in some ways it has always been like this! Sure, the recent horrible, disgusting suicide bombings have brought the current situation to a crucial juncture, but let me remind you that in February 1996 a suicide bomber blew up a Jerusalem bus, killing twenty-five innocent people. Two weeks later, a suicide bomber on the same bus route killed thirteen people. A day later in Tel Aviv, eighteen people were killed by a suicide bomber. Between 1967 and 1971, 120 civilians and 180 soldiers were killed in Israel. Indeed, the magnificent victory of the Six-Day War came at the expense of 777 Israeli soldiers. All that in the "good old days."

In January 1991, there was a luncheon honoring Avrum Harman, former Ambassador to the United Nations and president of the Hebrew University. A distinguished and eloquent spokesman for our people, Dr. Harman rose and said,

> If I have one regret in all that I have done for this country, it is the many times over the years that I addressed Jews and said to them: this is the most challenging time in Israel's history. This is the most dangerous time in Israel's history. This is the most exciting time in Israel's history. I've said that so many times over the years, in '48 and in '67, with the PLO and Lebanon and the Intifada, I regret having ever said it. Because the truth is, right now is the most difficult, exciting and challenging time in the history of the State of Israel.

That is the way it is with our people! We always think that today is the worst when compared to the past. "Those were the days, my friends."

So let me remind you, we survived Scud missile attacks during the Gulf War when Israelis had to lock themselves in secure rooms with gas masks. We survived a Yom Kippur War in which we lost 2,522 of our best and finest. We survived terrorist attacks in Munich and Maalot and in Kiryat Shemona and countless other places. We survived airplane hijackings and a Japanese Red Brigade attack at Ben Gurion Airport that killed twenty-one people. We did all that in the "good old days." We will do even better now — now that we are stronger than ever. Now, when Israel needs us, let us not fall into despair and hopelessness, thinking how it used to be better in the "good old days."

"Those were the days, my friends?" No, I think for all of us, as Americans and as Jews, as parents and as spouses, a much more appropriate song to reflect our beliefs is my mother's favorite song. That is one from the Broadway show "La Cage Aux Folles" — "The best of times are now." These are the best of times — yesterday's gone, tomorrow may never be, and all we have is today, now. So let us enjoy and cherish both our sushi and gefilte fish, the old and the new. Let us be grateful for all the good that we have in our lives. Rather than complain, let us proclaim the words of our daily prayer: "*Ashreinu mah tov chelkeinu u'mah naim goralenu u'ma yaffa yerushatenu* — happy are we, how good is our portion, how pleasant our lot, how beautiful our heritage."

June 9, 1991

DO YOU LIKE YOUR RABBI?

I know that many of you have a tendency to wait until the last minute, but it's not too late! When Shabbos, is over, you will still have time to do the necessary shopping for the special day on the calendar tomorrow: Clergy Appreciation Day. I am not too sure many of you were aware of that holiday. It certainly is not as popular as Mother's Day — the day on which the most long-distance phone calls are made. Nor is it even as popular as Father's Day —the day on which the most long-distance *collect* calls are made! But tomorrow really is Clergy Appreciation Day, and if you did not know about it, you should have! Just type in the words "Clergy Appreciation Day" on the Google search engine and you will find more than 37,000 entries. It is recognized as an official day in more than forty states. And yet, who even knows about it or much less celebrates it? That, in it and of itself, says something about how important clergy are to their congregants.

Even the way the holiday started tells you something. It began in 1992 when a lay person, Jerry Frear, who was brainstorming with church colleagues about how they might be of help to their minister, glanced at a calendar and noticed that it was almost Groundhog Day. He recalled, "I thought, if they have a day for groundhogs, there ought to be a day for the 375,000 clergy people in America." Groundhogs, clergy — you get the connection! Each should be seen once a year — at best.

Yet, it is nice to know that there are people out there who take this day seriously. A subsidiary of Hallmark cards now offers 120 Clergy Appreciation cards. You do not even have to go to a store to purchase one; they are available right on the Internet. In fact, based on my experience in past years when I did not receive a single card for this day, I decided this year to send myself one. I picked out one that I thought most appropriate and e-mailed it to myself. This is what it said: "Thank you, Pastor, for making a difference. You are a servant who is kind and sensitive to the needs of others. YOU ARE GREATLY APPRECIATED. We always thank God — the father of our Lord Jesus, when we pray for you."

Okay — it wasn't a perfect fit. But sending a card is the first thing I found on a Web page list of things to do for your clergy to show your appreciation:

1. The first — send a card. I already took care of that for you!

2. An afternoon or evening social. You really don't have to bother.

3. A bulletin board of your pastor's history at the church. Nice idea, but how many people are really going to look at it?

4. Altar flowers — we have them already.

5. Balloons. I think I'm getting a little too old for that!

6. A financial gift. Well, if you really feel you have to do something . . .

We can kid all we want, but I can tell you that, while I love being your rabbi, most clergy are not as happy as I am. Most feel unappreciated. The statistics show that. Seventy percent of clergy feel that they have a lower self-image now than when they entered their calling, 50 percent have considered leaving their position within the past three months, and 70 percent say they have no one they consider a close friend. It is not easy being a member of the clergy.

For some people, the rabbi never gets it right. Like the woman I saw during the High Holidays who, when I asked her how she was, angrily replied, "Now you ask? I was in the hospital for a week this year. Not once did you come to visit me." I apologized. I explained to her that I run to the hospitals constantly, but I just did not know that she was there. I told her, "You or a member of your family should have told me." To which she replied, "You should have known!" So innocently, I asked her, "How did your doctor find out that you were there?" End of conversation. "You should have known!" Rabbis are expected to know everything and be everything. And that is not easy to do.

I speak of all this today not simply because of Clergy Appreciation Day, but because of two popular books focusing on rabbis. One is entitled *Rabbis – The Many Faces of Judaism: 100 Unexpected Photographs of Rabbis with Essays in Their Own Words*. It is a picture book full of photos by one of the world's great sports photographers, George Kalinsky, who traveled around the world taking pictures of rabbis. When you look at the 100 he chose for his book, you cannot help but notice the incredible diversity among rabbis. There are photos of an Asian-American woman rabbi, guitar–playing rabbis, a surfing rabbi, a black Ethiopian rabbi, and a rabbi dressed in a cowboy hat and cowboy boots, with a guitar in hand and a horse beside him (who said Gene Autrey is dead?). And then there is a Lubavitcher rabbi sitting on a red Suzuki motorcycle.

In noting this rabbinic diversity, I thought of the other popular book about rabbis, a book called *The New Rabbi: A Congregation Searches for Its Leader*, written by Stephen Fried. Mr. Fried somehow was given an inside look at Har Zion Temple in Philadelphia as it went through a search for a new rabbi. Har Zion is one of our country's most impressive and important congregations, and its retiring rabbi, Gerald Wolpe, is acknowledged as one of the "giants" in the rabbinate. The book describes the intrigue, the in–fighting, the politics that went on at Har Zion during its search for a new rabbi and of how one candidate after another just was not considered good enough. One was not liked because of the way he positioned his yarmulke on his head. Another was immediately written off because he referred to Bob Dylan in one of his sermons. (They would have loved my Rosh Hashana sermon on the Grateful Dead. And the Yom Kippur sermon where I described the scene at my first Pink Floyd concert. At least Bob Dylan is Jewish.) It took them three years to find a suitable rabbi! You cannot help but wonder that, if one book shows you the wide diversity of rabbis, how come the people in the second book found it so difficult to find one suitable for them? Are there really few, if any, good rabbis out there, as some people feel? I do not think that is true! I think something else is at play here. And to understand it, we need to better understand a rabbinic disagreement about the man named Noach.

Noach built the ark that saved the world. Yet, the first sentence of today's Torah portion about him is the basis of one of the most famous rabbinic disagreements. "*Elah toldot Noach. Noach ish tzaddik tamim haya b'dorotov et ha-Elokim hithalech Noach* — These are the generations of Noach. Noach was a righteous man, wholehearted in his generation. Noach walked with God" (Genesis 6:9). This is a seemingly simple and clear-cut statement about the special nature of Noach. But that is not the way the rabbis saw it. The rabbis wanted to know what it means when it says that "Noach was righteous and wholehearted "*in his generation.*" The biblical commentator Rashi writes,

> Some of our rabbis explain it to his credit: he was righteous even in his generation; it follows that had he lived in a generation of righteous people he would have been even more righteous, owing to the force of good example. Others, however, explain it to his discredit: "In comparison with his own generation he was accounted righteous, but had he lived in the generation of Abraham he would have been accounted as of no importance."

This second interpretation has always bothered me. I can understand the rabbi who argued that this statement is to Noach's credit. After all, the Torah clearly says he was an "*ish tzaddik* — a righteous man." The Torah clearly says, "Noah walked with God." You cannot do better than that! Why should this rabbi, hundreds of years later, question Noach's credentials and say, yes in his generation he was considered good, but by the standards of Abraham's generation he would not have been considered much of anything. That is so unfair. That is, in fact, so un-Jewish! We are taught in the Ethics of the Fathers that every person should be judged on the scale of merit. Every person is entitled to the benefit of the doubt. So why doubt Noah? Why put his merit into question?

I think a case can be made that the judgments of the rabbis had little to do with Noach, but had a lot more to do with the rabbis themselves. According to the Talmud, it was Rabbi Yochanan who made light of Noach, and it was his disciple Resh Lakish who held Noach in high esteem. If you study their lives, you will notice how different in background they were. Reb Yochanan became an orphan at an early age, and his grandfather soon after placed him in the academy to study. From a very young age, Reb Yochanan was surrounded by students, scholars, and righteous people. For him, that was the norm. Resh Lakish, on the other hand, according to legend, started off as a robber. He also worked as a gladiator to support himself. Resh Lakish saw and experienced the world as it was. He knew of all of its allurements and enticements, and yet, he decided to become a talmudic scholar. Is it not possible that Resh Lakish defended the character of Noach because he could appreciate Noach's greatness? He could understand the challenge that Noach faced living in a sinful world while still remaining loyal and steadfast in his righteousness. Resh Lakish understood what Reb Yochanan perhaps could not have understood.

Let me take it one step further. There are many disagreements in the Talmud involving Reb Yochanan and Resh Lakish in addition to the one I just mentioned. Let me point out one other one. Says the Talmud, Reb Yochanan declared, "The least fingernail of the scholars of old was worth more than all of the whole bodies of those of today." Whereas Resh Lakish was of the opinion, "On the contrary, the worth of today's scholars is greater for they devote themselves to the Torah and they ignore the persecution of the government." Notice that Reb Yochanan who said the generation of Abraham was much better than the generation of Noach is the same Reb Yochanan who said the previous generations of scholars were far better than the present one — while the same Resh Lakish who praised Noach in the generation in which Noach lived, praised the scholars in the generation in which he himself lived as well. For Resh Lakish, the people of the day — whether Noach in his day or the sages in Resh Lakish's day — were to be praised and glorified. In contrast, to Reb Yochanan, the previous generation was better, the generation before that was better yet — in fact, anything was better than what you have right now.

I believe that people's attitudes toward rabbis can be divided into the school of Reb Yochanan and the school of Resh Lakish. When rabbis feel unappreciated, when synagogues have difficulty finding a suitable rabbi, that is not because of the rabbis themselves. There are plenty of good ones. It is because of people's attitudes and the way they view rabbis. Thank God, there are some Resh Lakishes — people who understand the challenges and difficulties a rabbi has to undergo and find good in each one of them. And then there are the Reb Yochanans — those who think that the rabbis of the previous generation were better, or those who feel a younger rabbi from the next generation will be better. Anyone and everyone would be better than the rabbis we have today.

There is an extremely important concept involved here that goes way beyond the rabbinate. It has to do with the way we make almost every judgment in life. For often our judgments are not based on the facts themselves — as I believe was the case with Noach — but rather on our own perceptions and preconceived notions and personal experiences. Let me show you what I mean.

I, thank God, receive many complimentary notes and e-mails on my sermons. Not that everyone always agrees with them, but the comments are always enlightening, sometimes challenging, but always respectful — except in two instances. One was when I spoke highly of President Bush as being such a good friend of Israel. Oh, there were people who did not like that! And they let me know it, telling me, "He's only looking for the Jewish vote." "You can't trust him; he's his father's son." "He has a long record of being no friend of the Jews." All kinds of accusations! But the fact is, George Bush has stood by Israel when most every other world leader has not. And although he certainly does not support every Israeli decision, the fact is that every Israeli leader praises George Bush as a true friend, with some declaring him "the best friend Israel has ever had in the White House." The facts are clear, and so why do these people see it differently? I will tell you why: because they are Democrats and they cannot — or do not want — to see anything good in George Bush.

Before Democrats get too upset, let me tell you about a similar experience I had after I delivered a sermon praising Hilary Clinton. In this 1993 sermon, I spoke of an article I had read about the last days in the life of Hugh Rodham, Senator Clinton's father. I spoke about how deeply touched and impressed I had been in reading that Hilary Clinton had stayed at her father's bedside for the last sixteen days of his life. I remarked that she did not have to be there; after all, as the father of the First Lady, he was going to have the best of care, and she could have traveled back and forth to see him with ease. How nice and praiseworthy it was that she had chosen to remain by his side. Then, in my Yom Kippur Yizkor sermon that year, I took note of the fact that our own Congressman Ben Cardin had sent a copy of the sermon to Hilary Clinton and she had sent me a handwritten note. And how nice I thought that was.

I might have thought that, but not those letter writers who accused me of being naïve and foolish and simplistic, pointing out that she and her husband are bums and nothing we read about them should be believed. Now you tell me, what do you think was the one thing all of those letter writers had in common? That's right — they were twisting the facts to fit their perceptions and preconceived notions.

This Republican/Democratic divide was clearly seen during the presidential race in 2000 when Al Gore plastered a kiss on the mouth of his wife Tipper at the Democratic Convention. It became the talk of the country: the kiss was too hard, too soft, too much, too little, spontaneous, well planned, appropriate, and unbecoming — everyone had an opinion. What did their opinion usually boil down to? Robert Novak, a political columnist who has not had a good word to say about a Democrat in the last half-century, labeled the kiss "disgusting." Columnists who leaned more to the left viewed it as a beautiful expression of love between husband and wife. All the while, everyone forgot the words of the great philosopher, Jimmy Durante, who sang, "You must remember this: a kiss is just a kiss."

Now, it is one thing when we allow our Democratic and Republican perspectives to color the way we view a kiss, but it becomes dangerous if that is what we do when we form our own personal judgments about the important issues confronting us and our country. We must learn to make judgments in the way God would want us to make them. It says it right there in the Torah after the story of Noach when we are told that the people built the Tower of Babel: "*Vayered Hashem lir-ot* — and God went down in order to see" (Genesis 11:5). God had to go down in order to see? What does that mean? Writes Rashi, "*Ba l'lameid l'dayanim* — this comes in order to teach a lesson to all judges." Whenever you make a judgment, you have to come down from your own bias, your own perspective, your own preconceived notions, and look clearly at the situation as objectively as possible.

So when it comes to judging President Bush or Hilary Clinton, or your rabbis, or your friends, remember the words of Dragnet's Sgt. Friday: "Just the facts, ma'am." It will not only help you appreciate your clergy better but it will also help people appreciate you better for being the kind of person who gives the benefit of the doubt, who judges on the scale of merit, who is not blinded by personal prejudices. It was Resh Lakish who taught, "When one wants to point out the shortcomings of another, he should be told, 'first cleanse yourself and then you can cleanse others.'" In judging others, let us make sure our vision is clear.

October 12, 2002

MR. KNOW-IT-ALL

Let me teach you a word. The word is *teiku*. If you go to Israel and you attend a soccer match and both teams score the same amount of goals, it is called a *teiku*. *Teiku* has become the Hebrew word for "tie," or a "draw" in chess. Yet, that is really not quite what *teiku* really means. Indeed, the word "*teiku*" is not really a Hebrew word. In fact, it is not even a word! It's an acronym. To understand it, let us examine the law of the red heifer.

Most everyone considers the law of the red heifer (Numbers, 19) the strangest, most incomprehensible of all of the 613 commandments. Every step of the way, it seems to make no sense. The law tells us that when a person comes into contact with a dead body, that individual becomes impure. To be purified the person has to go to the priest, who then takes a red cow that is without blemish. Why red? No one knows. Why a cow? No one knows. The cow is slaughtered and the priest takes some of its blood with his forefinger — why, no one knows — and sprinkles some of the blood toward the sanctuary — why, who knows — seven times, again no one knows why. Then, the cow is burned— why? — and the priest takes cedar wood and hyssop and crimson thread and throws them on the burning cow. Why? Why? Why? No one knows, knows, knows. This law becomes even more incomprehensible when we are then told how this special potion is sprinkled on the person who is impure, thus rendering him or her pure. To top it all off, the priest who performs this ritual becomes impure himself!

This law is so strange, so irrational, that our sages tell us that the nations of the world use it to taunt the Jewish people. No one could explain it — not King Solomon, the wisest of our people, and not the sages in the Talmud. Indeed, Rabbi Yochanan told his students, "It is not the corpse that causes contamination or the ashes of the cow that cause purity. These laws are decrees of God, and man has no right to question them." So that's it? We do it because God told us to. Period, end of story.

But there is one problem. It is found in a statement in the Midrash that reads as follows: "What does God care whether a man kills an animal in the proper Jewish way and eats it, or whether he strangles the animal and eats it? Will the one benefit God or the other injure God? Or, what does God care whether a man eats kosher or non-kosher animals? Learn from this that the commandments were given to refine God's creatures."

Here our sages are telling us something that is central to all of the mitzvot: from God's perspective, it really does not matter if you do the law this way or that way. From God's perspective, it does not matter if you properly slaughter an animal or improperly slaughter an animal. I guess from God's perspective, then, it would not matter if the red heifer was green or if it had been burnt by the priest or in a George Foreman grill — it really does not matter to God. Who it matters to are humans! The purpose of all the mitzvot, say our sages, is "L'tzaref et habriyot" — to refine the individual, to teach self-control.

I can understand how this principle works when it comes to the laws regarding slaughtering an animal. Yes, it may not matter to God, but the law insists that we must use the sharpest knife, one that does not have a nick in it, so that the animal suffers the least amount of pain; I can understand the lesson there for humankind. If we learn how to control our instincts when it comes to an animal, then we will be better able to control our instincts when it comes to our fellow human beings. If we learn compassion toward the pain of animals, that will inculcate within us compassion for the pain of a human being! But what can we possibly learn from the law of the red heifer? What lessons of control are found in it? What moral message can there be in a law that we do not understand every single step of the way? How can that make us a better human being?

With the law of the red heifer, perhaps our tradition is teaching us another important lesson, one that speaks to each and every one of us today. One of the most important lessons we can learn in life is that none of us is so smart that we know everything. The red heifer is an important lesson in humility and in sensitivity. Don't think that you're so smart that you know it all! Don't think that you are always right! Don't be so sure of yourself. There are some things that only God knows.

There is a great *bracha* in the Jewish tradition that we are supposed to say when we meet a Torah scholar: "*Baruch atta Hashem Elokeinu melech ha olam, sh' cholak meychochmato l'yere-av* — Blessed art thou, O Lord our God, ruler of the universe, who has given a *chelek*, a portion of his wisdom, those who fear Him." God has given a "portion" of His wisdom to human beings, not *all* of His wisdom. Nobody but God knows everything. Nobody knows it all, only God. The rest of us, no matter how wise, are capable of getting things wrong.

George Tenet, the former head of the CIA, might still be the head, had he not told President Bush that it was a "slam dunk" that Iraq had weapons of mass destruction. Why didn't he just say, "It looks pretty sure," "The evidence is strong," or "If I were a betting man." Didn't he know that in life there are very few "slam dunks?"

Every day I read the editorial page of six or seven newspapers, and I am always amazed: the editorial writers seem to know everything about everything. There is no subject they do not have opinions on: everything from cicadas to the Sudan to suicide bombers to saccharin to salaries to security. And they are so sure of themselves — they are so sure that they are right! This, despite the fact that often the editorials from the different newspapers disagree with each other. So how can they all be so sure? Wouldn't it be nice if once, just once, there was an editorial on a subject in which the editorial writer wrote, "I'm not sure what the right position is; I don't know the answer."

You know who would do that? Do you know who DID do that? Rashi, the greatest biblical commentator! It is almost impossible to study the Bible or the Talmud without referring to Rashi's commentary. Yet, in his commentary, more than one hundred times Rashi has written, "I don't know what this means." Now, Rashi did not have to admit his ignorance. He did not have to write anything, and we would be none the wiser. But then, we never would have known how great Rashi was. His greatness is reflected not only in what he knew, but in the fact that he was willing to admit what he did not know.

Do you know who was very lucky? Rashi's wife and children. One of the most negative comments you can make about people is to say that they are a Mr. Know-it-all. Many of us grew up with people like that in our lives. Many of us had a parent or teacher who was so dogmatic, so intransigent, so unwilling to allow for any discussion or give and take. In style and in substance, they were so smug, so certain, so authoritarian. There is a thin line separating love, caring, and concern from dominance, subjugation, and control, and they cross it. Do you know anyone like that? Someone who thinks they are always right? Do you *live* with someone like that? Many husband-wife relationships and parent-child relationships suffer from this syndrome, in which there can be no discussion over any disagreements. I suspect it was not like that in Rashi's household. He was "man" enough to admit that he did not know it all! Only God is infallible. We as finite, frail, limited, mortal human beings must always recognize that little in life is certain or immutable. We dare not be a Mr. Know-it-all.

You know who does not know it all? Me! I gave a lecture a few months ago, and during the question-and-answer period somebody asked a question to which I replied, "I really don't know." They were surprised that I — a rabbi — admitted that. And I told them that they would be amazed at how much I did not know! I always think of the words of the great writer, Isaac Bashevis Singer, who won a Nobel Prize and said, "Don't think I'm so smart, I still don't know why a magnet doesn't work on cottage cheese." Well, I do not know that either, and I do not know a lot more things. I am not even sure I know how I feel about the death penalty. A few weeks ago I read in the newspaper that one of the rabbis in our community was now against the death penalty because members of his congregation had a son who was found guilty of murder and put to death.   That rabbi, in dealing with the family, had become sensitized to the issue. Although he once believed in capital punishment, he no longer did. I find myself in the opposite position. We have members of our congregation who lost loved ones to brutal, barbarous killers. I know years later the pain they still feel, and I have become sensitized to their desire to have the killers put to death. So which rabbi is right, and which family is right? And should decisions be made based on our own personal experiences? I am not really sure.

I am also not really sure about my position regarding homosexuals. I know that my religion prohibits homosexuality, and I know that I am opposed to homosexual "marriage." But I also believe that biology plays an important role in homosexuality and if two homosexuals are living together, should they not be entitled to the same benefits enjoyed by a heterosexual couple? I am conflicted. I do not know. And there are lots of issues like this. For example, issues like how much pressure — or, if you want, call it torture — can be applied to a terrorist to obtain information that might save the lives of innocent people? Nobody knows for sure.

That is where *teiku* comes in. Teiku is an acronym of four Hebrew words: *tishbi yetaretz, kushyot vahavayot* — "Elijah the prophet will solve such puzzles and problems." The word *"teiku"* is used in the Talmud when there is a disagreement between two sages regarding an aspect of Jewish law and there is just no way to know who is right. And so the Talmud leaves it at that and says we will wait until Elijah comes. He will answer the puzzle.

Teiku reminds us that there are no slam dunks in life, and that other people have opinions that are as valid as ours. So when you disagree with your spouse, just say *"teiku,"* and leave it at that. It might be the wisest thing you ever did! When Elijah comes we will find out who was really right and then it won't matter, for that will usher in the Messianic era — an era with no conflicts — with the *"geulah sheleimah bimheiru b'yameinu* — the complete redemption, speedily in our time."

June 26, 2004

THE JOY OF SEX

In 1972, Alex Comfort wrote the book, *The Joy of Sex*, and it created a national uproar. Coming just at the time of the women's revolution and the sexual revolution, *The Joy of Sex* sold millions of copies with its frank and witty discussion of sexual issues. Now I must admit that I never read *The Joy of Sex*. I found The Joy of Cooking to be a book that spoke more to my needs and interests. Yet, recently *The Joy of Sex* was revised and reissued by Nick Comfort, the son of the original author, Alex, who is now deceased. While the book itself may not speak to me, there was something that Nick Comfort said during interviews about the book that I think speaks to all of us. Nick Comfort relates that his father spoke to him about sex only one time — and that was only because of the urging of his school principal, who told Alex Comfort that he ought to tell his child something about personal hygiene.

Can you imagine? Alex Comfort, the expert on sex, the man who spoke to the whole world about sex, hardly ever discussed it with his own son. How is that possible? But the more I thought about it, the more I realized that it is not only possible, but it is something that occurs frequently — and not just in regard to sex, but in all areas of life. Often, those who achieve acclaim or renown in some area of life end up being not much of an expert in that very same area when it comes to themselves and their own. Let us look at three examples that touch us as Jews and as human beings.

The first comes to us from "The Ethicist" in the *New York Times.* Every Sunday in its magazine, the *Times* publishes a column called "The Ethicist." It is written by Randy Cohen. People who have ethical questions write to "The Ethicist," and he gives them answers. The questions run the gamut from the one asked by a person who, on a rainy day left his expensive umbrella in a basket at the front of a store, and when he was leaving his umbrella was gone. He asked whether it would be ethical to take one of the other umbrellas that were there. There was the question from the teenager who said his parents did not mind if he sees "R"- rated movies, so was it alright for him to lie about his age at the box office? Randy Cohen is considered so knowledgeable and so capable in answering these questions that he has recently published a book entitled *The Good, the Bad and the Difference,* which is a collection of his ethical responses.

Recently, a woman wrote to "The Ethicist" with the following problem. She had hired a real estate agent to rent her house for her. The agent, in her own words, was "courteous and competent." However, when the transaction was completed, she reached out her hand to shake the real estate agent's hand, and he politely explained that he is an Orthodox Jew and does not shake hands with women. The woman wrote to "The Ethicist" expressing her conflicting feelings. As a feminist, she was offended. Yet, the Orthodox Jew's actions stemmed from his religious conviction. How should she feel? What should she do? Do you know what Randy Cohen, the ethicist, told her to do? He told her to tear up the contract! He wrote, "Sexism is sexism . . . even when it is motivated by religious conviction." In so doing, Randy Cohen, a Jew, showed that he is the ethical counterpart to Alex Comfort: knowledgeable abut the ethics of the world around him but ignorant of the ethics of his own people.

The unwillingness of some Orthodox Jews to shake the hands of members of the opposite sex is not "sexism." Quite the contrary, it is the ultimate act of respect. It is telling that other person, "I respect who you are. I respect your sexuality. I respect the sanctity of your body, and it is not for me to invade your space." Some Orthodox Jews will not touch any member of the opposite sex unless it is their spouse or their child. Of course, shaking hands is rather innocuous, and that is why many Orthodox Jews will, in fact, do that with others. But those who do not shake hands have established a high standard of ethical conduct for themselves. Believe me when I tell you, not shaking hands with a member of the opposite sex is not an ethical offense. Tearing up a contract is an ethical offense! Too bad Randy Cohen could not see that. Too bad that he is so knowledgeable about the culture of others but not of his own. Too bad that so many Jews are knowledgeable about so much — except about their fellow Orthodox Jews.

Another group that fits into this category are Hollywood Jews. It is well known that right from the very beginning a high proportion of Jews have been involved in the music, television, and movie industries. For some, this is a source of anti-Semitism. Yet, for most of us, as Jews, this involvement is a source of pride in our people's achievements. We can take pride not only in what many of our people have achieved as actors, actresses, producers, and directors but also in the causes that their fame and fortune have enabled them to endorse and advocate. From Rob Reiner to Barbara Streisand, from Ed Asner to Norman Lear, Hollywood Jews have raised their voices on every issue from gun control to taxes, to global warming and fur. On almost *every* issue — on every issue except one. An article in the *Los Angeles Times* spoke of the "silence of the Jews" — they were silent about what? Silent about Israel! During the years when Israel has been confronting the threat of terror to every one of its citizens, the Jews of Hollywood have remained silent. At a time when support for Israel is so crucial, in the words of Dennis Prager, "Far more has been said by Hollywood against potential threats to endangered insect or bird species than against actual attempts to render Israeli Jews an endangered species." Hollywood Jews — like Alex Comfort — have much to say to the whole world, but very little when it comes to their very own.

Many Jews are like that. They support the Zoo, the Philharmonic, the museums, the university — every one but their own. Almost every week I read of some Jewish philanthropist contributing a fortune to some cause, any cause but a Jewish cause. It is sad. Think of all the good these people can do to help their own people. There are so few of us in this world, and our needs are so great. Sure, we should help others; we must help others. That is part of our mandate, "L'takein *olam"* — to make this world a better place in which to live. But charity does begin at home!

The Alex Comfort syndrome is all around us — from the *New York Times* to Hollywood, from ethics to philanthropy. Perhaps, saddest of all, it is in our own homes. And perhaps one of the first who fell victim to this malady was our patriarch Jacob.

The Torah describes a poignant, heartbreaking scene in the life of Jacob. It tells of the many children that Jacob's wife Leah gave him. But his other wife, Rachel — Leah's sister — was barren. And the Torah tells us, "And Rachel saw that she had not brought children to Jacob, so Rachel became envious of her sister. She said to Jacob, 'Give me children, otherwise I am dead'" (Genesis 30:1). One can feel Rachel's pain. Her sister is having children — she wants to have children. Without them, she feels her life is meaningless. Now, if your wife said something like this to you, how would you react? What would you say? What would you do? Let me tell you what Jacob said and did. It is right there in the Torah: "*Vayichar af Yaakov b'Rochel* — Jacob's anger flared up at Rachel" and he said, 'Am I instead of God who has withheld from you fruit of the womb?' (Genesis 30:2).

What a harsh and terrible response. One would have expected Jacob to put his arm around his wife and to say something like this: "Rachel, it doesn't matter if you have children — you have me. And I love you and that's all that matters." One would have expected that. And while there are attempts by many of the commentators to try to put Jacob's response in a better light, our sages took Jacob to task, stating in the Midrash, "The Holy One, blessed be He, said to Jacob, 'Is this the way to answer an aggrieved person?' By your life, your children (by your other wives) are destined to stand humbly before her son Joseph."

Yes, Jacob was wrong for what he said. What made matters even worse was the fact that it was Jacob who was saying it! Jacob — the one who is described in the Torah as being the "*ish tam yosheiv ohalim* — the wholesome man, the dweller of tents." Jacob, the student, the scholar. It is the same Jacob who, when he appeared before his father disguised as Esau, his father said of him: "*Hakol kol Yaakov* — the voice is the voice of Jacob," upon which the biblical commentator Rashi notes that Isaac was sure it was Jacob speaking because the person was speaking in such a gentle and respectful manner. Gentle and respectful Jacob. This is the Jacob who gets angry and responds so harshly to his wife? Do you know anyone like that? If you don't, I bet your wife or husband might!

One of the seven blessings we recite when consecrating a marriage refers to a bride and groom as "*Reyim ahuvim* — beloved friends." Is that the highest and most noble title you can give to a bride and groom? Explained one rabbi, yes it is. For often we are nicer and more sensitive and speak more respectfully to our friends than we do to our spouses. To our friends, we put on our best face, always seeming sensitive and understanding, while our own spouses we tend to take for granted and we heap all our frustrations on them.

It is sad that a Nick Comfort remembers his father as an expert out in the world but not when it came to his own. Let us make sure that our families and our people will not think of us in the same way. Perhaps the saddest and most poignant words in all of biblical literature are those that came from the wisest of our people, King Solomon. In looking back on his life, he was forced to admit, "They made me keeper of the vineyards but my own vineyard I did not keep" (Song of Songs 1:6). Let all of us as Jews and human beings reach out to the world around us. Let us tend to those vineyards, but let us never forget that our own vineyard must be tended to first — whether it be our people, our family, or our tradition and heritage.

- So all of you out there who are Little League coaches, make sure you are there to coach your own kids with their homework as well!

- Supporters of museums and symphonies, make sure you take care of the needs of your people as well. Save the whales — but also save the Jews!

- Those who volunteer their time for worthy causes, make sure you give quality and quantity time for your family as well. They too are a worthy cause!

- And if you can put on a nice, friendly face for your clients and business associates who would drop you for a buck, make sure you put on a nice, friendly face for your loved ones who you know will always be there for you.

While Nick Comfort reaps the harvest from his father's book, *The Joy of Sex*, let us continue to learn from our book — *the* Book — the book that teaches us the most important joy, the joy of living, allowing us to fulfill the words of the Psalmist: "*Ivdu et Hashem b'simcha* — to serve the Lord in joy" (Psalms 100:2).

November 16, 2002

Part V:
My Own Life Lessons

A FORTIETH WEDDING ANNIVERSARY

Here it is, the month of June, and I have nothing to do! June is the month for weddings, and I have no weddings to officiate at this month, or next month for that matter! I always have weddings in June; every rabbi does! Some say the tradition of June weddings goes back to ancient Rome when the Romans believed that Juno — the Goddess of Marriage — would bring prosperity and happiness to all those who wed in her month. Still others find the roots of June weddings in the Middle Ages where people got married in June because they took their yearly bath in May and still smelled pretty good in June! However, because they were beginning to smell, brides were given a bouquet of flowers to hide the odor; hence, the custom today of carrying a bouquet when getting married.

Maybe I should have been carrying a bouquet! Maybe then there would have been one couple who wanted me to marry them in June. But in fact, I am not the only rabbi officiating at too few weddings these days. In honor of its centennial celebration, the American Jewish Committee sponsored a major survey of the American Jewish community, and do you know what was one of the most shocking results of that survey? More Jews between the ages of 18 and 40 are *not* married than *are* married! And one can understand why! The *New York Times* reports that on television not one of the twenty-five most popular programs features a happily married couple. The *Wall Street Journal* reports "Love Is a Four-Letter Word," and romance movies invariably deal with the troubles in marriages. These days most new books would lead someone to believe that marriage is futile and hopeless. This anti-marriage tirade began with *Men are from Mars, Women are from Venus*. It continued with *They Just Don't Understand*, and it is now embodied in the following new titles: *What Men Don't Want Women to Know: The Secrets, the Lies, the Unspoken Truth; He's Just Not That Into You; How to Heal the Hurt by Hating; How to Dump a Guy: A Coward's Manual*; and my favorite: *How to Make Your Man Behave in 21 Days or Less Using the Secrets of Professional Dog Trainers*.

Rabbi Jack Riemer asks, Would you want to get married under these circumstances? Too many risks involved. Right from the start you can get hurt. The very first call for a date you risk rejection. And the more dates, the greater the risk of getting hurt. It is this risk that underlies the story of the young man who wanted to ensure himself against rejection, so he first asked the girl, "If I were to kiss you, would you call for help?" And she replied, "Why? Would you need help?" But you do need help when you become involved with another person. You make yourself vulnerable when you tell someone, "I love you. I want to marry you and live with you for the rest of my life." That is quite a gamble! All too many have chosen not to marry — too great a risk of heartbreak and divorce, they claim.

Why do I tell you all this today? Because this week Sherry and I will be celebrating our fortieth wedding anniversary. I am reminded of an incident that took place when I was getting my hair cut, and the woman next to me told her hairstylist that she was celebrating forty years of marriage. To which the hairstylist asked, "To the same person?" Yes, to be married to the same person for forty years is quite an achievement these days. But in reality it should not come as a surprise for Sherry and me that we have been happily married for this long. If ever there was a marriage of two people who seemed to be meant for each other, it was ours! When we got married, we shared so much in common. We hung out with the same crowd, had the same friends, and went to the same camps. We grew up two blocks away from each other. Our brothers knew each other and went to the same schools. Our parents knew each other. Her parents were at my Bar

Mitzvah. Our mothers were pregnant with us at the same time. It was a perfect fit. That's what I thought!

Now, as much as I thought that Sherry and I had in common when we got married, if there is one thing I have learned in the last forty years (and what most of you have learned in your marriages as well), it is just how different we really are.

- I like to drive fast . . . Sherry slow.

- I like the television loud . . . Sherry low.

- On radio, she prefers NPR . . . I choose classic rock.

- She likes the air conditioning high . . . I like it low.

- I like the heat high . . . she, low!

- One of us is a spender . . . the other a saver. One enjoys shopping . . . the other does not. And many of you know who's who!

- Her second language is Hebrew . . . mine, Yiddish.

- She likes old movies . . . I have never seen *Gone with the Wind*.

- Sherry reads novels . . . I prefer nonfiction.

- She's brutally honest . . . and I'm . . . a rabbi!

So you tell me, how did we make it? I know another rabbi who celebrated his fortieth wedding anniversary, and when a congregant asked him what was the key to the success of his marriage, he replied, "My wife and I agreed long ago that no matter how busy we were, no matter what our professional obligations, once a week — no matter what — we would go out to dinner. She went on Wednesdays and I went on Mondays!" Now, that arrangement may have worked for him, but I never even thought of trying that!

So what kept Sherry and me together? The answer is that we did not know we had a choice. Sure, Judaism allows for divorce, and yes, sometimes a marriage just is not meant to be. But we never knew to even think like that because we grew up with a word that you rarely hear anymore. And that word is COMMITMENT. Today when you say someone is "committed," it usually means to a mental institution. We do not speak of commitment any more; rather, the word we hear today is one that I never heard when I was growing up. And that word is DISPOSABLE. When my mother brought something home in a bag from the grocery, after she emptied the bag, what did she do with it? That's right! She folded it up. And after the jar containing the food was empty, what did she do with it? That's right! She cleaned it and put it away. That is unheard of in the age of the disposable. Look at the advertisements on television, and you will see how one of the come-ons for products is stressing that they are disposable. We have disposable diapers, disposable cameras, disposable razors and lighters and contact lenses and cell phones. Do you know what? Today we have disposable people! There are hundreds of thousands of them in Darfur. Here in America there is a book entitled *The Disposable American*, which is about the many people who have been laid off from their jobs.

And today we have disposable marriages. That is what marriage has become for all too many. Marriage has changed from being a commitment into being a one-year lease with an option to renew. The reality is that, if you go into a marriage with the attitude that we will try it and if it does not work, if it becomes painful instead of pleasurable, then we can always go our separate ways — if part of you is in the relationship and part of you is standing outside the relationship evaluating it — you simply will not care enough to make it work out.

This, in some ways, helps explain my opposition to the "commitment ceremonies" now being proposed for homosexual and lesbian couples. This is another one of those issues that represents the cultural divide in our country. That this should not be considered a "marriage," even some of those in favor of such a ceremony agree. That this should not be prohibited by a constitutional amendment, even many of those opposed to such a ceremony agree. My concern is referring to it as a "commitment ceremony" to differentiate it from a "marriage ceremony." But what else is a marriage ceremony than a "commitment ceremony?"

The central idea of Shavuot is that, on that day, God gave us the Torah and entered into a covenant with us. He made a commitment that He would be our God, and we made a commitment that we would be His people — that's right — until death do us part. Do you know that when our rabbis wanted to underscore just how binding and powerful the marriage commitment is, they compared it to the giving of the

Torah on Sinai. The words describing Sinai, *"kafa aleihem hahar* — that Mt. Sinai was held over the heads of the people," are interpreted by the Kabbalists to mean that Mt. Sinai served as the *chuppah* under which God and His people were united eternally in marriage. Our tradition could think of no more powerful metaphor to express the commitment of the Jewish people to God and His Torah than to compare it to the commitment of husband and wife.

Do you know who understood this commitment? A man named Claude Brodesser. Every Sunday the *New York Times* features several pages of marriage announcements. If you want to be considered part of high society, you need to have your wedding announced in the *New York Times*. David Brooks, in his book, *Bobos in Paradise*, refers to the *Times'* marriage page as the "mergers and acquisitions" page! Each Sunday, the page is filled with short articles describing ten to fifteen weddings. But a recent feature of the *New York Times* is to take one of the weddings and highlight it, to give details about how the couple met and what made their wedding ceremony unique. On April 2, 2000, *The Times* featured the wedding of Cathy Akner and Claude Brodesser. Cathy Akner is an Orthodox Jew. Her grandfather was a survivor of the Dachau concentration camp.   She lives in New York, and in the fall of 2003 she hired Claude Brodesser, who was then a reporter for *Variety* in Los Angeles, to run a workshop for her business. Claude Brodesser's father served in the German army during World War II. Mr. Brodesser is not Jewish. I should say he was not Jewish. But he and Cathy fell in love. And these were the opening words in the *New York Times* describing their marriage: "There are many ways for a man to prove his commitment to his fiancé: diamond rings, love poetry, the occasional tattoo. One of the most sincere and certainly most painful is going through a religious conversion involving circumcision." "There is no way she wasn't going to marry a Jew," Mr. Brodesser said of the conversion late last year. And what of his visit to the mohel who did the circumcision? "It didn't tickle!" he said. "But for the first time I feel like I belong somewhere."

That is quite a commitment Claude Brodesser made to his marriage. So much less is asked of most all of us. Claude Brodesser and Cathy Akner had much less in common than Sherry and I had when we got married, but I have every reason to believe that their marriage will last as long as ours has.

Many rabbis conclude a wedding ceremony with the Priestly Blessing. What is the bottom line, the closing phrase, the be-all- and-end-all of this famous Priestly Blessing? "May the Lord bless you and keep you. May the Lord cause His face to shine upon you and be gracious unto you. May the Lord lift up His face unto you and grant you shalom, peace" (Numbers 6:24-26). And as to the phrase, "May the Lord give you peace," the Midrash adds these strange words: "Peace when you enter, peace when you leave, peace with every man." What does that mean? Explains the biblical commentator Ktav Sofer: "Peace when you enter means peace in your home. Peace when you leave means peace in your State. Peace with every man means peace in the world." Before you can tackle global issues of world peace, you must feel peace and security in your home.

We are all so concerned with the need for peace in this world. Yet, the reality is that our greatest need is for peace and harmony in our own homes. For forty years that need has been met in my home. May it be in yours, and may we all find fulfillment of the last of the seven blessings recited under the chuppah. May our marriages be blessed with *"Gilah rinah ditzah v'chedvah* — joy and song, delight and rejoicing; *ahavah v'achvah v'shalom v'reut* — love and harmony, peace and companionship."

June 10, 2006

On Turning Fifty: It's Never Too Late — It's Later than You Think

Scott Peck wrote a book, *The Road Less Traveled,* that has sold more than five million copies. Why was it such a success? What great wisdom does it contain? The first sentence of the book reveals what he believes to be the key to understanding life: "Life is tough." Five million copies for that *chochma.* Sometimes, it is the simple truths that say it all.

Today I am going to try to outdo Scott Peck. I have written not a book, but a card — not one sentence but two. Each sentence captures a simple truth of life, despite the fact that one sentence contradicts the other. I write these two sentences on a card to help mark one of the most unbelievable events in the history of humankind that is about to happen. It has never happened before. In a world filled with so many mysteries and wonders, this has got to be the most unbelievable of all. Next month I turn fifty! It is absolutely unbelievable! Me? Fifty? Unbelievable!

Of course, one birthday is no different from any other, but turning fifty does seem to mean that ominous doings lie on the horizon. I guess it is because with this birthday I start receiving the magazine, *Modern Maturity* and I become a member of AARP and Club Jubilee. I also know what the statistics tell us regarding the life-span of the average human being. At age fifty, like it or not, you are forced to admit to yourself that you have been here longer than you are going to be here. The end, as it would be put in Yiddish, is *shoin nenter vi veiter*. Of course, we do not like to think that way. That great *chochom* Woody Allen, when asked what he would like people to say about him a hundred years from now, replied, "I hope they will say 'He looks good for his age.'" That is how it is with us. Getting older is something we are anxious to do until we do it. But the reality is we are doing it — each and every one of us, each and every day of our lives.

No, there is nothing intrinsically momentous about the fiftieth birthday, except that it does represent another transition in our lives. A transition that comes earlier than fifty for some and later than fifty for others. It marks something we feel — physically and emotionally. We all have heard someone reading off that cute list, "You Know You're Getting Older When...," and then comes the series of instances: "You know you're getting older when your knees buckle and your belt doesn't. Your back goes out more often than you do. Everything hurts and what doesn't hurt doesn't work. You turn out the lights not for romantic reasons but for economic reasons." You know you're getting older when you hear that list, and rather than laugh you say, "Yeah... that's right." You begin forgetting the names of people you have known for years. Has this ever happened to you? Sometimes I find myself standing before the open refrigerator, just staring inside, wondering what it was I was looking for in the first place. Or, have you ever heard a voice answer the other end of the telephone and you have forgotten whom you called? For me, the realization set in this past summer when my kids asked me if I wanted to relive my youth and return to Woodstock of twenty-five years ago, and my first thoughts were, "Will they have valet parking?" "Do I really have to sit on the ground?" "What am I doing listening to rock singer Joe Cocker when I have so much more in common with his cousin, Alta?"

No, I am not a kid anymore. I am going to be fifty. Suddenly all around me I notice best-selling books that have titles such as *How We Die*, *The Tibetan Book of Living and Dying*, *Embraced by the Light*, *Death, The Trip of a Lifetime* — they sound like travel brochures. Was there so much being written about death when I was younger, or am I just more sensitive now? Only a few years ago it seemed that Erica Jong was writing her risqué *Fear of Flying*. This year she wrote her *Fear of Fifty*. Betty Friedan, who wrote *The Feminine Mystique*, this year wrote

The Fountain of Age. Last month the *New York Times* reported that Ms. Friedan held a party where all the guests ate from a buffet that had been prepared under the guidance of Dr. Roy Walford, who with his daughter had just written a cookbook called *The Anti-Aging Plan.* Dr. Walford claims that if people stick to his recipes they can live until 150. Those interviewed at the party who had tasted his recipes said they would rather die at 80.

Yes, all around me, all around all of us, there is this confrontation with our mortality. Time is marching on. And no matter how old we are, no matter what birthday we are celebrating, we are all part of a continuous process that begins at the cradle and ends at the grave. Gail Sheehy, in her classic book, labeled these ongoing transitions in our lives *Passages.* The actor Hugh O'Brien, who played Wyatt Earp on television, put it a bit differently when he called them "stages."

> I found out very early in my business that no matter who you are and no matter what business you're in, all of us go through five stages in life. The first stage is: Who is Hugh O'Brien? This is where you begin your journey, when you sow the seeds for success. The second is: Get me Hugh O'Brien. The third is: Get me someone like Hugh O'Brien. That's when you're really successful, when they can't afford you but they want someone like you. The fourth stage is: Get me a young Hugh O'Brien. And the fifth stage is: Who is Hugh O'Brien? No matter who we are, we all begin at stage one and we're all going to wind up eventually at stage five, back where we came from.

Judaism also speaks of stages in life; it also speaks of passages. And it speaks most forcefully of them today in the concluding service that is called *Neilah*, which literally means "closing." According to the Talmud, the *Neilah* service is meant to evoke the image of the closing of the gates of prayer, as the day of Yom Kippur fades into dusk. This is the last opportunity we have for our prayers of repentance and forgiveness to reach the Heavenly throne. The central prayer of the *Neilah* service seems to sound a note of great urgency, even anguish. "*P'tach lanu shaar* — open for us a gate, *b'ayt neilat hashar* — whenever a gate is closed." Some say this refers to the Gates of Heaven closing at *Neilah* time. Others claim it refers to the Temple gates closing.

But I think it is more than that. Life is a series of openings and of closings, of stages and passages. In a powerful way, this prayer is speaking about the gates of life through which we all must pass. Life is a succession of gates we pass through from youth to adulthood to old age, encompassing challenges, opportunities, and decisions. "Dear God, as we pass through life, as we hear each gate closing behind us, please God, let us hear another gate open." And you know what? Now that I am entering a new stage in my life as I turn fifty, I looked for a birthday card. I could not find anything I liked, so I went and printed my own. It is just a little business card for me to carry around in my wallet. I printed on it the words I think you will find written on every gate that closes in every stage of your life. You know what it says? IT'S LATER THAN YOU THINK!

IT'S LATER THAN YOU THINK sounds simple enough, but the gates keep saying them as they close because people have so much trouble hearing those words, really hearing them. For instance, some parents want to keep their children young forever and refuse to recognize that yesterday's infant is now a teenager or a young adult who can no longer be treated as a child. That young person is in the process of developing a sense of self and a sense of separateness. You can try to hold the process back if you want to, but if you do it will be to your harm and to your child's. You cannot stop your children from growing up and growing out, no matter how much you try. IT'S LATER THAN YOU THINK. And those people who are forty and yet dress and act as if they were twenty, and those who are sixty and dress and act as if they were forty — who do they think they're kidding? Only themselves. Don't they know IT'S LATER THAN YOU THINK.

And what about all those people who refuse to face up to the reality of life and death. I will never forget the following words. In a sense they were the most complimentary I have ever heard and were said of me on one of the most memorable nights of my life. On Sunday, December 13, 1992, I was honored by the Zionist Organization of America. Me — and Larry King. When I finished speaking, he got up to talk and his opening words — those of you who were there might remember — were, "If I die, get Wohlberg to do the funeral." I will never forget how those words struck me. They hit me on several different levels: as a compliment but also as a puzzle. "*If* I die?" Larry darling, it is when

— no ifs, ands, or buts about it. There is some of Larry King in so many of us. Those who forever put off buying a cemetery plot or insurance or avoid going for an annual physical — as if it will all go away if you just ignore it. You can try to live that way if you want to, but if you look at the sign on the closed gates of life's passages, you will accept the fact that IT'S LATER THAN YOU THINK.

Do you know who understands these words and lives by them? David Williams — who plays tackle for the Houston Oilers football team. Do you remember what he did? It was on page one of all the newspapers for a day or two, and then it was forgotten, but it should not be. His wife gave birth to their first child on a Sunday morning, the day his team was scheduled to play the New England Patriots in Massachusetts. Dave was present during the delivery, went through the entire experience with his wife, and then the baby was born and he had a choice. He could have arranged to get on a plane and been at the game in time to play, or he could have stayed with his wife. He chose to skip the game so that when his wife woke up he would be there and when his baby looked up for the first time he would be there. The Houston Oilers fined him $110,000 for missing the game, and that aroused a howl of protest. The reporters asked Williams, "If you had known that you were going to be fined $110,000, would you still have done it?" His answer was, "Of course, isn't family what the money's for?" It was not enough for him to be there for the birth. He wanted those first moments of deepest joy, of intimate sharing, of bonding with his child. "Isn't family what the money's for?"

The words of his statement deeply moved me. I know a rabbi, a rather successful one, whose wife gave birth. As soon as the doctor came out and said, "It's a boy and they are both well," that rabbi immediately left in order to officiate at a funeral. It never occurred to him not to leave. Dave Williams was smarter. Dave Williams knows what is important in life. He knows that there has to be a commitment to work, but there has to be an even greater commitment to family. He knows that being a football player is what he does for a living. Being a husband and father is what he is. And he knows that as a husband and father, IT'S LATER THAN YOU THINK. Somehow he was smart enough to know that,with your children, it is, "Sunrise, sunset, swiftly flow the years." Our kids are only ours for a short while, and there is always going to be something pulling us away from them.

Ask Dr. Jocelyn Elders, the Surgeon General of the United States. She is supposed to tell our country how to live a healthy life. Like the rabbi, she is supposed to know what's best. Two weeks ago her 28-year-old son Kevin was sentenced to ten years in prison for selling cocaine. In a letter to the sentencing judge, Dr. Elders said that, when her son needed her most, she was too busy with politics. "As I sat there watching my son, I thought of how much and how long he had suffered because at the time of his greatest need, we had not been able to communicate as a family. I was too busy with my confirmation hearings." She, the rabbi, and so many of us can learn from the football player the Number One rule in the game of life: IT'S LATER THAN YOU THINK.

There is a new item on the market that might help us remember the importance of this rule. It is in the Sharper Image catalog and is called the "Personal Life Clock." The watch contains a tiny computer into which you feed your age, medical history, lifestyle, and gender. The watch uses actuarial data to compute your life expectancy and then displays the actual hours, minutes, and seconds remaining in your statistical lifetime, counting down to zero. So imagine walking down the street and someone asks you the time. You glance at your watch and say, "Oh about 27 years, 110 days, 21 hours, 4 minutes, and 42 seconds until I die." That is a lot more interesting than saying "3:45." According to the Sharper Image catalog, this clock reminds you to live life to the fullest. But there's several problems with the clock. First, it costs $100. Second, you really do not need it. All you need is a card that says IT'S LATER THAN YOU THINK.

There is another problem with the clock: it does not always give the correct time. Just ask a dear family friend of ours, Pearl Bassan. Her daughter Rachel lived in Israel and developed a rare form of cancer. They brought her back to America to the University of Rochester Medical Center, where her only chance for survival was to have a bone marrow transplant. The cost was approximately a quarter of a million dollars. Her family and friends across America attempted to raise the funds, and Rachel had the bone marrow transplant. In February 1994, a few months short of her 32nd birthday, Rachel Bassan Hurwitz, wife, daughter, mother of three, died — from complications, they said. But her personal life clock would have said she had a lot more time. Don't you know people like that? You see, the clock is not always right. At all stages of life, only the card is right: IT'S LATER THAN YOU THINK.

Just ask a woman named Jacqueline Kennedy Onassis. Shortly before she died, she said to a friend, "I don't get it. I did everything right to take care of myself and look what happened. Why in the world did I do all those push-ups?" Yes, you can be Jackie Kennedy, you can be in the best of shape, and yes, you can be young, but there are always gates closing shut. The clock is always ticking, and you can never be sure when it will stop.

I am always struck when I am called to the home of someone who has just died, and there I sit, in a living room, and the couch has plastic covers on it. Yes, it is a living room, yet it was anything but that. You were not supposed to step into it, and you were not allowed to sit on the couch. It was all being saved for some special time. Now it is going to look so nice and fresh and clean when people come to pay condolence calls. What were the people waiting for? Didn't they know at every stage of life that IT'S LATER THAN YOU THINK.

Please, if at this point you are a little depressed, that is not my intention. If you think you are listening to the morbid ramblings of a rabbi preparing to face a midlife crisis, you are wrong. Quite the contrary. I speak to you about this theme this morning because I think the message of the *Neilah* prayer is a powerful one and an important one — and a significant, uplifting one. Sure, gates are constantly closing, telling us IT'S LATER THAN YOU THINK. But at the same time that prayer reminds us of the all-important message that, as God closes one gate in our life, He opens another one. This is a message of hope and anticipation and excitement for what lies ahead. For strangely enough, while our physical energy diminishes, our insight and wisdom seem to increase. As we get older, we realize that many of our childhood dreams would not have made us happy. We discover a painful truth that purpose and meaning in life are not defined by the size of our house or by the make of the car we drive or by the number of shoes we own. Other things become important — more important things. And that is the beauty of life.

The closing gates tell us IT'S LATER THAN YOU THINK. Yet, those gates that open proclaim the sentence that I put on the other side of my custom-made birthday card: IT'S NEVER TOO LATE. It's never too late to learn, to be, to reach out, to love, to grow. You remember that rabbi who, when his son was born, rushed away to a funeral? His sons are now in their twenties, and when his youngest son asked him this June if he would like to go to Philadelphia one night for a concert, the rabbi looked at his calendar for that day and saw he had a full schedule in one of the busiest times of the year. But that did not matter. He closed the datebook, and off he went with his son to Philadelphia to see Pink Floyd. It was quite a night. There we are, in line with a huge crowd outside of Veterans Stadium, and my Jonathan turns to me and says: "Dad, I think you're going to be the only rabbi here tonight!" But that was alright. I was with my kids! Inside the stadium a more shocking realization hit me. I looked around at the sold-out crowd. 70,000 people strong, and I was the oldest man in the place. Oh, how depressing. Until the show started. The band came out and I realized, "They are older than me." (Did I enjoy the concert? Well two weeks later I went with my boys to New York to see them again.) That scene took place all across America this summer. Pink Floyd, the Rolling Stones, the Eagles, Billy Joel, and Elton John — it was referred to as the summer of "Geezer Rock."

Yes, IT'S NEVER TOO LATE to teach an old dog new tricks. Sure we have to surrender to life's decrees when they are inevitable. But perhaps they only become inevitable after we surrender to them. Sure we have to accept the verdict of fate once it has come, but until then why can't we fight as long as we can and as well as we can? When you really come to think of it, perhaps we ought to try to be twenty at forty, forty at sixty — to the extent that our bodies will let us. Perhaps we ought to try to live as well and as much as we can for as long as we can, despite the clock and the calendar. It is worth a try.

That is the spirit in which we ought to live. IT'S NEVER TOO LATE. Right up to the very end. Did you read about the wedding that took place when Playmate of the Year, Anna Nicole Smith, married 89-year-old billionaire Houston tycoon, J. Howard Marshall II? Newspapers reported that the 26-year-old bride wore a low-cut satin gown, while the groom was in a wheelchair. Commentators pointed out that this proves that where there's a will there's a way. Yet, I don't know if that comment is fair to either of the people involved. IT'S NEVER TOO LATE.

It is never too late to get married, and do you know what? It is never too late to become happily married. I know of many husbands and wives who are living lives of quiet desperation and despair. No, they are not divorced. They are married, living under the same roof, but in two different worlds. Behavior patterns become entrenched over the years. Every disagreement, every argument becomes part of the Hundred Years War. I know a man who says that every time they have a fight his wife becomes historical. I said, "You mean hysterical." He replied, "No, historical. She begins to scream about everything I've done wrong over the last twenty years." Yes, we do fall into modes of behavior that seem impossible to change. "That's the way I am," says he or she. "Like it or not, take it or leave it." Yet, "that's the way I am," is not necessarily the way you have to be. No matter how many years you have been married, no matter how right you may think you are, no matter how set in your ways you claim to be, remember these words: IT'S NEVER TOO LATE. Never too late to change.

Professor Abraham Joshua Heschel spoke from the Jewish tradition when he said, "A stone is characterized by its finality, whereas man's outstanding quality is his being a surprise." Yes, we are capable of surprising ourselves. We place a stone as a monument to those who are gone for they, like the stone, can no longer change. But we, the living, can, because the reality is we are constantly changing. It has been said that no woman can be married to the same man for twenty-five years. After twenty-five years he is not the same man, nor is she the same woman, and that is true. We are constantly changing. In a modern novel a husband and wife are having an argument when the husband says sadly, "You should have married a better man," to which his wife replies: "I did." Yes, he had changed — in the wrong direction. It is never too late to change in the right direction. Try therapy. Speak to a counselor. Look in the mirror. IT'S NEVER TOO LATE.

If people who for twenty years smoked two packs a day can change and stop, if alcoholics of twenty years can change and stop, if people who for twenty years stuffed themselves with fats and cholesterol can change and stop, then you — who twenty years ago looked at that person lying in bed next to you with such love, feeling that there is no one in this world you would rather spend the rest of your life with — can change and start feeling that way once again. No, it is not easy, but it can be done. It has been done. People are constantly changing.

At the age of eighty-five, you know who is one of the most outspoken advocates for accepting homosexuals in the military? A man named Barry Goldwater. He has changed. In his eighties, Justice Harry Blackmun, after twenty-five years on the Supreme Court voting in favor of capital punishment, said he would never do so again. He changed. I know of a man who made his living as a smuggler and a crook, who cheated on his wife with every floozy he could find, who wheeled and dealed and bribed his way through life, and who indulged in good food, fine wine, and fine women. One day he changed, and he set himself to saving the lives of 1,100 Jews. His name? Oskar Schindler. Never too late. Never too late to change. Never too late to become real husbands and wives to each other. Never too late to become good parents and children to each other.

Most all of us, as parents, get a second chance in life when a new child enters our family, a child who is not really a child. He or she is called a son-in-law or daughter-in-law. They marry our children, but we come along as part of the package. Some call us Mom and Dad. Some do not know what to call us. And some call us things that would be best left unsaid. But how do we react to them? After all, we are older, and we are supposed to be smarter. And we share something in common with our sons-in-law and daughters-in-law: they now have to do something that we once had to do. They have to put up with our kids, and we know how hard that can be. Our son-in-law and daughter-in-law could use a little help; they could use a little support. They could once in a while use a little bolstering-up, a little love, a little unconditional love from us.

I had a mother-in-law who gave that to me — Helen Kwestel, of blessed memory. She died this year, and she was mourned, truly mourned, not just by her four children but also by me, her son-in-law, and her three daughters-in-law, because she was the kind of woman for whom it was never too late to be a mother. She was like a mother to all of us. I remember the first time I dated Sherry. We only lived two blocks away from each other on 15th Avenue in Brooklyn, and when the date was over that night, I walked home and I looked over my shoulder. I saw Helen Kwestel standing on the porch, watching to make sure that I got home safely. For more than a quarter-century I felt like I had a second mother, always watching to make sure that I was okay, and because of that, there are lots of us who will never ask, "Who was Helen Kwestel?"

Every day I read the obituaries in the *New York Times*. That is how I know which important Jewish figures have died, because Jewish organizations place the obits in that newspaper. It is said that if you're Jewish and there's no obituary for you in the *New York Times*, then you did not really die, no matter what the medical examiner says. Be that as it may, I was struck on July 26th of this year by the obituary notice for a Zachary Feinstein. There were no notices from any organizations, which means he could not have been very wealthy, but there was this one: "Zach, you were the father I no longer had. I love you and will miss you forever. You were my friend, my support, my inspiration. Always remember, I'm crazy about you, Dad. You will remain in my heart everyday for the rest of my life. Love, your daughter-in-law Jill." Wow! For a daughter-in-law to feel that way! Zach Feinstein was a smart man. He knew that it was never too late to be a father and a father-in-law. And because of that, contrary to what Hugh O'Brien said, as the gates of life closed for Zach Feinstein, no one asked, "Who is Zach Feinstein?"

Yes, it's never too late. Our sons and sons-in-law, daughters and daughters-in-law can always use a little love and attention and devotion. And you know what? So can we — from them.

No guilt trips, but as I am getting older I realize more and more that parents get a bum deal in life. Some of it is our fault. We just cannot help it. In America today it is considered neurotic or at least unhealthy to teach children that they owe us for their orthodontia, their college tuition, their very lives. The model of a sacrificial parent waiting for a return on her investment has become a satire. Raising children is supposed to be a free act of love. So we tell our kids we need nothing in return. Indeed, we set as our goal in life that old Jewish wish: "*Tzum eltern yahren zol min nit darfen ohn-kummen tzu die kinder* — In our old age we should never have to depend upon our children." Let them take care of their own; we will take care of ourselves. So we prepare for our own old age — buffer our lives against needing — with IRAs and Social Security, with health insurance and Medicare.

And then one day we wake up and realize that Social Security does not make visits or send cards and that it is very rare for a person to leave this world without becoming somewhat dependent on others, especially their children. Our shame about aging prevents us from admitting to ourselves that we are not as independent as we had hoped we would be; it prevents us from telling our children the dirty little secret of our human existence: we need them. We need to lean on them. To most everyone else, we are just another name: a patient, a Social Security number, a medical card, a room number in a hospital or convalescent home. The doctors and nurses? They will try to be nice, try to make us comfortable, try to make us feel at home. They will even call us by our first name — though they hardly know us. They know our blood pressure and cholesterol count. But the real me? As one elderly patient wrote:

> I am not the stroke in Bed 2
> Or the hip replacement in room 4
> Or the Foley that needs changing in 7
> I AM ME
>
> I used to have responsibilities like you
> There were people dependent on me
> I had a wife
> I raised 7 children
> I have made decisions
>
> My body was young and strong
> I ran, I flew, I made love
> I ran with the wind
> Skimmed the lake in a sailboat
> I have lain alone on smooth grass
>
> I have kissed hurts away from skinned knees
> And felt a baby's face nuzzling into my neck
> I remember the fragrance of baby powder
> I have been brave
> I have won honors

I have failed in some things
But please see ME
You will be old someday just like ME
Then you will understand how I want you to know ME
But then it will be too late.

For us as children, it is never too late to be there for our parents when they need us. It is nice if we help pay their rent and arrange for their care. It is nice if we remember to send them flowers and cards. But that is not what our parents really need. What they really need is us. "*Al tashlicheinu l-et zikna* — Let us not be cast off in our old age." "*Kichlot kochainu al taazveinu* — When our physical strength fails let us not be abandoned emotionally." They are living longer these days, so now more than ever IT'S NEVER TOO LATE to be a good child. A good kid when you are five or fifteen years old? That counts. But to be a good kid, a devoted child, when you are forty-five or fifty— that is when it really counts. IT'S NEVER TOO LATE.

Not in life and not in death. That is the beauty of Judaism. That is the beauty of this Yizkor service. You see, for us, death is not the end of the story. Death, for us, is but another passage. This world, taught our sages, is only a vestibule before the palace of the world to come. When the gates close on the vestibule, it opens into the palace. Most Jews are not aware of this teaching. Most do not know that Judaism very strongly believes that there is life after life. Yes, the best-seller lists today are filled with books about death and the hereafter. We Jews are always reading what others have to say, but we forget what we say.

What words are we about to say? "*Yizkor Elokim et nishmat avi mori imi morati* — Remember, O Lord, the soul of my mother and my father." For many, these words are nothing more than a way of expressing our honor and respect for a deceased parent. But they are so much more than that. They are very much a statement that their souls do, in fact, live on — literally — and that, for us, it is never too late to reach out to them so that we can uplift them and they can uplift us. We come to a synagogue to say Yizkor in order to say to God and to say to our parents: "You haven't been forgotten. You're not Hugh O'Brien. You were a mother or father who inspired me enough to want to come to a synagogue and say Yizkor." Yes, it is never too late for us to be able to make our parents proud of us.

At the same time, it is never too late to be inspiring parents to our children. Arthur Ashe reminds us of that. Arthur Ashe was the great tennis player who died this year from AIDS. Before he died, he established a foundation for urban health so that others can live healthy lives after his death. But the most important thing that he did in the last days was write a letter to his daughter, Camera, who was just three or four years old at the time. It is a letter meant for her to read when she is old enough. It is a lovely letter and it contains much wisdom about life. He ends his letter this way — with a declaration of his love and devotion:

> Don't be angry, Camera, with me, if I am not there in person when you need me. Don't feel sorry for me that I am gone. When we were together I loved you deeply and you gave me much happiness. Camera, wherever I am, when you feel sick at heart and weary of life, or when you stumble and fall and feel that you can't get up again, think of me. I'll be watching and smiling and cheering you on.

Arthur Ashe knew. IT'S NEVER TOO LATE. Even after you are gone, you can be a parent. Your influence can be felt.

Did your parents leave you such a letter? Did your parents write you such beautiful words to remember after they were gone? Of course, they did. They may not have been as sophisticated and educated as Arthur Ashe to put their words and feelings on paper. So all they could do is transcribe them in your heart. Our parents speak to us everyday from beyond the grave. Inside each of us there speaks a small voice, part of which is a father, a mother, or some other loved one. Ten years later, do I not hear my father saying to me, "*Derech Eretz?*" What do you hear? What do you remember from your parents? What will your children remember from you? And believe me, not everything we remember and hear in our inner ear are positive lessons.

Yes, in this never-ending dialogue we have with our parents, we continue to learn from them — learn from them both what they did right and what they might have done wrong. If we listen carefully, we can hear them admit to some mistakes. Memories of failures are also precious. Our parents lived their lives very differently than we do. Many of us are still bothered by the gnawing feeling that our parents did not allow themselves to enjoy life to its fullest. They worked and skimped and saved, and then they worked and skimped and saved some more. They didn't *fargin* themselves much, not in the way of clothing or vacations or some of the simple pleasures in life. Many of us are bothered by our parents' inability to express the words of love and provide the acts of affection we yearned for. We think they were not as generous with us, with others, or with themselves as they should have been. If we listen carefully, perhaps they are telling us now that we should understand that they were products of a different time. It was not cheapness or stinginess that dictated their actions; it was fear, it was insecurity. And they would be the first to tell us to go and enjoy and to do! To show our love and express it, to take the plastic off the couches, to live in the living room, to use the good dishes and silverware more often. Live and give and enjoy what you have, while you can. IT'S LATER THAN YOU THINK. Our parents would be the first to tell us: do what you can now, while you can. Do what you can to make sure that those whose lives touch yours will never have to ask who you were.

Yizkor beckons. We pause to remember. As I get older, my memory at Yizkor has been affected. Once Yizkor recalled my relationship with my father. Now it makes me think of my relationship with my sons. I remember so many moments in my father's life. Now, I wonder what moments my children will remember of me — what stories will they tell their children of me.

So yes, I am turning fifty. I hear gates closing, but I hear gates opening. I am growing old. IT'S LATER THAN YOU THINK. But I am also growing up, and it's never too late for that. I am a husband, a father, a son, a brother — but there is still a little boy in me. I still like getting birthday cards and giving them too. So I made one for myself and I printed up a few extra — not five million — just enough to share with all of you. The ushers have them, for your birthday and mine. At every birthday, indeed everyday, may you be young enough to feel that it is never too late and may you be old enough to know that it is later than you think.

Scott Peck is right: Life is tough! But that's okay. It is also exciting and challenging and meaningful and can be beautiful if we work at it each and everyday of our lives. Thank you, God, for the lives of those who preceded me, for the lives of those who will follow me, and thank you, God, for my life as well.

My first birthday was spent in the hospital connected to life support systems. An emergency tracheotomy had been performed in an attempt to keep me alive. They did not think I would make it. When I did, they were sure my vocal cords had been damaged and I would never be able to speak. On my thirteenth birthday, at my Bar Mitzvah, my father, of blessed memory, reminded me of that and challenged me to use my voice to speak the words of God and Torah. And here I approach my fiftieth birthday, able to do just that to this glorious, marvelous congregation that I love. Thank you God, "She'hechiyanu v'kiymanu v'higiyanu lazman hazeh — for giving me life, for sustaining me, and for enabling me to reach this milestone in my life."

Yom Kippur, September 15, 1994

Death of a Mother

It was on a Friday afternoon, shortly after Sherry and I got married. Sherry had decided to make chopped liver for Shabbos, but when she broiled the piece of liver it seemed to have a green coloring on top. She asked me if I thought the meat was okay. I told her I didn't know, but I was calling my parents to wish them a good Shabbos and I would ask my mother. Sure enough, I get on the phone, and I say, "Ma, Sherry is making her own chopped liver, but the meat looked a little green. Do you think it's okay?" And she replied, "Oh, that's no problem. Sometimes when it's broiled it has a greenish cast." I tell this to Sherry and I continue the conversation with my mother. And then, a few minutes later, Sherry picks up the extension and says, "Mitchell, the chopped liver is ready." To which my mother shrieks, "Mitchie, you're eating that liver? Don't touch it!"

On May 15th of this year, I lost the woman who sought to protect me from Sherry's chopped liver — the woman who warned me not to eat it, who warned me to buckle my seat belt, who warned me to stay out of the sun, who warned me not to shovel the snow, who warned me not to eat too many carbohydrates, who warned me not to eat too many proteins, who warned me not to over exercise, who warned me to stay inside when there was lightning, who warned me to stay out of deep water, who warned me not to smoke, who warned me not to overwork (despite the fact that I was a rabbi), who warned me to stay away from wild dogs, who warned me about the dangers of syphilis, gonorrhea, AIDS, and bubonic plague, and, of course, who warned me to stay off of Old Court Road. I lost my mother — the woman who sought to protect me, her baby, throughout her entire life.

That desire, that need, indeed, that obsession to protect her children was just one manifestation of the fact that Jessie Wohlberg was not just a mother — she was a Jewish mother! I was deeply, deeply touched by the hundreds and hundreds of visits and expressions of sympathy I received from all of you when my mother passed away. I was deeply, deeply comforted by the many of you who said that, although you had never met my mother, you felt as though you knew her through the many stories I told about her in my sermons. The fact is, you knew her because, in many ways, you had a mother just like her! For better and for worse, my mother was a Jewish mother!

Recently, I came across this list of "Things a Jewish Mother Would Never Say:"

"Be good, and for your birthday I'll buy you a motorcycle!"

"Run and bring me the scissors! Hurry!"

"I don't have a tissue with me — just use your sleeve."

"Of course you should walk to school and back. What's the big deal about having to cross a few main streets?"

"My meeting won't be over until late tonight. You kids don't mind skipping dinner, do you?"

"Don't bother wearing a jacket; it's quite warm out."

"Well, if Timmy's mom says it's okay, that's good enough for me."

No, what was good enough for Timmy's mother was never good enough for my mother! Never good enough for the Jewish mother!

That is another trait associated with a Jewish mother: whatever her children do isn't good enough, and so she's never satisfied; she is always kvetching. Listen to another list, this one called "Statements from Famous Jewish Mothers:"

MONA LISA'S JEWISH MOTHER: "After all that money your father and I spent on braces, that's the biggest smile you can give us?"

COLUMBUS'S JEWISH MOTHER: "I don't care what you've discovered; you still could have written!"

MICHELANGELO'S JEWISH MOTHER: "Can't you paint on walls like other children? Do you have any idea how hard it is to get that stuff off the ceiling?"

NAPOLEON'S JEWISH MOTHER: "All right, if you aren't hiding your report card inside your jacket, take your hand out of there and show me."

THOMAS EDISON'S JEWISH MOTHER: "Of course I'm proud that you invented the electric light bulb. Now turn it off and get to bed!"

ALBERT EINSTEIN'S JEWISH MOTHER: "But it's your senior picture! Couldn't you do something about your hair — styling gel, mousse, something — ANYTHING?'

The Jewish mother is the butt of jokes, the Sophie Portnoy, the overprotective, overdemanding, self-sacrificing, guilt-inducing martyr. There was a lot of that in my mother. It was hard to argue with her or disagree with her when she would respond, "Don't worry — you won't have to put up with me much longer." Yes, there's a strong case to be made that Jewish mothers are experts at causing guilt in their children. Again, the joke: A mother brings her son two ties for his birthday. He puts one on, and what does she say? "What's the matter? You didn't like the other one?" But let us remember, there is guilt — and there is guilt! There is good guilt and there is neurotic guilt! If a mother says, "If you don't do what I say, I'm going to put my head in the stove," that's neurotic guilt! But many of today's "guilt-free" kids would be a lot better off if someone had made them feel guilty once in a while.

Similarly, in regard to the charge that Jewish mothers are overprotective, my mother certainly was. She got up early to put our underwear on the radiator so we would be warm when we got dressed. All I can tell you is it felt so good — better overprotection than underprotection. How good it is to know that there is someone you can depend on in your life — someone who loves and cares about you no matter what, someone who makes you feel important and thus fortifies your own self-esteem. Sure, some Jewish mothers have been known to be more than overprotective, to be smothering. Yet, I maintain that too much is still a lot better than too little.

The fact is, whether your mother was guilt inducing or not, whether your mother followed Spock or Shlock, whether she practiced mother-love or smother-love, who among us sitting here in these moments before Yizkor would disagree with the words of that well-known song:

My Yiddishe momma
I need her more than ever now.
My Yiddishe momma
I'd love to kiss her wrinkled brow.

Oh, I know that I owe what I am today
to that dear lady so old and so gray,
to that wonderful Yiddishe momma,
momma mine.

Yes, there is something about mothers, Jewish and non-Jewish alike. Just ask Paris Hilton. You would never think of her as being a "momma's girl," but she is! When the judge ordered the 26-year-old back to jail, she cried, "Mom!" And when she was released from jail, it was into her mother's arms that she ran. There is something about that umbilical cord that really never gets fully severed. I was taught that by my son, Jonathan. It was during one of our first trips to Israel when Sherry and I had taken Andrew and Jonathan along with us and Jonathan must have been all of ten years old then. Sherry and I had our room in the Laromme Hotel, and the kids had their room a couple of doors down. One night Jonathan was sick, and as he got into bed I asked him if I should stay in the room with him that night — just in case. And he said, "Yeah dad, that's a good idea. Because in case I wake up in the middle of the night feeling sick, you can go and get Mom."

Don't get me wrong; not all mothers are candidates for sainthood. Look at Tony Soprano's mother! She tried to kill him! And don't get me wrong, not all children are angels. Look at Britney Spears. She wrote a poem describing how much she hates her mother! If life was fair, it would have been nice if Livia Soprano had been Britney Spears' mother. They certainly deserve each other.

What mothers do deserve is our gratitude. Being a mother is no easy task; in fact, it is a thankless task. You are on duty 24/7; you get no training, no health benefits, no salary — you pay them! Most of the time you get no thanks. Even worse, you have to do something that goes against your very nature, your very instinct. Again here is a joke, a sick one: What's the difference between a Rottweiler dog and a Jewish mother? Eventually, the Rottweiler lets go!

Rabbi Norman Lamm writes how Erich Fromm, in his book, *Sane Society*, underscores the deeply tragic character of Mother Love. The dilemma is this: love normally seeks to hold tight, to grow closer. In the love between husband and wife, for instance, they look forward to an ever-growing closeness as the years go by. With a child, however, it is different. The mother loves the child passionately. Yet this love is doomed from the outset because the mother cannot expect to grow constantly closer to the child as time goes on. A mother's love that holds tight must learn to let go. The mother must help the child grow away in order to grow up.

Of course, in some ways we never let go. An op-ed article in the *New York Times* entitled "A Parent is Always a Parent" told of a successful psychiatrist who, in his fifties, took his mother, who was almost an octogenarian, to a performance given by the Metropolitan Opera in New York's Lincoln Center. After the last curtain came down and they were making their way out the lobby to his Mercedes, she turned to him and said, "Did you go to the bathroom?" Some things never change! But when it comes to our children, many things have to as they grow up.

Children are given to us by God in trust to raise — for them to grow up, to grow out, and to grow away from us as time goes on. That is the only way they will be able to fulfill themselves. It is a process that begins right at the beginning with the cutting of the cord. And it continues slowly but surely ever after. It is a process that goes on — like it or not — all the days of the child's life. Think about it: it starts the first day you bring your child to preschool, and you have to let go of his hand and he doesn't want you to. And it continues with the child wanting to cross the street by herself and you don't want to let go of her hand. It is very hard when a parent has to let go of the keys to their car and give it to their 16-year-old kid. And it is even harder later on in life when an 86- year-old parent has to let go of the keys to his car and give it to his adult child. And when we march our children down the aisle at their wedding, it is very hard letting go of their hands, knowing that when they walk back up the aisle they will be holding someone else's hand.

Yes, at some point we have to let go of our children and that is not easy. And it is not easy letting go of our dreams for our children. What is it that we dream of having from our children? All sorts of answers: success, marriage, children, happiness, fame — we Jews have one word that says it all. What do we want from our children? We want *nachas*! That is the dream, but what is the reality? The reality, as I have told you many times before, is that our children are not "*nachas*-producing machines." Look, even Baby Einstein turned out to be no Einstein! Our children are real human beings, and, like us, they have their virtues and their flaws, their strengths and their weaknesses. At some point, we have to be able to let go of some of our dreams for our children and trade them in for other dreams.

One of the most powerful things I ever read was written by Emily Perl Kingsley, a woman who gave birth to and was raising a child with a disability. She was asked what it was like and how it felt. And this is what she wrote:

When you're going to have a baby, it's like planning a fabulous vacation — to Italy. You buy a bunch of guidebooks and make your wonderful plans. You will see the Coliseum, the Michelangelo, David, the gondolas in Venice. You may even learn a handy phrase in Italian. It's all very exciting.

After months of eager anticipation, the day finally arrives. You pack your bags and off you go. Several hours later, the plane lands. The stewardess comes in and says, "Welcome to Holland."

''Holland?" you say. "What do you mean, Holland? I signed up for Italy! All my life I've dreamt of going to Italy."

But there's been a change in the flight plan. They've landed in Holland and there you must stay. The important thing to remember is that they haven't taken you to a horrible, disgusting, filthy place. It's just a different place.

So, you must go out and buy new guidebooks. And, you must learn a whole new language. And, you will meet a whole new group of people you never would have met.

It's just a different place. It's slower-paced than Italy. It's less flashy than Italy. But, after you have been there awhile and you catch your breath, you begin to look around and notice that Holland has windmills, Holland has tulips, Holland even has Rembrandts.

But, everyone you know is busy coming and going from Italy, and they're all bragging about what a wonderful time they had there. And, for the rest of your life, you will say. "Yes, that's where I was supposed to go. That's what I had planned..." The pain of that will never, never, ever go away because the loss of that dream is a very significant loss. But, if you spend your life mourning the fact that you didn't go to Italy, you may never be free to enjoy the very special, the very lovely things about Holland."

Great lesson! Our children are not made in one-size-fits-all. They each have their own quirks and needs and desires, and those may be very different from ours. We can either go through life bitter and resentful about what they did not turn out to be or we can try to enjoy who and what they are — our own flesh and blood.

Our people have a tradition that when we come to a cemetery for the burial of a loved one, as we carry the casket to its final resting place, we pause and make seven stops along the way. There is a beautiful and relevant explanation for this ritual. The seven stops are meant to represent the seven stages in life that we pass through from birth till death; for each one of these stages, we are being taught that we have to learn to stop and let go before we can move on to the next stage in life. From childhood to adolescence, to early adulthood to middle age, to old age, to all points in between, there come moments in life when we must face up to the fact that time moves on, and so must we. And in order to do this in a well-adjusted manner we have got to let go of that previous stage in life that is no more.

One of the reasons why we do not want to let go of our children and of our dreams for our children is because, in so doing, we have to accept that we are letting go of our own youth, that we are not so young anymore. In our youth-obsessed culture, that letting go is very hard to accept. You have difficulty letting go of the youthful you who was, but will never be again. It used to be that children tried to dress like grown-ups. Now, grown-ups try to dress like children! It is hard to let go of that picture of ourselves that we had in our youth. Indeed, it is hard to let go of the dreams that we had for ourselves in our youth, but there comes a time in life when we have to accept that they are not going to come true anymore. We all start out with dreams of what our life is going to be like — dreams of love and beauty, fame and fortune, happiness and achievement — but in case you have not noticed, not all of our dreams come true. Some people are shattered by that because they can never let go of their dreams. Others learn to change their dreams for new ones. Golda Meir was called lots of things in life, but no one ever called her a "babe," no one ever called her "sexy," no one ever called her "good looking." That must have been very hard for her in her youth. But she writes in her autobiography,

> I was never a beauty. There was a time when I was sorry about that. When I was old enough to understand the importance of it and looking in the mirror I realized it was something I was never going to have … it was much later that I realized that not being beautiful was a blessing in disguise. It forced me to develop my inner resources; I came to understand that women who cannot lean on their beauty and need to make something on their own have an advantage.

It was not a matter of Golda Meir learning to "settle" for what she was; it was a question of Golda Meir learning to be happy with what she was.

I think my mother was good at doing that. My mother started off in life with a "silver spoon" in her mouth. She was the oldest of the four children of Anna and Max Turoff, who were highly respected members of the Bronx Jewish community. My grandfather, Max Turoff, was a leader of his congregation and well known for his philanthropy. My mother graduated from New York University in the 1920s, when few women could afford to do that. My mother and her siblings had every reason to expect to marry "well." Well, my mother married my father, a Hungarian immigrant who came to our shores as an eighteen-year-old with a black hat and black coat and *peyos* — and nothing else! He spoke not a word of English. He paid his rent by packing matzoh at the Horowitz & Margarten matzoh factory. Somehow, he swept my mother off her feet. This was a marriage that never could have happened through JDate! Let me tell you something: being married to a rabbi was a step down for my mother in her standard of living. Her siblings — and their spouses — were always more affluent, while my mother had to run a small catering place in the basement of our house to help make ends meet. Yet, I never heard my mother complain — never, ever. I never heard my mother express any envy — never, ever. She had managed to trade in a dream of a high standard of living for a high standard of life. The youthful dream of affluence was traded in for the dream of a family. My father was not much as a breadwinner, but my mother treated him as if he was the richest man on earth. Up to the day she died, there was hardly ever a day that my mother did not speak of my father who had died twenty-three years earlier.

I think my mother and father provide a good lesson for all married couples. It is a lesson that is a modified version of what those great scholars, the Rolling Stones, sing: "You can't always get what you want. But if you try sometime, you just might find you get what you need." When we get married, we think our dream has come true. We think we are getting exactly what we want. But in case you have not noticed, it does not always work out that way. Sigmund Freud, who knew a little something about human relations — even more than do the Rolling Stones — once wrote that there are four people involved in every marriage: the woman, the man she thinks she is marrying, the man, and the woman he thinks he is marrying! Yes, soon enough we all learn that the person we married is not quite the person we thought he or she was. And Freud writes, "This realization of the difference between fantasy and reality is the first crisis of a marriage; a crisis every married person faces." I have to believe my parents, coming from such different backgrounds and having such different aspirations, at some point had to let go of the dream that their spouse was exactly what they had wanted. But they never even dreamed of letting go of each other, because they came to understand that in each other they got what they needed. I think many of us sitting here this morning would do well to do the same.

Moses dreamt of entering the Promised Land. Martin Luther King had a dream. Some dreams come true, and others we have got to learn to let go of. The truth is that some of us drive ourselves crazy by constantly going back in time and thinking what could have been, what should have been. In July of this year Albert Ellis passed away. Ellis was described as the "Lenny Bruce of psychotherapy." He had written seventy-four books including one of his most popular, *How to Stubbornly Refuse to Make Yourself Miserable About Anything. Yes, Anything!* He believed that each of us has the power to influence our own thinking and not to allow ourselves to make ourselves miserable. He wrote,

> Some of us walk around all day long getting on our own cases: "I've got to do this, I've got to do that, I should have said this to that person, I need to be more, I ought to be more organized, I should be more attractive, intelligent, witty, popular and personable. I ought to be more assertive. I need to be less aggressive. I've got to speak up more. I really need to keep my mouth shut ... some of us "should" on ourselves all day long!"

Good advice. Stop "shoulding" on yourself. "Should have, would have, could have" — there comes a time when you have to learn to let go and move on. You know what they say, It is what it is.

So yes, our dreams must sometimes be traded in for different ones. And the same must be done with some of our realities. All of us have our hurts, and all of us have had our quarrels. They are very real and very painful. What do we do with them? Do we hold onto them? Or do we let go? My mother, I am sorry to say, was one of those who held onto them. You know the concept of "forgive and forget?" Well, there are some people who can forgive, but they never forget! And there are some people who, strangely enough, can forget but never forgive! I am married to one! Many years ago I did or said something to Sherry that really hurt her, and she said she would never forgive or forget what I said. Well, as the years have gone by, she has forgotten what it was, but you know what? It doesn't make a difference — she still doesn't forgive me! My mother did not forgive or forget. My brothers and I thought about this when we were sitting *shiva* for her; we thought back to when we had all sat *shiva* for my father and someone had commented to my mother what a beautiful tribute it was to him that so many people came and expressed their condolences. They said, "I'm sure you'll always have a list in your heart of those who came." And my mother replied, "Yes, but I'll always have another list in my heart of those who didn't come!"

Many of us have such lists — lists of those who hurt us, who slighted us, who insulted us, who were not there for us; lists of those whom we cannot forget or forgive. Some of us are like the child who wrote the letter to God: "Dear God, If we come back as something, please don't let me be Jennifer Horton, because I hate her. Signed, Denise." Yes, some of us take the hurt and hatred to the grave. And I ask you, What for?

Let me tell you a story of two monks on a pilgrimage who came to a ford of a river. There they saw a beautiful, voluptuous girl dressed in a flowing, silk dress who could not figure out what to do since the river was so high. Without a thought, one of the monks lifted her onto his back, carried her across the river, and put her down on dry ground on the other side. Then the monks continued on their way. After two hours of walking in silence, the second monk couldn't stand it anymore. He turned to the first and complained, "How could you carry that woman, when it is against our sacred vows to even touch a woman?" The monk who had carried the girl across the river replied, "I set her down by the river two hours ago. Why are you still carrying her?"

How many of us are like that monk, carrying around our silent resentments, hour after hour, day after day, year after year? It is told of the Ari, the great kabbalist and Chasidic master, that every night before he went to sleep he would say, *"Hareini mocheil l'chol Adam shechata k'negdi hayom* — I hereby forgive whoever has hurt me this day." He said that every single day. You know his reward? A good night's sleep! It is not easy letting go of our anger and resentment. The English poet, Lord Byron, once said, "Hatred is by far the longest pleasure; men love in haste but they detest at leisure." Yes, we are so slow in letting go of our hurts, but do you know what? You would be better off doing it sooner rather than later, because sooner or later, you are going to have to let go of life itself.

Letting go of a loved one is something that we all know intellectually we are going to have to do at some point in life. But emotionally we are never really prepared for that day. It matters not whether our loved ones pass on when they are young or old, suddenly or after a long illness — there is no such thing as a "happy" ending. Yet, my mother's ending came as close as possible to a happy one. I had been in Israel, and I was coming home that night. I was walking through the Old City doing some last-minute shopping. I called my mother on my cell phone just to say hello. She was fine, sharp as a tack, eating her breakfast. I told her I would call her in the morning when I landed. I hung up, walked back to my hotel, and then got a phone call that she had passed away. Her last words were, "Please get me some ice cream." Not bad for a woman who was going to be ninety-five! She had always told her boys she would do her best not to die when it would require cutting short a vacation. And she did! She made it easy for us to let go.

But you know what? It was not so easy. This summer my brothers and I went to Florida to break up her apartment. At first, it started humorously as we ransacked her drawers and looked in her dresser to see if she hid some money. But then, it turned very serious. It was hard to throw anything away. Every piece of paper was a part of her, a piece of her life. The letters from my father, her diploma, pictures of her on the Queen Mary, invitations to family simchas, her phone book — who needed them? But how could we throw them away? How could we let go? The three of us, as rabbis, recognized that what we were experiencing was a rather mild form of what many experience at the time of death of a loved one. Many choose to leave the house exactly the way it is, in the very real expectation — not hope — but expectation that their loved one is going to be returning. Their lives become obsessed with this expectation. Joan Didion, the noted writer, won the National Book Award last year for the way she described this feeling in her book appropriately titled *The Year of Magical Thinking*. While her ill daughter, who later died, was in the hospital, one night her husband, suddenly from out of nowhere, died. As she writes it, "Life changes fast. Life changes in an instant. You sit down to dinner and life as you know it ends." But it is hard to accept, hard to let go. Her book describes her year of "magical thinking" — the thinking that her story can be revised, her husband will return alive! At first, she did not want the death notice to appear in the newspaper. That would mean he was really dead. In her words, "I needed to be alone so that he could come back. This was the beginning of my year of magical thinking."

I think Jewish tradition shows keen insight in dealing with this reaction. For one year, it has me coming to shul to say *kaddish* for my mother. From the perspective of the mystics, this helps elevate her soul. But do you know that saying the *kaddish* does something for me? For an entire year, my schedule is based on being in a shul every morning and every evening to say *kaddish*. Wherever I go, my plans revolve around being near a shul every morning and evening for the kaddish. All of her life, my mother's world revolved around her children. Now, for one year, our entire world evolves around her.

But the months of saying *kaddish* must come to an end. And holding onto a life that revolves around a loved one must come to an end as well. My mother showed us that. After my father passed away, my mother moved to Florida where her siblings lived. She was ready to purchase a one-bedroom apartment at Tower Forty One in Miami Beach. It was a lovely apartment with a terrace overlooking Collins Avenue and the ocean. But when she walked out onto the terrace, she said she couldn't buy that apartment because she could see the street where she and my father used to walk together during the winter months, and it would be too painful for her to see that without him. So she took another apartment, one not as nice, facing toward the city. But a year later, she moved into that first apartment. She knew that at a certain point in life she had to go on with her life. Toward the conclusion of her book, Joan Didion writes, "I know why we try to keep the dead alive: we try to keep them alive in order to keep them with us. I also know that if we are to live ourselves, there comes a point at which we must relinquish the dead. Let them go ..."

Yes, there comes a time when we must do that. And it is often at the time of death of a loved one that we learn to let go of something else. We learn to let go of God — the God we thought we knew. As children, we grow up being taught that God is good, God is just, God is merciful. We grow up thinking that God will take good care of us — if we are good, all will be well, and no harm will come to us. I grew up thinking that, didn't you? But as I grew older I began to wonder. I saw too much that made me question. And when my father died there were no more questions. I knew I had to let go of my childish view of God. Here was my father, who had been such a great spokesman for God, now so weak that he could hardly speak more than a few words at a time. Here was my father who did not have a bad bone in his body, who now had those bones filled with cancer, making it impossible for him to move without being in pain. This is justice? This is mercy? This is God taking care of good people? For some it is that confrontation that causes them to lose faith in God. But I did not, because my father did not as he lay on his deathbed with his yarmulke on his head saying the *Shema*. He lost his father at the age of four, and soon thereafter he and his siblings were separated and raised by aunts and uncles. He understood early on in life what I had come to understand a bit later: belief in God cannot guarantee that nothing bad will happen to you. The God who created this world created it with tumors and infections and viruses and drunk drivers and murderers and mad men — just as He created it with men and women who have made vaccines and medications and works of art and beauty. Faith in God does not guarantee that nothing will go wrong in your life. What it does guarantee is that you will never walk alone, that you will be able to cope, you will be able to carry on, you will be able to make your life worth living, no matter what.

Just ask Tony Snow. Tony Snow was George Bush's press secretary (don't hold that against him). Snow, age fifty-one, thought he had beaten colon cancer two years ago only to find out it returned and spread to his liver. Rather than wallowing in self-pity and questioning God, Tony Snow has found this experience moving him closer to God.

He says that the illness has deepened his religious faith and made him more purposeful about life. In a wonderful article in the July issue of *Christianity Today*, Mr. Snow writes, "We want lives of simple, predictable ease — smooth, even trails as far as the eye can see — but God likes to go off-road.... He provokes us with twists and turns. He places us in predicaments that seem to defy our endurance and comprehension — and yet don't. By His love and grace we persevere."

Yes, even in the valley of the shadow of death, we can persevere. It is not easy to die. Our sages point out that when we come into this world, our fists are clenched tight, symbolizing our desire to conquer, to acquire, to possess everything we can get our hands on. But when we die, our palms are opened, teaching us that we are going to have to let go of it all. Yet, none of us wants to let go of life. Dylan Thomas told his old, suffering father: "Do not go gentle into that good night ... rage, rage against they dying of the light." We did not have to tell that to my mother. She used to tell us, "When you get to the end of the rope you tie a knot and hold on for dear life." Sure, none of us want to let go, but I have found, in my experience as a rabbi and in my experience as a son, that letting go of life is much easier for those who have lived the way God wants us to live, for those who have lived good lives, meaningful lives, for those who were able to cherish each and every day of their lives.

Tony Soprano's mother, Livia, died as she lived — bitter and angry. As she approached death, her parting words to her grandson were, "It's all a big nothing." My mother did not die feeling that way. My mother loved life and lived it to its fullest. She lived in keeping with the words that Tony Soprano's psychiatrist quoted to him from the poet Carlos Castaneda: "Live every moment as if it were your last dance on earth." That is the way my mother lived. And because of that, she died a happy woman. How do I know? Because she told us. In going through her papers, we came across a copy of a letter she had sent to each of us twenty years ago when she turned seventy-five.

On the occasion of my 75th birthday I have many things to be grateful for. One: I am grateful to the Almighty for my wonderful children and grandchildren. Two: I am grateful for having loved and been loved for fifty years by your wonderful father, of blessed memory. Three: I am also grateful that I have kept fairly well physically so that I have not been a burden on you and have never *'farshtert'* on your *simchas*. I think that I have lived a full and wonderful life. I make every day count. I never took anything for granted. I always try to do the things I enjoyed most. As the New Year approaches, let us hope that we all keep well for many years and that your children should give you the respect and *nachas* that you gave to Daddy and that you continue to give to me. Love, Mommy.

It is a blessing to have such a mother. It is a blessing to be such a woman. In her later years of life, when she knew the day would come when she would have to let go, she lived at peace — at peace with herself, at peace with her family, at peace with God, appreciating each and every day that she had.

We can do the same. It requires letting go — letting go of a lot of our "should haves," "would haves," "could haves." It requires letting go of a lot of our anger and resentment. It requires letting go of some of our dreams of childhood and trading them in for more realistic, more mature dreams. It requires our accepting our parents for who they were and what they were, just as we wanted them to accept us for who and what we are. It requires moving on and making every day count, knowing that we are all going to have to let go some day. Knowing the time will come when we must surrender so much that is so very precious to us — our parents, our children — should spur us on to enjoy them while they are ours: to be with them, to share with them, to embrace them, to love them — before we have to let go.

How important it is to call them while we still can. I have made my peace with my mother's death. I have accepted the reality of it. But I still have her number on the speed dial of my cell phone. That was my umbilical cord that I cannot yet let go of. I cannot help it. I have lost my mother, and I will never have another one. There will never again be anyone who will say I am their child. The only person who was there when I came into the world has left this world. There will never again be anyone who will endearingly call me "Mushkilah." Nobody will ever again ask me about my children and grandchildren like she did. I am no longer a child — anyone's child.

But that is alright. I may no longer be a child but now I'm a "Pops!" My future is bright, and my past is connected to my future. Morrie said it so well in the book, *Tuesdays With Morrie*: "Death ends a life but it doesn't end a relationship." No, I cannot call my mother anymore, but as I have pointed out to you so many times before in these moments before *Yizkor*, that is what *Yizkor* is all about. It gives us an opportunity to speak to our loved ones once again. They may not be here, but they hear us. What will you say to your loved ones who are gone? I don't know but I hope they are words of love. I know exactly what I will say to my mother during the moments of *Yizkor*. My brother, Saul, in eulogizing my mother, reminded us that every night before we went to sleep, my mother said the exact same words to us: "Good night, sleep well. I love you."

Mommy, good night, sleep well — I love you.

Yom Kippur, September 22, 2007